Latino Boom II

Latino Boom II

CATCH THE

BIGGEST

DEMOGRAPHIC

WAVE SINCE

THE BABY BOOM

Chiqui Cartagena

A CustomWorthy Edition
published by
Worthy Shorts, Inc.
39 Crosby
New York, NY 10013
www.worthyshorts.com

Cartagena, Chiqui
Latino Boom II
CW109

ISBN 978-1-937504-51-9

Manufactured in the United States of America,
or in the United Kingdom when distributed elsewhere.

*Dedicated to all the people who
help elevate the conversation
about the growing importance
of the Latino community*

〜〜〜

CONTENTS

Foreword   xi

Introduction   xiii

1   The Latino Effect   3
    Yo Decido   7
    Decoding Latino Culture   11

2   A Brief History of Latinos in the United States   17
    The Discovery   17
    The Hispanic Tipping Point   19
    Historical Perspectives of Mexicans, Puerto Ricans
        and Cubans   20
    Florida's Mambo   21
    Puerto Rico: The 51st State?   22
    Toss Out the Melting Pots and Salad Bowls   25

3   Portrait of Latino U.S.A.   31
    Hispanic Population Growth   34
    Breakdown of Hispanics into Country Subgroups   35
    Geographic Concentration   38
    Distribution of Latinos by Region   41
    Youth: Our Secret Sauce   43
    Hispanic Household Incomes   47
    Shift From Foreign-Born To U.S.-Born Latinos   51
    Language Preference   51

Are There Spanish Dialects?   55
Hispanic Buying Power   56
Education   57
Employment   61

4   How To Capitalize on the Hispanic Opportunity   71
Snapshots of the Seven Sectors For Growth   75
Sizing The Prize   88
Multicultural Organizational Structures   91

5   The Top Eight Hispanic Markets   99
Los Angeles, California   102
New York, New York   105
Miami-Ft. Lauderdale, Florida   109
Houston, Texas   113
Chicago, Illinois   117
Dallas-Ft. Worth, Texas   121
San Antonio, Texas   125
San Francisco, California   129

6   Hispanic Identity   135
Are You Talking To Me?   139
The Importance of Culture To Identity   141
Politics, Values, and Religion   142
The Influence of Culture
In Hispanic Identity   149

7   The Changing Media Landscape   159
A Brief History of Hispanic Media in the U.S.   161
Chronology of Spanish-Language Media in the United States   164
Overview of Media Landscape by Industry   172
The Telenovela Phenomenon   177
Cable TV   181
Digital Cable TV   184

Spanish-Language Radio 185
Spanish-Language Print 191
Newspapers and Magazines Ad Revenue 192
Profile of the Hispanic Magazine Reader 195
Key Players 197
Hispanics Online 198

8 The Hispanic Advertising Industry 209
History of Hispanic Advertising 210
Total Market Strategy Roadmap 215
Who's Got Game? 217
What About Creative? 224
The Rise of Content Marketing 228
A Final Thought 230

9 Your Roadmap To Success 233
Five Rules for the Road 235
A Word of Caution About Research 238
The Rise of Marketing Accountability 243
Brand Measures 244
Creative Effectiveness 245
Sales Metrics—Opportunities and Challenges 246
Test Markets—Do's and Don'ts 248
Putting It All Together: 249

10 The Big Picture 253
The Four Ps 255
People 255
Press 256
Politicians 257
Presidents 259

Resource Guide   **261**

    Research Companies   261

    Nonprofit Research Centers   263

    Government Offices   264

    Hispanic Market Publications   265

    Trade Associations   266

    Hispanic Associations   267

    Recommended Conferences   270

Acknowledgments   **273**

FOREWORD

By Randy Falco
President and CEO
Univision Communications, Inc.

Are you bullish on the future? I know I am because I see the potential of our future in our talented group of professionals and in the community we serve at Univision. I see Hispanic professionals and leaders like Latino Boom II author, Chiqui Cartagena, every day, individuals with strong work ethic and an entrepreneurial spirit, who are driving the economic growth of our country. These individuals are why I know the future of America is one of solid growth and prosperity. The Millennial Generation, 85 million strong, will slowly replace the aging Boomers and their incremental demand for a wide variety of goods, products, and services will continue to make the United States the economic engine of the world.

Just look at the Hispanic consumer who makes up more than 20 percent of all millennials and who, as everyone already knows, is growing faster than any other group in America with 50,000 Hispanics turning eighteen every month. It is not just about the numbers; Hispanics are making a positive impact on our country, contributing socially, politically, and economically. Take last year's presidential election in which Hispanics proved that they have the political clout to elect the next president of the United States. One candidate ignored this, at his peril. Business leaders need to realize that they, too, can no longer ignore the Hispanic community or consider it a niche market. Whatever category your business is in, there is no doubt that the future demand for your product or service will be largely coming from Latino families.

Just as in the presidential election, we are seeing some companies who understand the opportunity and others who have a long way to go.

Hispanics are leading the growth of the multicultural consumer sector, which also includes African Americans and Asians, of course. In fact, according to the Latinum Network, by 2026 multicultural consumers could represent 33 percent of total expenditures in the United States, potentially adding $2.7 trillion to the American economy. Half of that growth in spending, 15–16 percent, could come from Hispanics alone.[1]

Understanding how culture affects consumer behavior is important not only to grow your businesses with multicultural markets inside the United States, I believe it can help America be more competitive in the global economy. So as leaders in Hispanic media, we try to help our clients and business partners with thought leadership about the Hispanic consumer.

We believe that elevating the conversation about Hispanics in the United States benefits us all, which is why the new edition of Latino Boom, written by Chiqui Cartagena, one of the leading Hispanic marketing experts in the US and Vice President of Corporate Marketing at Univision, is a resource every CEO, business leader, and marketer should read. This new edition is a follow-up to her first book and creates a compelling story from all the data that is out there about this community. It also deciphers the biggest trends in the Hispanic community to help you better understand this constantly changing marketplace. Latino Boom II will give you the knowledge and tools you need to start growing your business with Latinos and help you capitalize on this once-in-a-lifetime opportunity which is being brought on by the biggest demographic wave since the Baby Boom.

NOTES

1. "The Big Shift: How the Multicultural Segment Is Driving Consumer Spending," Dec. 13, 2012 Latinum Market Dynamics Model, Latinum Network © 2012

INTRODUCTION

In spite of all the talk about the rise of the BRIC countries (Brazil, Russia, India, China), in his book *The Next 100 Years: The Forecast for the 21st Century,* historian George Friedman contends that America will continue to be the dominant superpower of this relatively new century. America's greatness is not only based on its military and economic supremacy around the globe, according to Friedman, America will continue to be powerful because of its people and the strength of our democracy. Of course, at the heart of this great country is the indomitable spirit of its citizens who came here looking for life, liberty, and the pursuit of happiness. Let's not forget that since its very beginning, this country has been built on the strength of immigrants. For the past nearly 230 years, the people who have come here from all over the world searching for their American Dream have made America stronger and better. No country is more diverse than the USA, and nowhere is this more visible than during the Olympics. In the parade of nations, the athletes wearing red, white, and blue uniforms are a manifestation of who we are: a truly multicultural America.

The multiculturalism that is celebrated in the sports arena has not yet permeated the political or business worlds of America. On the contrary, over the past decade the political rhetoric has taken on an extremely divisive tone. We talk about our country in terms of red states and blue states, and at heart of this clash are two demographic trends that experts say will reshape the America of the twenty-first century: on the one hand, you have an increasingly young and diverse population (in large part fueled by the Latino Baby Boom) in which minorities will soon make up a majority of the country; and on the other hand, you have the Baby Boom Generation (four-fifths of whom are white) that is massively moving into retirement after having recently suffered one of the worst economic downturns in their lives. Below the surface of these two demographic shifts are undeniable racial and cultural tensions that, according to William Frey, a demographer at the Brookings Institution, have already formed a "cultural generational gap" that will "rattle American politics for decades," because the attitudes, needs, and priorities of each group seem to be diametrically opposed in terms of policy choices.

During the 2012 presidential elections, we saw how this cultural generational gap has started to affect the political discourse. But if you look closely, this cultural generational gap has been fueling the so-called culture wars Americans have been living over the past decade, the victims of which have often been women, gays, and now immigrants. But now this cultural generational gap is coming to a head, and as Ronald Brownstein wrote a few years ago in the *National Journal*, "the twist is that graying white voters who are skeptical of public spending may have more in common with the young minorities clamoring for it than either side now recognizes. Today's minority students will represent an increasing share of tomorrow's workforce and thus pay more of the payroll taxes that will be required to fund Social Security and Medicare benefits for the mostly white Baby Boomers."[1]

This is not a political book, but as Washington discovered in 2012, Latinos are no longer a constituency they can continue to ignore. Likewise, business leaders need to understand that the Latino community is the business opportunity they must start focusing on if they are looking for growth for their companies. The goal of this book is to help put in perspective the positive impact the growing Latino population will have on the future of America. Beyond the census numbers, there is a lot of cultural context and information that one needs to understand in order to *win* with the Hispanic consumer, and this book sets out to help you do just that. This book does contain a lot of charts and data that can help anyone start a project with the Hispanic community in mind. From business to politics to marketing, Latinos are the most sought after opportunity this country has, and yet we are still viewed myopically by many, if not most, Americans. My hope is that this book will help change that…at least a little.

A lot has changed since I wrote my first book in 2005. In July of that year, News Corp. acquired MySpace for $580 million, signaling for the first time the importance of social networking in the media ecosystem, even though Twitter didn't yet exist.

Six years later, News Corp. sold MySpace for $35 Million, Twitter became the media darling *du jour*, and Facebook became the billion-dollar baby that it is today.

Many of these changes are fueled by advances in technology in smartphones and tablet computers. Google, with its Android platform (Google acquired Android Inc. in August 2007), and Apple make products that are not only beautiful (the iPhone came out in July 2007 and the iPad was launched in September 2010) but user-friendly, and consumers have adopted them very, very quickly.

The media industry, rightfully, first viewed these advances with trepidation but has learned to embrace them so they are not left behind as the music industry was with the rise of Napster a decade earlier. In May 2007, ABC started offering online streams of some of its most popular television shows, including *Desperate Housewives* and *Lost*, for free the day after they first air on broadcast TV. At the time, analysts said it was a very bold move that had the potential of shaking up the TV industry because it gave consumers control of when and how they wanted to watch TV. Today consumer control is a given and it has become the biggest challenge *and* opportunity facing media companies.

The American consumer has also changed fundamentally, thanks to the extreme highs and lows we have experienced in both our economy and politics. Led by Wall Street greed, the housing bubble burst, sending this country—and the whole world—into the deepest recession it has seen since the market crash of 1929. As a result, the unbridled American consumer spirit is now cautious about spending and rethinking why and how they buy products and services at every level. But as the Baby Boomers start retiring at the rate of 10–15,000 a day, the

Millennial Generation will take center stage and become the backbone of the American economy. And who is at the very heart of this new American consumer? The Latino community. Did you know that Latinos already make up 21 percent of the Millennial Generation? In fact, 29 percent of all Hispanics are millennials and researchers agree that Latinos are among the leading trendsetters of this generation, creating new trends from food to fashion.

On the political front, of course, Barack Obama became the first black president of the United States of America in 2008 by harnessing grassroots support from a broad spectrum of Americans including youth, Latinos, women, and even whites.

The 2012 presidential election proved to be a historic political year for Latinos. As early as November 2011, David Alexrod, Obama's chief campaign strategist, opined that "there isn't a swing state in the union more important than the Latino community in the 2012 elections." Latinos became an integral part of the political conversation as media coverage of the 2012 election swung into full gear, and campaigns competed for the Hispanic vote. Indeed, as election-night ballots were tallied, Mr. Axelrod's prescient comment, which was also a key insight into the campaign's winning strategy, was proved true when, for the first time, Latinos became the deciding factor in a presidential election, returning Obama to office for four more years.

The fact is that we are at the dawn of a new reality in America. This new reality is reflected in the way we look, the foods we eat, and even the way we dance. For some, the recognition of the increasing role minorities are starting to play in America today is long overdue. For others, however, this new multicultural America is very scary. When you hear them talk on the radio or on TV, saying that the best days of America are behind us because—for them—a future in which the hegemony of white, Anglo-Saxon men is over makes them cringe.

That fear, not surprisingly, is promulgated through disinformation about the state of our country by disingenuous politicians and conservative talk radio and television show hosts and then disseminated even further by other media outlets that care more about ratings and filling their airtime with anything that is thinly veiled as "news." Charles Garcia wrote about this recently for the *Huffington Post Latino Voices*, citing a study from 2010. Professors Sei-hill Kim of the University of South Carolina and John Carvalho of Auburn University researched, with others, newspaper articles and television transcripts from between 1997 and 2006 and found that the terms "illegal alien," "illegal immigrant," or just plain "illegals" are everywhere on television, in newspapers, and on talk radio. They also discovered that journalists attracted the largest audiences with crime stories, so linking immigrants to a crime drama was preferred because it increased ratings and profits.[2]

A more recent study conducted by Latino Decisions for the National Hispanic Media Coalition, published in September 2012, concluded that "media portrayals of Latinos and immigrants are fueling rampant negative stereotypes among the general population that are diminishing perceptions of these groups throughout the United States." Case in point: although 85 percent of all Hispanics in the United States are either American citizens or here legally, by associating Latinos with the issue of illegal immigration, this study found that "30 percent of respondents believed that a majority of Hispanics (50 percent or greater) were undocumented."[3]

More on that later, but I blame both the conservative and the liberal media for not getting our story right. The truth is that our country is changing. We are experiencing tectonic demographic shifts, but the spirit of America has not changed, and the foundation on which the future America is built remains the same: a belief in hard work that allows our families to get ahead and a respect for one another allows us all to pursue our American Dream. If you look beyond the divisive talk and instead focus on what really matters, you will see what I see, which is a huge opportunity to catch the biggest economic wave since the baby boom.

In a report published in spring 2012, the Nielsen Company described the change like this: "The country's vibrant demographic composition, with its healthy multicultural dynamic and youth, is a critical American asset in the global economic competition. At the heart of this asset, both now and over the next several decades, is the Hispanic population... Latinos are no longer just a sub-segment of the economy, but a prominent player of American life."[4]

Over the next ten chapters, I hope to show you the amazing opportunity the Hispanic community represents for this country and its future. I will help you take advantage of this opportunity by sharing insights about this consumer group, by sharing with you organizational models that drive to best-in-class Hispanic marketing practices, and finally by sharing research that I believe will help you understand how both culture and language must be at the heart of everything you do to win with Hispanics.

Yes, you may have to change the way you do things. But change, while sometimes difficult, is always for the better. The definition of insanity is doing the same thing over and over again and expecting different results.

NOTES

1. Ronald Brownstein, "The Grey and the Brown: The Generational Mismatch," *National Journal*, June 24, 2010. http://www.nationaljournal.com/magazine/the-gray-and-the-brown-the-generational-mismatch-20100724.

2. Mass Communications and Society, The View of the Border: News Framing of the Definition, Causes, and Solutions to Illegal Immigration DOI: 10.1080/15205431003743679 Sei-hill Kim, John P. Carvalho, Andrew G. Davis & Amanda M. Mullins, pages 292-314.

3. The Impact of Media Stereotypes on Opinions and Attitudes Towards Latinos, National Hispanic Media Coalition/Latino Decisions, September 2012, pg. 5.

4. *The State of the Hispanic Consumer: The Hispanic Market Imperative*, Quarter 2, 2012 Copyright © 2012 The Nielsen Company.

Latino Boom II

1

THE LATINO EFFECT

You can stop by McDonald's and order a tropical smoothie or walk into a Panera Bread and order your favorite Cuban chicken panini. That's the Latino Effect.

You can go to Sephora and see the new face of L'Oreal, Jennifer Lopez, telling you that the secret behind her beautiful skin is that she is "100% Puerto Rican." You can buy a Bud Light Lime or clean your home with Lavender Fabuloso®, a line of cleaning products imported from Mexico by Colgate over a decade ago. That's the Latino Effect.

Or you can attend ComicCon and hear David Marquez, one of the hottest names in comics today, talk about how he and some friends launched their alternate universe comic book "to be more representative of both those who make and read them," referring to the new Ultimate Comics Spider-Man series, in which Peter Parker is replaced by Miles Morales, who is biracial, African American and Puerto Rican. Now that's the Latino Effect!

From food to fashion to financial services, the rapidly growing Latino population will have a huge and positive impact in the United States not only in the next five years, but for decades to come. According to Nielsen population estimates, Hispanics will contribute over 60 percent of the total population growth over the next five years,[1] even though immigration is down sharply. And yet most American companies are

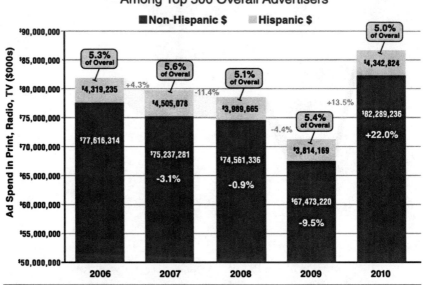

Hispanic Ad Spend Allocation
Among Top 500 Overall Advertisers

Figure 1.1

Source: Advertising 2011 Budget Alignment, Association of Hispanic Advertising Agencies. Ad Spend Analysis conducted by Santiago Solutions Group with Neilsen Ad Spend 06–10

still not taking advantage of this opportunity. According to the latest study by the Association of Hispanic Advertising Agencies, from 2006 to 2010 only 5 percent of the top 500 advertisers' advertising dollars was dedicated to actively marketing their products and services to the Latino community.[2]

In 2010, I wrote a blog post for *Advertising Age* titled "Add an 'H' to Your BRIC Strategy," where I urged American corporations to count not only on BRIC countries for future growth, but to look domestically for new growth opportunities as well. Now Nielsen is telling its clients the same thing. "Many companies believe that significant growth opportunities come from outside the U.S., but the Hispanic market offers unique growth prospects within our borders," says the 2012 Nielsen report, *State of the Hispanic Consumer: The Hispanic Market Imperative*. "What's more, the per capita income of U.S. Hispanics is higher than any one of the coveted BRIC countries. Despite the recession, U.S. Latino households that

A Country Within A Country

	Brazil	Russia	India	China	U.S. Hispanics
Total Population (In Millions)[1,2]	197.5	142.5	1,189.1	1,336.7	52
GDP (Current Dollars)[3,4]	$2.28T	$2.38T	$4.46T	$11.29T	$1.1T
GDP Per Capita (PPP)[3,4]	$11,600	$16,700	$3,700	$8,400	$31,135*
YOY Pop Growth	0.9%	-0.1%	1.4%	0.5%	3.2%**

Source: 1) U.S. Census Bureau International Database Division. Population Estimates for 2011. 2) U.S. Census Bureau. 2011 Population Estimates. Released May, 2012 3) CIA Fact Book. Country rankings based on 2011 Estimates. 4) IHS Global Insight – 2010 Hispanic Market Monitor. Based on 2011 Estimate. *Based on average Hispanic household income in 2010. **Based on U.S. Hispanic population growth from April 1, 2010 to July 1, 2011. Country population growth based on % growth in total population by country 2010 vs 2011.

Figure 1.2 Hispanic Per Capita Income vs. BRIC Countries

earn $50,000 or more are growing at a faster rate than total households," they add. In fact, according to the CIA World Fact Book, if it were a stand-alone country, the U.S. Hispanic community's buying power would make it the sixteenth largest economy in the world, ahead of Turkey, Australia, Argentina, Saudi Arabia, and South Africa![3]

In addition, according to the census, the Hispanic population growth is projected to outpace all other ethnic groups in the U.S. over the next forty years (Figure 1.3). So why aren't more companies doing more in this space? I've got three words for you: Ignorance (and I mean that in the nicest way), Fear (and we all know how paralyzing that can be), and Avoidance (meaning "not on my watch, buddy"). But the days of saying, "I don't care, it's not big enough to matter" are over. As the Selig Center for Economic Growth said in its 2010 report *The Multicultural Economy*, "The Hispanic market's sheer size, growing clout, and buying power . . . of $1.5 trillion by 2012 require thoughtful understanding about what the market represents to a company's bottom line."[4]

Beyond the numbers, which we will get into much more in Chapter 3, what business leaders fail to understand is that the *influence* Latinos

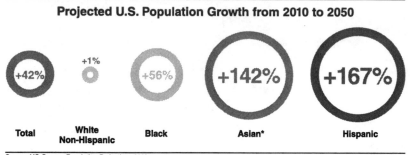

Projected U.S. Population Growth from 2010 to 2050

Total	White Non-Hispanic	Black	Asian*	Hispanic
+42%	+1%	+56%	+142%	+167%

Source: US Census Population Projections 2012
*Excludes American Indian, Alaskan Native, Hawaiian & other Pacific Islander

Figure 1.3

have in the U.S. is not only limited to them. A recent study by Experian Marketing Services, in collaboration with the Hispanic agency Wing, set out specifically to determine just how much Latinos are influencing non-Latinos in the United States and how the influence is expressed in actual consumer behavior of non-Latinos. The Latino Influence Project (http://www.experian.com/simmons-research/latino-influence-project-report.html), which was published in November 2012, shows us just how much Latinos are influencing their non-Hispanic neighbors in a wide array of consumer areas, such as technology, fashion, food, beverages, sports, music, and travel. The study encourages marketers to consider "how to leverage Hispanic insights in general market communications, taking advantage of 'Hispanic influencers' as brand ambassadors and focusing on Hispanic markets as hotbeds for cultural activity and interaction."[5]

According to Nielsen, global companies such as P&G, Coca-Cola, Unilever, and Walmart have already made the Latino market "an imperative for growth" because they have realized that Hispanics will be "the dominant and in many cases the only driver of domestic CPG sales growth" in the United States.

For the first time since it started in 1978, the 2012 Customer and Channel Management Survey (CCMS), which analyzes the practices of top-performing CPG companies and is conducted in a collaboration with McKinsey & Company, Nielsen, and the Grocery Manufacturers of America, added a new module on the Hispanic market. According to this study, winning CPG companies were "three times more likely to invest in emerging channels and the Hispanic market." And those who did invest in the Hispanic market "grew sales to Hispanics by 2.5 percentage points more than category average and also achieved higher rates of Hispanic household penetration, beating out their peers by 2.9 percentage points."[6]

So you can either be the person who treads water and really does nothing to move the needle for your company or you can be the person who actually drives results by trying something new: capturing a greater share of the American market and growing revenues by capitalizing on the Latino Boom. Don't worry, there will be people along the way to help you get it right, starting with me.

YO DECIDO

In March of 2012, *TIME* magazine proclaimed on its cover "Why Latinos Will Pick the Next President," using a Spanish headline, "Yo Decido" (I Decide) and a mosaic of Latino headshots to make their point even stronger. According to census data, every month 50,000 Latino citizens turn eighteen and are therefore eligible to vote. The American electorate is growing by the minute. And it's not only about presidential politics. Did you know that Hispanics already account for more than 50 percent of the adults in the eighteen-plus population in twenty-five congressional districts? Those kinds of numbers can swing an election, and politicians know it.

The growing importance of the Latino vote and how the candidates courted or alienated the Latino community became an important narrative during the 2012 presidential campaign and had political pundits scrambling to sound intelligent about what impact the Latino vote might have. Blatantly missing across all networks were Latino journalists who could intelligently talk about the issues that really mattered most to Latinos as well as how they would vote and why. There are very few prominent Latino journalists in network or cable news, which just adds to the overall invisibility of Latinos in American culture. I hope that will change in the next five years, especially since Univision recently announced a joint venture with ABC News to launch a twenty-four-hour cable news and lifestyle network directed to bilingual or English-dominant Hispanics. The new network, called Fusion, will be launched in 2013 and will help elevate our voices in English-language media. But we are a long way from where we need to be.

Case in point is that much of the coverage around the Latino vote in 2012 was singularly focused on the immigration issue—not on what candidates were saying about their political platforms regarding jobs, health care, and education—which were the top issues for Latinos. What most people inside the beltway fail to understand is that immigration is not strictly a Latino issue, it is an American issue. However, for Latino citizens—not only the recent arrivals, but those who may be generations removed from their families' migration—immigration becomes a personal issue because of the anti-Latino rhetoric and hate speech that surrounds much of the discussion of the topic these days. It's kind of hard not to get your back up when Bill O'Reilly agrees with a caller on his radio program, *The Radio Factor with Bill O'Reilly*, that illegal immigration "has the same impact as a major terrorist attack" that surpasses the impact of 9/11, and that immigrants are "biological weapon[s]." Or when Michael Savage on his radio show, *The Savage Nation*, says that "[t]he immigrants, when they take over America, won't be as enlightened as the (European) people running America today. There is a racial element to the 'immigration invasion.'"[7]

In the end, what we do about the 11.1 million undocumented people who are living in the shadows in the United States *is an issue all Americans have to figure out*. And, ultimately, how we treat this issue says a lot about who we are as a country. Let me just remind you what Alexis de Tocqueville once said: "America is great because she is good. If America ceases to be good, America will cease to be great."

Besides the immigration issue, clearly the Washington establishment—as demonstrated by the Commission on Presidential Debates—did not grasp the importance of the Latino community in the future of American politics. In August, when they announced the names of the four journalists selected to moderate the 2012 presidential and vice presidential debates, people were up in arms about the fact that there were no people of color among moderators for the first time since 1996. "I am writing to express disappointment on behalf of the millions of Hispanics who do not have a voice in the upcoming presidential debates as evidenced by the selected moderators announced yesterday," wrote Randy Falco, CEO of Univision in a letter to Janet Brown, head of the Commission on Presidential Debates. Both Mitt Romney and Barack Obama, however, knew that they had to do something for Latino voters and a week later agreed to appear at the first-ever Meet-the-Candidate events hosted by Univision and Facebook to directly address topics of importance to the Hispanic community. The interviews, conducted in Spanish and English, were moderated by Emmy award-winning journalists Maria Elena Salinas and Jorge Ramos, who asked the candidates very tough questions that, in fact, helped define the candidates' positions on key issues such as jobs, health care, and immigration reform.

In addition to the very different positions each candidate had on important Latino issues, perhaps the biggest lesson learned from this past presidential cycle was that you must talk directly to the Hispanic community consistently, authentically, and in their language of preference, which is still predominantly Spanish. Obama's team understood that Hispanics were disillusioned with him, so they started investing in Spanish-language media (broadcast television, radio, and online) as early as March 2012 with messages about what he had been able to accomplish in his first term, which, as we all know, did *not* include immigration reform. Obama's accomplishment message was also being delivered for him by high-profile Latino celebrities like Ricky Martin and Cristina Saralegui, who even spoke at the Democratic Convention. In the end, according to Joe DelGrosso, EVP Managing Director for Univision's Political and Advocacy Group, "direct spending by the Obama campaign garnered a 62 percent share of voice advantage on Univision properties compared to 38 percent for Romney's campaign effort." In Miami, Obama's positive messaging ran unopposed in Spanish language *exclusively* for nearly six months! There is no doubt that this was a key to his winning Dade County and the state of Florida. Romney's combined campaign and affiliated SuperPAC spending in the final four weeks of the campaign slightly offset Obama's share of voice advantage and, according to sources inside the campaign, showed Romney's messaging gaining momentum fast with Hispanics but, by then it was too little and too late.

On Election Day, the Latino vote effect was resounding. "Defying predictions that their participation would be lackluster, Latinos turned out in record numbers on Tuesday and voted for President Obama by broad margins, tipping the balance in at least three swing states and securing their position as an organized force in American politics with the power to move national elections," wrote Julia Preston and Fernanda Santos on November 7, 2012 in *The New York Times*. "Overall, according to exit polls not yet finalized by Edison Research, Mr. Obama won 71 percent of the Hispanic vote while Mitt Romney won 27 percent. The gap of 44 percentage points was even greater than Mr. Obama's 36-point advantage over John McCain in 2008," they added.

When you analyze the data on how the Latino vote helped Obama win key swing states, you realize the *real power* of the Latino vote. As we all know by now, in the key states of Florida, Ohio, Colorado, Nevada, and New Mexico, the Latino electorate overwhelming helped Obama win. Obama took Florida with 58 percent of the Hispanic vote, which raised quite a few eyebrows since much of the pro-Obama vote came from younger Cubans, a community that has traditionally been staunchly Republican. In Ohio, a state in which Latinos only represent 3 percent of the total electorate, 82 percent of Hispanics voted for Obama. According to data from the ImpreMedia-Latino Decisions election night exit poll, the number of votes Obama needed to win Ohio was 103,175 and the number of votes he got from Latinos in Ohio was 103, 481. According to the Speak Our Language Project, a study funded by the United States Hispanic Chambers of Commerce (USHCC) to track political advertising spending in the Hispanic market in 2012, Spanish-language spending on the presidential race was largely confined to ten markets, with most of the money going to Denver, Las Vegas, Miami, Orlando, and Tampa. The total spend in Spanish-language advertising was only 6.2 percent of all the monies spent on the presidential race by both parties. When you remove combined spending by both parties in hotly contested Miami, the combined investment in Spanish-language advertising drops to a paltry 5.4 percent in the remaining markets, where Hispanics represent nearly 16 percent of the total electorate. To put a finer point on it, Obama only lost one swing state, North Carolina, which also happens to be the only swing state where he did *not* spend any money in Spanish-language media, even though the Romney campaign did! Obama needed 97,465 Latino votes to win, and he got only 80,176 Latino votes. Coincidence? I think *not*. If that doesn't send chills down your back, I don't know what will.

But many experts say 2012 was only the tip of the iceberg. According to Pew Hispanic Center projections, Hispanics will account for 40 percent of the growth in the eligible electorate in the U.S. between now and 2030, at which time forty million Hispanics will be eligible to vote, up from 23.7 million now.

The Pew study, *An Awakened Giant: The Hispanic Electorate is Likely to Double by 2030*, published the week after the election, went on to say that "if Hispanics' relatively low voter participation and naturalization rates were to increase to the levels of other groups, the number of votes that Hispanics actually cast in future elections would easily double within two decades."[8]

DECODING LATINO CULTURE

Before we delve deeper into the many aspects of Latino consumers that you must understand in order to win your fair share of the Hispanic wallet, let's first take a step back, way back, and look at the intersection of the American culture and the Hispanic culture in the United States. One of the best parts of my job is working with our research department and other partners who help us uncover unique Hispanic insights that we can use to drive innovation across the enterprise and also share with our clients. In 2011, Truth Consulting NY Inc.,[9] an independent consultancy that helps brands stay culturally connected in order to move businesses forward, conducted a study, "Decoding the Hispanic Culture," to understand how Hispanic culture intersects and coexists with general American culture. Obviously, I will not be able to share with you the whole Truth Culture Decoder™ study, but I will be giving you an overview of what the study uncovered. This study used semiotics, which is the study of how things get to mean what they mean. It analyzes the way signs create meaning in culture. Used for years by consumer product companies in the U.S. and abroad to inform product development and marketing, semiotics is only now being introduced to media and entertainment brands. Semiotics is the art and science of reading, analyzing, interpreting, and explaining the unwritten cultural codes that guide our daily routines and attitudes. For example, the color red in Western cultures signifies danger. In Eastern cultures, the color red signifies good luck; it is a symbol of richness. How the color red is used by brands affects how consumers perceive that brand in the respective cultures. People are usually unaware of these cues, but they can sense when messages are right—or feel dated. By using semiotics to decode a brand's meaning within a larger cultural context, brands gain insight into what consumers expect and want from them. Studies like these keep brands relevant and enable them to lead rather than follow when the culture shifts and society changes.

The objective of this study was to map the shared cultural mindset at the intersection of Hispanic culture and general market culture today. This study examined patterns in culture today and divided them into two different kinds of codes: dominant and residual codes.

Residual codes reflect what is considered the "entrenched mentality" in the U.S. It may not be how *you* think, but it certainly is how *many* people today think. Residual codes aren't necessarily bad, but they are fading into the past. These are ideas that tend to appeal to older, more conservative, less sophisticated, suburban, and rural types of people. They are ideas that have been around for a long time and, by the way, some of these entrenched notions are even shared by the Hispanic community. They are not threatening the status quo, and because of that, they are ripe for use in comedic and satirical contexts.

On the other hand, dominant codes reflect what the world looks like today. They are those things that everyone recognizes, enjoys, and celebrates, even if they don't necessarily like them. They are so prevalent in society today that they dominate the conversation.

Dominant and Residual Views of Hispanic Culture

The residual view of Hispanic culture is that Hispanics live in a world apart. In this view, Latinos are often seen or portrayed as being in opposition to American culture. This residual view of Hispanics is based on fear and helps perpetuate a win/lose notion of culture, where one culture has to lose (American) for the other one to win (Hispanic).

This way of viewing Latinos is very dated and often uses semi-racist Hispanic imagery in mainstream culture, which is still out there. For example, the character of "Chuy Bravo" on *Chelsea Lately* or the over-the-top characters of the now defunct ABC situation comedy *Ugly Betty* are examples of these stereotypes. This comedic version of what Hispanics are goes back as far as the 1970s as evidenced in the "Killer Bees" sketches on *Saturday Night Live*[10] that were satirizing people's fears and playing on cultural stereotypes. Even the adorable Sofia Vergara character on *Modern Family* is residual—so everyone can safely laugh at her. Whenever you see these kinds of tacky Hispanic images—from Hollywood to advertising to TV news—you are seeing residual codes at work.

The dominant view of Hispanic culture is that in which Latinos bring optimism and a sense of belief in the future of America. In the dominant view of Hispanics, Latinos are an important part of America and are often seen or portrayed as those who will make this country stronger and better in the future. When dominant codes are used, you see Latinos and Anglos having fun together, as we see when Cuban-American rapper, Pitbull, appears on the fourth hour of the *Today* show talking to Hoda and Kathy Lee as part of their "Girls Gone Latina" segment[11] or when Tom Hanks went on *Despierta América,* to promote his new movie and ended up dancing with cohost Chiquinrina Delgado while doing the weather with her in Spanish! By the way, the videoclip of that appearance went viral by the time Hanks went on the *David Letterman Show* to promote his movie so he ended up talking about it more than the movie.[12]

The New American Reality™ is: Americaña

So the intersection of where Hispanic culture meets American culture is what Univision calls the New American Reality™. And this reality is best represented by a concept this research calls Americaña. This is not bad Spanglish. Americaña is about being bullish on both cultures. It takes the essence of what we all know as Americana and lifts it to a new level by adding a Latin twist. Americaña is a win-win culture where one can be 100 percent American and 100 percent Latino at the same time. One culture does not succeed at the *expense* of the other. The New American Reality™ is additive, not subtractive.

Truth Consulting visualizes the concept of Americaña with a picture of Justin Bieber and Selena Gomez at a Hollywood movie premiere. They are dressed in black tie and a red gown, looking young and beautiful. Justin and Selena perfectly represent the idea that these two cultures can coexist without conflict. If you think about it, the old Hispanic paradigm was represented by another couple, this one from the '50s: Lucy and Ricky Ricardo. But the *I Love Lucy* show was all about one culture dominating the other. Justin and Selena are Americaña because they are equals. Theirs was a win-win relationship.

There's a new kind of wholesomeness to the New American Reality™ that this country has forgotten about. What you see with Americaña is the Hispanic community embracing the bedrock American values of life, liberty, and the pursuit of happiness through family, home, and hard work. These values are American values that we all believe in, but the way of expressing them in the Hispanic community is slightly different, and that difference is what this study calls Americaña, with an "ñ."

The study examines nine other themes (family, self-image, work, community, pop culture, money, food, men and women, and youth) to

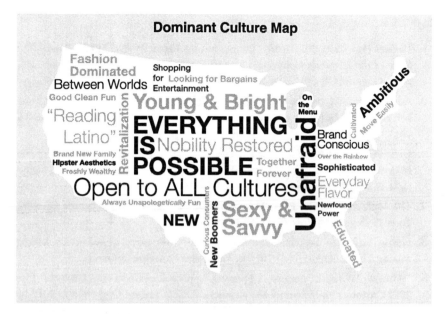

Figure 1.4: The New American Reality: Dominant Culture Map

help us look at today's society with a new set of eyes, one that understands residual and dominant codes. What is more important, you can strive to use these new dominant codes as part of brand communications to establish a stronger connection to today's Hispanics.

Key Takeaways:
- Latinos are no longer an isolated, niche segment; they are a fundamental part of America and a key to the future growth of American business.
- U.S. Hispanics have higher per capita income than all the BRIC countries.
- The Latino vote will be critical to every election cycle going forward.
- There is no longer a mainstream without the Hispanic sensibility.
- The Hispanic community is embracing the bedrock of American values—family, home, and hard work—while exhibiting significant cultural sustainability.

NOTES

1. Nielsen Pop-Facts 2011-2016, "Population by Ethnicity and Single Race," *The State of the Hispanic Consumer: The Hispanic Market Imperative*, Quarter 2, 2012, Copyright © 2012 The Nielsen Company.

2. Advertising 2011 Budget Alignment: Maximizing Impact in the Hispanic Market. Published by the Association of Hispanic Advertising Agencies, www.ahaa. org.

3. CIA *WORLD FACT BOOK*, Estimates Online 2011 cited in *The State of the Hispanic Consumer: The Hispanic Market Imperative*, Quarter 2, 2012, Copyright © 2012 The Nielsen Company.

4. The Multicultural Economy Report 2010, Selig Center for Economic Growth, Terry College of Business, University of Georgia.

5. Latino Influence Project: How Latinos are Influencing Non-Latinos Living Among Them, Copyright © 2012 by Wing and Experian Simmons.

6. "Winning Where It Matters: A Focused Approach to Capturing Growth," The 2012 Customer and Channel Management (CCM) Survey, Copyright © 2012 by the Grocery Manufacturers Association, McKinsey & Company, and Nielsen.

7. Fishel, Ben, "Burn the Mexican Flag!," *Media Matters for America*, March 31, 2006. http://mediamatters.org/research/2006/03/31/savage-burn-the-mexican-flag/135297.

8. Taylor, Paul, Ana Gonzalez-Barrera, Jeffrey S. Passel and Mark Hugo Lopez, An Awakened Giant: The Hispanic Electorate Is Likely to Double by 2030, Copyright © 2012. Published by the Pew Hispanic Center, November 14, 2012. www.pewhispanic.org/2012/11/14/an-awakened-giant-the-hispanic-electorate-is-likely-to-double-by-2030

9. "Decoding the Spanish Culture," *Truth Culture Decoder ™*, Copyright © 2012 Truth Consulting NY Inc., www.truthco.net.

10. "The Killer Bees," *Saturday Night Live*, NBC, www.nbc.com/saturday-night-live/video/the-killer-bees/29161.

11. "Pitbull Beto Perez," *Today*, NBC, www.aoltv.com/2011/08/03/kathie-lee-and-hoda-pitbull-and-beto-perez-today-video.

12. "Tom Hanks Explains His Univision Dance Party," *David Letterman*, CBS, http://gawker.com/5816530/tom-hanks-explains-his-univision-dance-party-to-david-letterman.

2

A BRIEF HISTORY OF LATINOS
IN THE UNITED STATES

Before we talk about the growing Hispanic opportunity, I think some historical context is necessary. Throughout this book you will read about the strong bond Latinos have with the Spanish language and Hispanic "culture." But to fully understand the Hispanic culture of Latinos living in the United States, one must also realize that this culture has also been shaped in part by the historical and political relationship of Spain with Latin America. So, allow me first to take you through a quick review of the history of Spain in Latin America, and how the politics and beliefs of the Spanish empire have come to influence many aspects of today's Hispanic culture, including some very deep-rooted issues of race and class.

THE DISCOVERY

The Spanish conquistadores who came to the Americas were often the sons of noblemen who were not going to inherit titles, lands, or fortunes in Spain; so they ventured to the New World in search of new riches and titles. They were not alone, of course. With them came religious missionaries, military personnel, and seamen whose only desire was to get rich. But the real base of political power always remained in Spain. For more than three hundred years, all the decisions on how to settle, govern, and exploit the New World came directly from the Spanish court in Madrid, subjugating both the colonizers and the colonized to a higher power: the king of Spain and through him, of course, God. So, from the very beginning, class issues permeated the colonization of the Americas. Unfortunately, these class issues still remain today, with 90 percent of the political and economic power concentrated in the hands of 10 percent of the population—the so-called 150 families—who more often than not are the direct descendants of light-skinned Spaniards or other European colonizers.

In terms of race, Latinos have a colorful and seemingly contradictory history. Although Spaniards participated in the slave trade, it was a Spanish slave owner turned missionary who, as early as 1524, became the strongest advocate for the rights of Indians. Bartolomé de las Casas successfully convinced the Spanish Crown to recognize that African slaves and American indigenous peoples had "souls" and that, therefore, the Holy Roman Catholic empire of Spain should grant them human rights. As a result, the Spanish Crown recognized the rights of Indians for the first time in 1542, when the Law of the Indies was enacted. The mixing of races that ensued created the many beautiful shades of brown that now exist across all of Latin America and, of course, in the United States. This mixture of races, once lauded as "the cosmic race" by the great Mexican writer and intellectual Jose Vasconcelos, led the Spanish to an obsession with racial purity, which was demonstrated by the often insulting terms used to "classify" the mixing of racial groups in the New World.

At the top of the list are, of course, the *criollos* or Creoles, the descendants of Europeans who were born in the New World. Although criollos were usually not racially mixed, they were deemed as "less than" by Spaniards since they would never have the power of the peninsular Spaniards or other Caucasian Europeans and, therefore, needed to be classified differently. "The *mestizo* was the child of a white and an Indian," says Carlos Fuentes in his wonderful book, *The Buried Mirror: Reflections on Spain and the New World,* commissioned by the Spanish government to commemorate the 500th anniversary of the discovery of the Americas in 1992. "The *mulatto* (the offensive name was derived from the Spanish word for mule) was the child of a black and a white. The *zambo* was the offspring of an Indian and a black."[1] The terms go on and on, getting more offensive at each turn. Five hundred years of intermarriage and racial mixture in Latin America have created a "brown" skin tone that for many Hispanics no longer has any kind of racial implication. It's simply part of what makes us beautiful. However, when Hispanics come to the United States, they are confronted with America's racist baggage and are often forced to self-identify as belonging to one or another race. This causes a lot of confusion to Latinos who have never been asked questions about their race. The question of race in this country turns even the simplest acts of life—getting a driver's license or registering your kids in school—into a black versus white paradigm that is difficult for Hispanics to understand. That is why Hispanic identity is more closely aligned with country of origin than with ethnic or racial composition, as we will discuss in more detail in Chapter 6.

THE HISPANIC TIPPING POINT

Fast-forward now to the year 2000, when the press touted the crossover success of Ricky Martin, Jennifer Lopez, and Marc Anthony as a "Latin Explosion." The truth is that we've been around for a while. In 1985, when I was fresh out of college, people were calling the eighties the "decade of the Hispanic," but nothing ever came of it, mainly because the Hispanic population hadn't reached "critical mass." Well, now that the 2010 census reaffirmed the incredible growth that took everyone by surprise in 2000, it is evident that while the U.S. population is graying, the youthful Latino population has become the primary feeder of workforce growth and of new consumption in a vast array of categories.

Clearly the influence of Latinos on mainstream America can no longer be denied. But before we get into what that really means, let's take a short trip back in modern history to better understand how current perceptions and stereotypes of the Latino community *in this country* have been formed over the years.

HISTORICAL PERSPECTIVES OF MEXICANS, PUERTO RICANS AND CUBANS

The perception is that Latinos are the latest immigrant group to come to the United States. The reality is that Hispanics have been a part of the fabric of America since before pilgrims landed in Plymouth Rock in 1620. In fact, the city of Saint Augustine was established by Spaniards in 1565 and the city of Santa Fe in 1598. But those facts were rarely mentioned in U.S. history books until well into the twentieth century.

Historically speaking, the first sizable group of Latinos who became "Americans" were of Mexican or Spanish descent. They did so through the conquest and annexation of the American Southwest in 1848, including much of the present day states of New Mexico, Colorado, Utah, Nevada, Arizona, and California. During the California gold rush that followed, thousands of Anglo settlers came west, too. "The mass Anglo-American migration to the West turned the native Spanish-speaking population into a marginalized minority whose 'Americanness' would be challenged well into the next century," writes Gregory Rodriguez, the Director of the Center for Social Cohesion at the New America Foundation, in an essay in *The New York Times*.

People sometimes forget that America is a country of immigrants, and while all immigrants to the United States have had to face prejudice after their arrival, Rodriguez argues that Latino Americans have had to endure wave after wave of anti-Latino sentiment. "Because Mexican labor has been recruited into the United States during boom times and expelled during busts, native-born Mexican Americans have suffered the fallout from campaigns ostensibly aimed at their foreign-born cousins. In the 1930s, the fear that Mexicans were taking jobs from 'real' Americans led to the deportation of more than one million people," adds Rodriguez, who is also the author of *Mongrels, Bastards, Orphans and Vagabonds: Mexican Immigration and the Future of Race in America* (Pantheon). Some scholars now believe that up to 60 percent of those "Mexicans" forced to leave were actually American citizens. As a result of these strong and continuous waves of anti-Latino sentiment, Rodriguez says that many Latino immigrants, especially

Mexicans, were forced to conceal their cultural heritage in order to get ahead. For decades, it was not uncommon for Latinos to claim to be of Italian or Spanish descent in order to avoid hostility while living in the United States.

Between 1965 and 1970, California experienced another surge of growth among its Mexican population, most of it due to the Bracero Program sponsored by the State of California from 1942 to 1964. The Bracero Program allowed "guest" workers to legally come into the United States to live and work. These workers came and stayed for decades, but were never counted in the U.S. Census. For more than twenty years, a good chunk of the population of California officially didn't exist. After the program finished, most of these workers were "invited" back by their employers to become American citizens. As a result, in the census of 1970, the population of the State of California practically doubled.

FLORIDA'S MAMBO

Another state that literally grew overnight was Florida. In the 1960s, hundreds of thousands of Cubans fled to Miami after Fidel Castro took power on December 31, 1959. The sudden influx of many well-to-do Cuban professionals in this sleepy retirement state—until then the playground of rich and famous northerners—began to drastically change Florida forever. Thanks in large measure to the entrepreneurial spirit of its Latino immigrants, Miami today has become the vibrant "Gateway to the Americas." It may have first been the Cubans in the sixties, but in the eighties and nineties many other Latin American groups made Miami their home. In the late seventies and early eighties, after the defeat of the Somoza regime in 1979, well-to-do Nicaraguans began moving to Miami. The eighties also brought another huge wave of Cuban immigrants, this time by way of the Mariel boatlift, as well as a significant increase in the number of well-to-do Colombians fleeing the drug wars back home. Most recently, Miami has become home to wealthy Venezuelans, Mexicans, and Argentines, who are also fleeing the political and economic instability of their homelands. Unlike the

Mexican immigrants of the southwest, the Latino immigrants in the southeast largely comprise educated professionals, business people, and political refugees escaping repressive left-wing governments in Latin America (which broadly explains why Latinos in Florida have gravitated to the Republican Party).

PUERTO RICO: THE 51st STATE?

I am half Puerto Rican and half Spanish. I am very proud of my heritage, but when I talk about Puerto Rico, people seem to be really confused about what Puerto Rico really *is*, besides an island where they can go on vacation without having to take their passports. For the record, Puerto Rico is a commonwealth of the United States, which means it is neither a state nor a sovereign country.

Puerto Rico became a military possession of the United States in 1898, when Spain ceded its colony to the American government at the conclusion of the Spanish-American War. Almost twenty years later, in 1917, Puerto Ricans were given restricted American citizenship via the Jones Act. This meant that Puerto Ricans on the island were considered American but did not have full American citizenship rights, such as the right to vote for the president of the United States. Why would the American government do that? Because they were desperate to find workers who could work in tropical climates, where 'American' workers were dropping like flies, to help out with the construction of the Panama Canal. But it wasn't until the late 1940s that Puerto Ricans started migrating to the United States in droves in search of a better life. They were, however, encouraged by the U.S. government's "Operation Bootstrap" to come and help build New York City. And so more than one million Puerto Ricans came to New York, and quickly became the backbone of the city's manufacturing workforce and subjects of Hollywood films such as *West Side Story*.

At the same time a strong movement toward independence from the United States was growing on the island of Puerto Rico. The U.S. government did not pay too much attention to this movement until

1950, when two men who claimed to be Puerto Rican *independentistas* assaulted the White House in a vain attempt to assassinate President Truman. What ensued was a political debate that tried to appease both sides and ended up creating a unique political status for the island: the commonwealth. The Puerto Rican Constitution, which was ratified by the people of Puerto Rico in 1952 and later approved by the U.S. Congress, states that as a commonwealth, Puerto Rico is an unincorporated territory of the United States that is "free of superior authority in the management of its own local affairs but is linked to the United States of America and hence is part of its political system in a manner compatible with its federal structure." If you are a bit confused by what that exactly means, well, join the crowd.

Here's what you need to know about the commonwealth status. What it really means is that Puerto Ricans are governed by a popularly elected Governor but are subject to U.S. federal laws, although island residents are exempt from some federal taxes. (These tax exemptions helped the island attract many U.S.-based businesses for decades, but as labor costs went up, American businesses moved their operations to lower-cost areas in the Caribbean or Latin America). However—and this is where it gets tricky—Puerto Ricans living on the island cannot vote for the president of the United States, but Puerto Ricans living in the United States *can* and, of course, do exercise their right to vote in whichever state they happen to live. In Congress, the Commonwealth of Puerto Rico is represented by one non-voting member called the resident commissioner. But the truth is that, to this day, Puerto Ricans who live on the island are not even considered part of the population of the United States. (Even the census counts them separately!)

The political status of the island, including the possibility of statehood or independence, has been fodder for heated debates among Puerto Ricans over the past fifty years. In fact, Puerto Ricans have put the question to vote via nonbinding referendums in 1967, 1993, and 1998, with Puerto Ricans always narrowly voting against statehood until last year. Although the Puerto Rican vote for statehood was overshadowed by President Obama's reelection in 2012, it is historic in many ways. On the November 6, 2012 ballot in Puerto Rico, there was a two-part question addressing this issue. The first part of the question asked whether Puerto Ricans supported the island's status as a commonwealth and for the first time 54 percent of Puerto Ricans said no. The second part of the question asked voters to select an alternative and offered three choices: statehood, a semi-autonomous "sovereign free-association," or complete independence. On this part of the question, 61 percent of Puerto Ricans voted for statehood, 33 percent voted for "sovereign free-association," and 6 percent voted for independence. However, one-third of the votes cast on the second question were left blank, leading some to criticize the results (or at least the phrasing of the question on the ballot) and argue that this vote does not really mean Puerto Ricans want to become the fifty-first state. The matter, however, is not entirely up to the Puerto Ricans; in order for Puerto Rico to become the fifty-first state, Congress must act. Statehood for the island would require a two-thirds affirmative vote in each chamber.

The question on many people's minds is, why now? In an interview with CNN two days after the election, Puerto Rico Secretary of State Kenneth McClintock offered some answers. "I think people just came to realize that the current relationship simply does not create the number of jobs that we need," McClintock said, noting that 58 percent of Puerto Ricans now live on the U.S. mainland, in part due to a troubled economy in which there is a 16 percent unemployment rate and few job opportunities for the relatively well-educated population. "When you have a political status that scares away half of your population, it is time to reject that political status," he said.[2] Ironically, Puerto Rico's pro-statehood governor, Luis Fortuño, lost his bid for reelection last November, putting the Popular Democratic Party candidate Alejandro García Padilla—who wants to maintain the commonwealth status—in the governor's office, so once again the path ahead for Puerto Rico is unclear.

But let me leave you with one last thought. Political analysts in both parties should seriously think about what the consequences to the balance of power could be if Puerto Rico became the fifty-first state.

TOSS OUT THE MELTING POTS AND SALAD BOWLS

Latinos are not assimilating as quickly as past groups of immigrants. According to Nielsen, "Hispanics are the largest immigrant group to exhibit significant culture sustainability and are not disappearing into the American melting pot."[3] The "melting pot" theory has been around since the 1870s but became popular around the 1960s. It basically states that the longer an immigrant group stays in the United States, the more it assimilates, melting into the American culture by adopting cultural traits and values of its host country and leaving behind cultural traits and values of its home country. The "salad bowl" theory is more recent and espouses the idea of acculturation, whereby immigrants who come to the United States keep *some* aspects of their culture and values intact while adopting other cultural aspects and values from the United States. Acculturation is one of those terms that I used widely in my last book but now find to be troublesome, mainly because acculturation is an individual process that can not be measured because it involves too many variables: your place of birth, age at emigration, educational background, where you live, and on and on.

The traditional theories—the melting pot and the salad bowl—do not truly reflect what really has happened with multiculturalism in the United States. However, I have found a newer theory that I believe does a better job explaining what really happens to the immigrant and to the host country in this process of assimilation. In their great new book, *Marketing to the New Majority*, David Burgos and Ola Mobolade from Millward Brown, propose a new way of looking at this process, which they call "chicken soup," to stick with food metaphors.

"The problem with the melting pot metaphor is that it tends to reflect more of a historic ideal than the reality of our modern, heterogeneous national identity. The truth is, while many minorities do become part of mainstream American culture, it is often at the expense of their ethnic identities. The salad bowls have a nuanced but decidedly different take on American multiculturalism. They see our society as a mix of distinct but complementary cultures, which together produce a final product that is flavorful and vibrant. But in this metaphor, the individual taste and appearance of each ingredient remains intact after being folded into a larger whole . . . What if we thought of America's multicultural society as a chicken soup? The broth would represent the predominant American ethos, seasoned with distinct cultural influences over the years and now representative of those things we have come to associate with classic Americana—like baseball, hot dogs, and apple pie. The other ingredients, which make the soup substantial and textured, would represent America's ethnic populations."[4]

I love this new metaphor because I believe it more accurately reflects the duality that all immigrants have and that Latinos in particular don't want to let go of. This duality is born from the need to preserve deep-rooted aspects of our native culture, which forms the core of our identity, and the need to adopt some aspects of the culture and values of our new host country which is now our new home. Acculturation is not a linear journey. It is an ongoing and ever-changing process with no particular endpoint; Hispanics don't necessarily want to reach a "fully assimilated" destination.[5] This helps explain why Latinos actively try to keep their culture alive by maintaining their cultural traditions, by teaching their children Spanish, and by keeping in touch and traveling back home. That is why it is better to say that Hispanics are acculturating and will continue to do so for the next fifty years.

All immigrants do this, not only Latinos, so when Burgos and Mobolade say, "We can envision how the natural by-product of America's increasing cultural diversity is the influence of these cultures on one another and on the predominant national culture," I couldn't agree more, just as we saw in Chapter 1 with the Truth Culture Decoder™.

There are many reasons Hispanic immigrants are not assimilating into the American mainstream as fast as other immigrant groups. One reason is the geographic proximity of their homelands, not to mention the shared border between Mexico and the United States, and the relative ease with which travel and commerce between the U.S. and Latin America keeps the Hispanic culture alive. The second reason Latinos have been slower to assimilate than other immigrant groups has been our ability to preserve our language and culture through a strong and growing Spanish-language media. The fact that just in 2012 several large media companies like Fox and CNN have announced major investments in new Spanish-language channels, websites, etc., is an indicator of the strength of Hispanic media within a media landscape that is fragmenting more and more. And of course, technological advances like Skype and social media platforms like Facebook and Twitter help knit an even stronger relationship between people who may be geographically separated but want to stay in touch.

The third reason is obvious: Let's not forget that a steady flow of immigrants also brings approximately 500,000 Spanish-speaking immigrants to this country every year.[6] And finally, as mentioned earlier, the Hispanic community, generation after generation, fiercely holds on to its language and culture. In spite of the fact that 63 percent of Latinos currently are born in the United States versus being foreign-born, 78 percent of Latinos speak Spanish at home, according the Global Insights' Hispanic Monitor.[7] Being Latino and speaking Spanish is now cool and seen as a thing of pride, as opposed to how it was viewed during my parents' generation.

But that doesn't mean we don't fully embrace our American side or refuse to learn English, a popular misconception spread by, well, you know who. In the 2011 National Survey of Latinos, the Pew Hispanic Center noticed some interesting trends in language usage among Latinos. According to the survey, 87 percent of Hispanics believe Hispanic immigrants need to learn English to succeed in the U.S.. But at the same time, nearly all (95 percent) Hispanic adults believe it is important for future generations of Hispanics in the U.S. to be able to speak Spanish. While the figures around the importance of learning English among Hispanic immigrants have not changed since 2002, what is interesting is that the importance of keeping or learning Spanish has increased. "These findings may reflect a recent shift in priorities among Hispanics," says the study. "Today's young Latinos are encouraged to speak Spanish more so than their parents when they were young."[8]

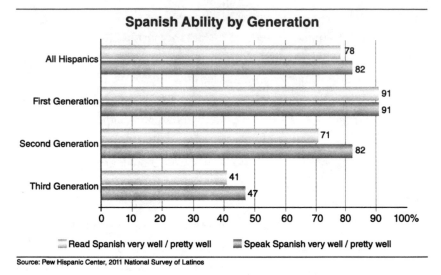

Figure 2.1 Spanish Speaking and Reading Ability by Generation

Even Hispanic millennials (ages 18–34) are holding on to their culture and language. In a first-of-its-kind study about Hispanic millennials published by *Advertising Age* in May 2012, a whopping 85 percent of millennials surveyed said that the language they preferred to speak at home was Spanish and 35 percent said that they often used Spanish to connect and make friends.[9] We will discuss Hispanic millennials and their culture connection in more detail in Chapter 8.

The fact that Hispanics have been able to hold onto their language and their culture has also allowed for Hispanic identity to remain strong with Latinos living in the United States. Hispanic identity is another one of those issues that has been around for a long time and is constantly evolving. "It wasn't until the 1960s and early 1970s that Hispanics started to assert their ethnic identities," says Gregory Rodriguez. "They began to coin terms like 'Chicano' and 'Latino' and used them with pride to identify themselves."

In his book *The Rise of the Hispanic Market in the United States*, Louis E. V. Nevaer explains how the term "Hispanic" first came to be used in the United States. The term was coined by the U.S. Census

Bureau during the Nixon administration, when for the first time it set out to identify and "understand the phenomenon of a permanent Spanish-speaking population." In one fell swoop, the U.S. government began classifying all Hispanics under this generic term, which helped obscure important and fundamental differences between the main subgroups of Latinos in the United States: Mexicans, Puerto Ricans, Cubans, and other Latin Americans. Once they were all grouped under this "Hispanic" label, in the minds of other Americans, Latinos all became one and the same.

As we saw in Chapter 1, the residual notion of Latinos today is that of migrant workers with little or no education who come to America purely for economic reasons. No one can deny that there are some Latinos who fit that description. But that group of Latino immigrants is not the *only* segment of Hispanics in the United States. In fact, the largest segment of Hispanics living in the United States today is made up of predominantly young, educated Latinos who were either born or raised in the United States and who are bilingual and bicultural, representing the dominant notion of Latinos today. But before we get into the nuances of the different segments of Latinos, let's take a look at the big picture: Latino U.S.A.

Key Takeaways:
- Latinos have been part of America since the very beginning of our nation's history; in fact, before America became America.
- The history of the different Hispanic subgroups in America: Mexican, Cuban, and Puerto Rican is important to understand.
- Acculturation is not a linear journey. It is an ongoing and ever-changing process with no particular endpoint, so toss out your melting pot and your salad bowl and embrace the new "chicken soup."
- While identifying as American, Latinos actively try to keep their culture alive by maintaining their cultural traditions, by teaching their children Spanish, and by keeping in touch with friends and family back home.

NOTES

1. Fuentes, Carlos, *The Buried Mirror: Reflections on Spain and the New World*, Copyright © 1992 by Carlos Fuentes. First Mariner Books Edition published 1999. http://books.google.com/books/about/The_Buried_Mirror. html?id=wXuqPwAACAAJ.

2. Castillo, Mariano, "Puerto Ricans Vote for Statehood for the First Time," November 8, 2012, CNN www.cnn.com/2012/11/07/politics/election-puerto-rico/index. html.

3. *The State of the Hispanic Consumer: The Hispanic Market Imperative*, Quarter 2, 2012, Copyright © 2012 The Nielsen Company.

4. Burgos, David and Ola Mobolade, *Marketing to the New Majority, Strategies for a Diverse World*, Copyright © 2011 Millward Brown.

5. Eleta, Graciela and Liz Sanderson, "Hispanic 411: Insights to Grow Your Business," Univision Communications, Inc., Copyright © 2012. http://corporate. univision.com/2011/press/univision-study-reinforces-deep-emotional-connection-bilingual-hispanics-have-with-language-and-culture/#ixzz2EUKByflP.

6. U.S. Census Bureau 2008 National Projections, Released August 14, 2008. Based on Projected Components of Population Change 2010-2050.

7. IHS Global Insight, Hispanic Market Monitor 2011. Based on 2010 Estimates Language Spoken At Home Among Pop 5+. www.ihs.com/products/global-insight/index.aspx.

8. Taylor, Paul, Mark Hugo Lopez, Jessica Hamar Martinez and Gabriel Velasco, "When Labels Don't Fit: Hispanics and Their Views of Identity," Copyright © 2012. Published by the Pew Hispanic Center, April 2012. www.pewhispanic.org/ files/2012/04/PHC-Hispanic-Identity.pdf.

9. Ruiz, Roberto, SVP Brand Solutions, Univision Communications Inc., Hispanic Millennials: Ambassadors of Your Brand, June 2012. http://corporate.univision. com/2012/content-types/articles/hispanic-millennials-ambassadors-of-your-brand/#axzz2J7BMvWE1.

3

~~~~~~

PORTRAIT OF LATINO U.S.A.

The question I get asked most often is: What is the difference between Latino and Hispanic? Let's go straight to
the dictionary and see what it says.

Hispanic (hɪ spænɪk)—**adj** 1. of or relating to the people, speech,
or culture of Spain or of Spain and Portugal 2. of, relating to, or being
a person of Latin American descent living in the United States; *especially*: one of Cuban, Mexican, or Puerto Rican origin.

Latino (læ ti n)—**n** (U.S.) 1. a native or inhabitant of Latin America
2. a person of Latin-American origin living in the United States. Origin:
American Spanish, probably short for *latinoamericano* Latin American.
First Known Use: 1946[1]

The 2010 census has its own definition for these terms, which they
use interchangeably, making things even more confusing:

Census definition: "Hispanic or Latino refers to a person of Cuban,
Mexican, Puerto Rican, South or Central American, or other Spanish
culture or origin regardless of race."[2]

But if you ask me where I am from, I'll probably say I'm Spanish
(because of my mom) or Puerto Rican (because of my dad). You see,
we generally don't use the terms "Hispanic" or "Latino" to identify ourselves. These are terms used by other people to refer to us. Like most

Which term do you use to describe yourself most often?

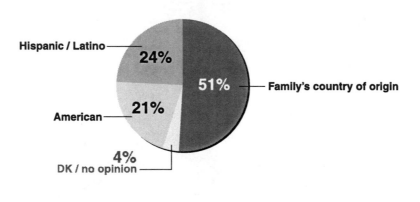

© PEW RESEARCH CENTER

Source: When Labels Don't Fit: Hispanics and Their Views of Identity. Pew Hispanic Center, April 4, 2012

Figure 3.1 Latinos Identify by Country of Origin

immigrants, we usually identify ourselves by our country of origin, the place the family calls home.

In a study published in April 2012, the Pew Hispanic Center found that "nearly four decades since the United States government mandated the use by federal agencies of the terms 'Hispanic' and 'Latino' to categorize Americans who trace their roots to Spanish-speaking countries, about half (51 percent) identify themselves by their country of origin. Only about one-quarter (24 percent) of Hispanic adults identify themselves by Hispanic or Latino."[3] Another 21 percent identify as American (see Figure 3.1). Keep in mind that the term "Latino" appeared on the census form for the first time in the year 2000.

But where all this gets *really* interesting is when we talk about race. According to the Pew Hispanic Center, "When Congress passed Public Law 94-311 in 1976 . . . it was the first and only time in the nation's history that an ethnic group had been singled out in this manner (Rumbaut, 2006). Government agencies also collect data on white, blacks, and Asian Americans, but unlike Hispanics, they are all categorized by the U.S. Bureau of the Census as racial groups. Hispanics are categorized as an ethnic group—meaning they share a common language, culture, and heritage but not a common race."[4]

So when the census and the Pew Hispanic Center asked Latinos how they self-identified in terms of race, the answers they got were very different. Results from the 2010 census indicate that a majority (53 percent) of Hispanics self-identified as white, 37 percent selected "some other race," 6 percent checked the box "two or more races" and 3 percent selected black. But when the Pew Hispanic Center asked a similar question: Which of the following describes your race? 26 percent of Hispanics selected "some other race," 36 percent said they were white, 25 percent said their race was Hispanic/Latino and 10 percent checked the box for Black/Asian, or mixed race. Maybe in our case, race is in the eye of the beholder, but clearly this is a subject that will need further exploration, since as we become a multiracial and multicultural nation, it seems that the labels used by the government simply don't fit as well as perhaps they used to.

How we are categorized is one thing, but what we believe in is an even more important part of who we are. Latinos believe in the same values that all other Americans believe in, starting with the importance of hard work. Like all Americans, we cherish the opportunity to get ahead and raise our children well by giving them a good education. And finally, Latinos believe that, in order to be a better society, we must believe in family and in the idea that we all have an obligation to help those in need.

This chapter will take you through some of the basic demographic data you need in order to better understand the impact that the Hispanic population can have on your community or business. First, we will go over the population growth and geographic distribution of Latinos in the United States, which garners the most media attention. Then, we will briefly go over the major statistics that define this community, such as language usage, household income, buying power, and levels of education, as well as data on employment in the United States.

HISPANIC POPULATION GROWTH

According to the 2010 census, the Hispanic population accounted for 56 percent of the total population growth in the United States, growing from 35.6 million in 2000 to 52 million in 2012. The Latino growth rate from 2000 to 2010 was 47 percent, which is four times the growth rate for the total U.S. population, which was only 5 percent during the same period. In terms of share of population, Hispanics accounted for 16.3 percent of the total U.S. population in 2010, up four percentage points from 2000. African Americans comprised 12.2 percent of the total population, down slightly from 2000, and Asians totaled 4.7 percent of the total population, up from 3.8 percent in 2000. The census projects that the Latino community will continue to grow at a much faster rate than any other group in the United States for the next several decades and will reach 66 million by 2020 and 108 million by 2040. Figure 3.2 gives you the latest snapshot of the racial composition of the United States today and Figure 3.3 shows you the projected growth rates through 2050.

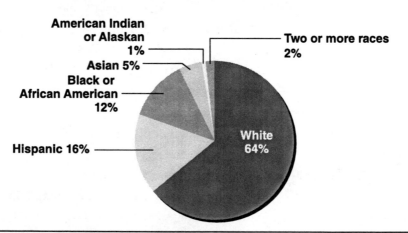

U.S. Population 2010 by Race/Ethincity

Source: US Bureau of the Census 2000 and 2010 Decennial Census.

Figure 3.2 U.S. Population 2010

Hispanic Population
Projected to Be 30% of Total Population by 2050

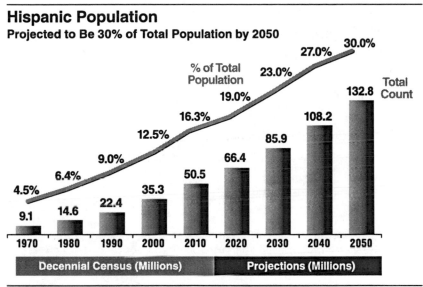

Sources: U.S. Census Bureau, 1970, 1980, 1990, 2000 and 2010 Decennial Census.
U.S. Census Bureau Projections by single year, age, sex, and Hispanic origin Released Auigust 14, 2008

Figure 3.3 Hispanic Population Growth: 1970–2050

Since I wrote my first book in 2005, the Bureau of the Census has revised the projected date by which 51 percent of the U.S. population will be multicultural from 2050 to 2040. As my good friend and fellow author M. Isabel Valdés says in her new book, *Win the Hispanic Market, Strategies for Business Growth*, the 2040 future multicultural consumer is already here, so companies that want to win their fair share of this new consumer's wallet have to start acting now!

BREAKDOWN OF HISPANICS
INTO COUNTRY SUBGROUPS

In an effort to better track the composition of the Hispanic population in the United States, the census has been changing the way it asks the question of "Hispanic origin" with each decennial census. According to the 2010 Census Brief on the Hispanic population, "the 2010 census question on Hispanic origin included five separate response categories and one area where respondents could write in a specific Hispanic origin group. The first response category is intended for respondents who do not identify as Hispanic. The remaining response categories ("Mexican, Mexican Am., Chicano"; "Puerto Rican"; "Cuban"; and "another Hispanic, Latino, or Spanish origin") and write-in answers can be combined to create data for the Office of Management and Budget's category of Hispanic. Yep, it is confusing to understand. So I thought it might help to show you how the question actually appeared on the last census form (see Figure 3.4).

→ **NOTE: Please answer BOTH Question 8 about Hispanic origin and Question 9 about race. For this census, Hispanic origins are not races.**

8. Is Person 1 of Hispanic, Latino, or Spanish origin?

☐ **No,** not of Hispanic, Latino, or Spanish origin
☐ Yes, Mexican, Mexican Am., Chicano
☐ Yes, Puerto Rican
☐ Yes, Cuban
☐ Yes, another Hispanic, Latino, or Spanish origin — *Print origin, for example, Argentinean, Colombian, Dominican, Nicaraguan, Salvadoran, Spaniard, and so on.* ➤

9. What is Person 1's race? *Mark ☒ one or more boxes.*

☐ White
☐ Black, African Am., or Negro
☐ American Indian or Alaska Native — *Print name of enrolled or principal tribe.* ➤

☐ Asian Indian ☐ Japanese ☐ Native Hawaiian
☐ Chinese ☐ Korean ☐ Guamanian or Chamorro
☐ Filipino ☐ Vietnamese ☐ Samoan
☐ Other Asian — *Print race, for example, Hmong, Laotian, Thai, Pakistani, Cambodian, and so on.* ➤ ☐ Other Pacific Islander — *Print race, for example, Fijian, Tongan, and so on.* ➤

☐ Some other race — *Print race.* ➤

Figure 3.4 Race Classification Question on 2010 Census Form

What they were trying to get at was a more accurate breakdown of Latinos by country of origin—based on self-reported responses—and hoping to capture any preference for different "labels" that help people identify themselves, like Chicano or Mexican American versus just Mexican, so I applaud them for the effort. The census also added "negro" to the classifications on the census, which had the black community up in arms and forced Director Robert Graves to issue an apology.[5] These are very touchy issues and, in fact, the idea that the census is only interested in the country of origin of Hispanics also offended some of my Anglo friends who thought their country of origin or heritage was also important.

How the Hispanic origin question is asked is always highly debated because nobody seems to be happy with the results. Of course, the only thing that *really* matters here is race, because the decennial census is used to allocate congressional apportionment, electoral votes and government program funding. Which is why how the question is asked is just as important as how it is answered. But let's not get political.

As we already discussed, for the past four decades, the census has mainly been tracking Hispanics coming from three countries: Mexico, Puerto Rico, and Cuba. All other Hispanics have been lumped together into one group clumsily labeled "other Hispanics." Not surprisingly, this "other" group of Latinos has become increasingly important as it has dramatically grown in size over the past two decades. In fact, today "other Hispanics" represent the second largest subgroup of Latinos in the United States. Unlike the other segments, this "other" group comprises people from many countries in Central and South America, so it is hard to really even consider it a group. Nonetheless, the size of the group is important to note, and depending on what city you are doing business in, it is important to keep in mind the composition of this "other" group (for example Colombians in Miami or Salvadorans in L.A.) as they should be taken into consideration to insure that your hyper-local efforts within the Hispanic market are successful.

Figure 3.5 shows you the current breakdown of Hispanics by country of origin. Figure 3.6 gives you more detail on the total population

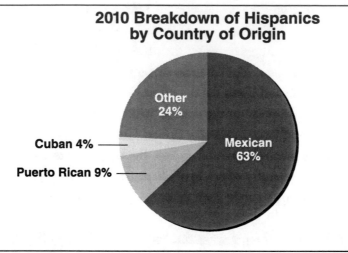

2010 Breakdown of Hispanics by Country of Origin

Other 24%

Cuban 4%

Puerto Rican 9%

Mexican 63%

Source: 2010 Census Briefs, Hispanic Population, issued May 2011

Figure 3.5

counts per country, as well as the change seen from 2000 to 2010, with Mexicans leading the pack, representing over 31 million Latinos in the U.S.

When analyzing the 2010 census data, it is interesting to note that the three main country groups actually increased in size from the 2000 census, in spite of the fact the immigration nearly came to halt during the Great Recession. That just speaks to the power of the Latino baby boom. The total Mexican population increased 54 percent to 31.8 million, from 20.6 million in 2000. Puerto Ricans grew 36 percent, from 3.4 million in 2000 to 4.6 million in 2010, and the Cuban population increased 44 percent, from 1.2 million to 1.8 million in 2010. The "other Hispanics" group slowed down significantly from 2000–2010, only growing by 22 percent, from 10 million to 12.3 million.

GEOGRAPHIC CONCENTRATION

The geographic concentration of the Hispanic population has always been an advantage for marketers, because it enables them to reach this

Hispanic or Latino Origin Population by Type: 2000 and 2010

(For information on confidentiality protection, nonsampling error, and definitions,
see www.census.gov/prod/cen2010/doc/sf1.pdf)

Origin and Type	2000 Number	2000 % of Total	2010 Number	2010 % of Total	Change, 2000 to 2010 Number	Change, 2000 to 2010 %
Hispanic or Latino Origin Total	281,421,906	100.0	308,745,538	100.0	27,323,632	9.7
Hispanic or Latino	35,305,818	12.5	50,477,594	16.3	15,171,776	43.0
Not Hispanic or Latino	246,116,088	87.5	258,267,944	83.7	12,151,856	4.9
Hispanic or Latino by Type Total	35,305,818	100.0	50,477,594	100.0	15,171,776	43.0
Mexican	20,640,711	58.5	31,798,258	63.0	11,157,547	54.1
Puerto Rican	3,406,178	9.6	4,623,716	9.2	1,217,538	35.7
Cuban	1,241,685	3.5	1,785,547	3.5	543,862	43.8
Other Hispanic or Latino	10,017,244	28.4	12,270,073	24.3	2,252,829	22.5
Dominican (Dominican Republic)	764,945	2.2	1,414,703	2.8	649,758	84.9
Central American (excludes Mexican)	1,686,937	4.8	3,998,280	7.9	2,311,343	137.0
Costa Rican	68,588	0.2	126,418	0.3	57,830	84.3
Guatemalan	372,487	1.1	1,044,209	2.1	671,722	180.3
Honduran	217,569	0.6	633,401	1.3	415,832	191.1
Nicaraguan	177,684	0.5	348,202	0.7	170,518	96.0
Panamanian	91,723	0.3	165,456	0.3	73,733	80.4
Salvadoran	655,165	1.9	1,648,968	3.3	993,803	151.7
Other Central American	103,721	0.3	31,626	0.1	−72,095	−69.5
South American	1,353,562	3.8	2,769,434	5.5	1,415,872	104.6
Argentinian	100,864	0.3	224,952	0.4	124,088	123.0
Bolivian	42,068	0.1	99,210	0.2	57,142	135.8
Chilean	68,849	0.2	126,810	0.3	57,961	84.2
Colombian	470,684	1.3	908,734	1.8	438,050	93.1
Ecuadorian	260,559	0.7	564,631	1.1	304,072	116.7
Paraguayan	8,769	—	20,023	—	11,254	128.3
Peruvian	233,926	0.7	531,358	1.1	297,432	127.1
Uruguayan	18,804	0.1	56,884	0.1	38,080	202.5
Venezualan	91,507	0.3	215,023	0.4	123,516	135.0
Other South American	57,532	0.2	21,809	—	−35,723	−62.1
Spaniard	100,135	0.3	635,253	1.3	535,118	534.4
All Other Hispanic or Latino	6,111,665	17.3	3,452,403	6.8	−2,659,262	−43.5

Source: 2010 Census Briefs: The Hispanic Population 2010

Figure 3.6

market more efficiently. However, the 2000 census revealed for the first time a new pattern of growth of Latinos in nontraditional areas. This speaks of the entrepreneurial spirit of this community, willing to go to new places like Virginia and Ohio in search of their American Dream. The 2010 census has seen this pattern continue, and the results can be

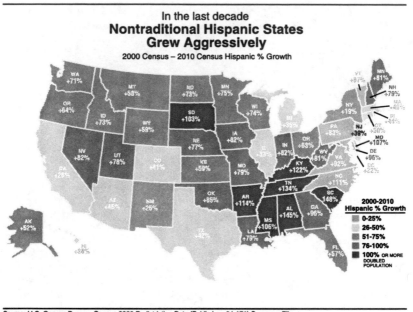

In the last decade
Nontraditional Hispanic States
Grew Aggressively
2000 Census – 2010 Census Hispanic % Growth

Source: U.S. Census Bureau, Census 2000 Redistricting Data (Public Law 94-171) Summary File,
Tables PL1, PL2, PL3, and PL4, and 2010 Census Redistricting Data (Public Law 94-171) Summary File, Tables P1, P2, P3, and P4

Figure 3.7 Growth of Hispanics in Nontraditional Areas

observed most at the state and local level (see Figure 3.7)—which, as we saw in Chapter 1, were also felt at the political level.

While the geographic dispersion in nontraditional areas is an important phenomenon to continue tracking and will most certainly affect specific areas where the Latino population has seen double- or even triple-digit growth, the reality is that the majority of the Latino population is still concentrated in the top eight traditional states. For marketers of national consumer products—goods and services—the good news is that you can still reach 75 percent of Hispanics by focusing your marketing efforts in the eight states with Hispanic populations of one million or more (California, Texas, Florida, New York, Illinois, Arizona, New Jersey, and Colorado). See Figure 3.8. I included Puerto Rico, even though it is not a state, just for comparison purposes.

But it's not only about reaching Latinos in large numbers, it's about the consumer trends that are emerging in those areas, which smart marketers can use to get ahead of the curve and learn from. According

State	2010 Census Hispanic Population Count	2010 Census Hispanic Share Of Total State Population
California	14,013,719	37.6%
Texas	9,460,921	37.6%
Florida	4,223,806	22.5%
Puerto Rico	3,688,455	99.0%
New York	3,416,922	17.6%
Illinois	2,027,578	15.8%
Arizona	1,895,149	29.6%
New Jersey	1,555,144	17.7%
Colorado	1,038,687	20.7%

Sources: U.S. Bureau of the Census, Census 2000 Summary File 1 and 2010 Census Summary File 1

Figure 3.8 States With 1M+ Hispanic Population

to Nielsen, in certain areas within the states with much higher concentrations of Latinos, such as Texas (38 percent), Florida (23 percent), Colorado (21 percent), New Mexico (46 percent) and Nevada (27 percent), "marketers can analyze communities and anticipate new trends that affect a growing portion of their business. In a very real sense, Hispanics are the bellwether for the rest of the country's future."[6]

DISTRIBUTION OF LATINOS BY REGION

While Hispanics can now be found just about anywhere in the United States, Mexicans, Puerto Ricans, and Cubans are all concentrated in different areas. As would be expected, the largest concentrations of Hispanics are in the West (41 percent) and the South (36 percent), followed by the Northeast, home to 14 percent of all Latinos and the Midwest coming in at 9 percent. See Figure 3.9

The most aggressive growth, however, came from the southern states, as seen in Figure 3.10, where eight out of eighteen states saw triple-digit growth rates from 2000.

A word of caution for national marketers doing regional Hispanic efforts: You must keep in mind that even within the key eight states there

Region	Hispanic Population 2000	Hispanic Population 2010	% Change (from 2000 Census)
Northeast			
Northeast Total	5,254,087	6,991,969	33.1%
Region Share of Total	15%	14%	
Midwest			
Midwest Total	3,124,532	4,661,678	49.2%
Region Share of Total	9%	9%	
South			
South Total	11,586,696	18,227,508	57.3%
Region Share of Total	33%	36%	
West			
West Total	15,340,503	20,596,439	34.3%
Region Share of Total	43%	41%	
Total U.S. Hispanic	35,305,818	50,477,594	43.0%

Source: U.S. Bureau of the Census 2000 and 2010 Decennial Census.

Figure 3.9 Hispanic Population by Region.

are important differences among Latino concentrations. While Mexicans certainly dominate much of the South and the West, there are pockets of Salvadorans, Guatemalans, and other Latin Americans to keep in mind. In the Northeast, Puerto Ricans, Dominicans, and Cubans are equally important to keep in mind. And finally, in Florida it would be a mistake to only target Cubans. While still the largest group of Latinos in Miami, Cubans are just one part of the larger mosaic of Latino cultures thriving in the Sunshine State. This does not mean you'll need different creative executions for each group in your advertising efforts. But it does mean that you must be careful with your marketing communication efforts to make sure to use culturally relevant messaging that will resonate with all

South	2000	2010	
Delaware	37,277	73,221	94%
Maryland	**227,916**	**470,632**	**106.5%**
District of Columbia	44,953	54,749	21.8%
Virginia	329,540	631,825	91.7%
North Carolina	**378,963**	**800,120**	**111.1%**
Georgia	435,227	853.689	96.1%
South Carolina	**95,076**	**235,682**	**147.9%**
Florida	2,682,715	4,223,803	57.4%
Kentucky	**59,939**	**132,836**	**121.6%**
Louisiana	107,738	192,560	78.7%
West Virginia	12,279	22,268	81.4%
Mississippi	**39,569**	**81,481**	**105.9%**
Tennessee	**123,838**	**290,059**	**134.2%**
Alabama	**75,830**	**185,602**	**144.8%**
Oklahoma	179,304	332,007	85.2%
Texas	6,669,666	9,460,921	41.8%
Arkansas	**86,866**	**186,050**	**114.2%**
South Total	11,586,696	18,227,508	57.3%
Region share of Total	*33%*	*36%*	

Source: US Bureau of the Census, Census 2000 Redistricting Data (Public Law 94-171) Summary File, Tables PL1, PL2, PL3, and PL4, and 2010 Census Redistricting Data (Public Law 94-171) Summary File, Tables P1, P2, P3, and P4)

Figure 3.10 Growth of Latino Populations in Southern States 2000–2010

Latino groups. As long as your message is based on real Hispanic consumer insight, you will be able to effectively communicate with all groups. Don't worry, we will get into creative best practices in Chapter 8.

And finally, according to Nielsen, the Hispanic growth through 2016 in the top Hispanic demographic metropolitan areas or DMAs (a term used by Nielsen to identify an area of counties in which the home market television stations hold a dominance of total hours viewed) "is approximately two or more times larger than the total population growth, demonstrating their growing influence across many of the country's major markets." See Figure 3.11

YOUTH: OUR SECRET SAUCE

According to the Bureau of the Census, the median age for Hispanics is almost ten years younger than that of the overall U.S. population

Top Hispanic DMA® 2011 and 2016

	2011		2016		2011 to 2016	
	2011 Hispanic Pop. (000)	2011 Total Pop. (000)	2016 Hispanic Pop. (000)	2016 Total Pop. (000)	Present Hispanic Growth	Percent Total Pop. Growth
Los Angeles	7,961	17,741	8,839	18,752	11.0%	5.7%
New York	4,466	21,050	4,788	21,369	7.2%	1.5%
Miami	2,051	4,368	2,269	4,531	10.6%	3.7%
Chicago	1,939	9,742	2,157	9,953	11.2%	2.2%
Houston	2,175	6,333	2,560	6,906	17.7%	9.1%
Dallas	1,979	7,283	2,394	7,936	21.0%	9.0%

Source: Nielsen Pop-Facts, 2011

Figure 3.11 Projected Growth of Top Hispanic DMAs

(median age of Hispanics was 27.7 versus 36.8 for non-Hispanics). When you look at Figure 3.12, you can see how multicultural communities are literally changing the face of the nation's youngest people.

Here's a sobering statistic: in 2010, whites made up 56 percent of young people and 80 percent of seniors. So while the overall U.S. popu-

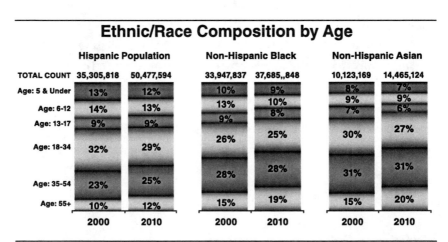

Source: U.S. Decennial Census 2000-2010

Figure 3.12 Comparison of Age/Race Composition-Hispanic, Black and Asian

lation is graying, over 65 percent of Latinos are under the age of 35, and 75 percent are under the age of 45. In fact, Latinos are growing faster than the total population among all age groups, especially among kids under the age of six, teens thirteen to seventeen, and adults thirty-five to fifty-four, as you can see in Figure 3.13.

A different way of looking at these numbers is to look at the share the Hispanic population represents in each age group (Figure 3.14). What's amazing about looking at the data this way is that you can clearly see that, although Latinos overall represent 16 percent of the total population, in every age group from birth through thirty-five years of age, our share per age group is above 20 percent and in the birth to five age group, we represent 25 percent already, according to *Ad Age*'s 2012 Edition of the Hispanic Fact Pack, which analyzed Bureau of the Census data from the 2010 American Community Survey (ACS).

In 2004, the big news demographically was that Hispanics had surpassed African Americans as the largest minority group in the country, several years ahead of when the census had predicted. As

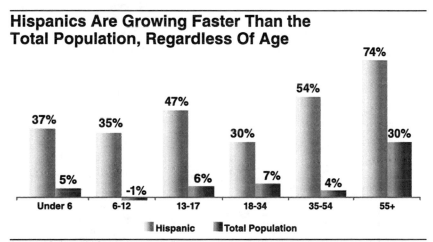

Hispanics Are Growing Faster Than the Total Population, Regardless Of Age

Source: U.S. Decennial Census 2000-2010. Please note some minorities may be experiencing growth, but the Non-Hispanic White population causes decreases for the whole total population.

Figure 3.13

I write this book, the historic demographic shift is that for the first time, in 2012, the total number of births from racial and ethnic minorities have surpassed the total number of births of whites in the United States.

"This is an important landmark," said Roderick Harrison, a former chief of racial statistics at the Bureau of the Census who is now a sociologist at Howard University, in an article published by the *Huffington Post*. "This generation is growing up much more accustomed to diversity than its elders."[7] Hispanics are certainly

Share of 2010 Hispanic Population by Age		
Age	U.S. Hispanic Population in Millions	Hispanics as % of U.S. Population
Under 5	5.1	25.3%
5–9	4.8	23.8
10–14	4.6	22.1
15–19	4.5	20.6
20–24	4.4	20.2
25–29	4.3	20.3
30–34	4.1	20.7
35–44	7.4	17.9
45–54	5.5	12.2
55–64	3.2	8.9
65–74	1.7	7.7
75–84	0.9	6.6
85+	0.3	5.2
Total	50.5	16.3

Source: *Advertising Age*'s Hipanic Fact Pack 2012, Published July 2012

Figure 3.14

Hispanic Growth Is Fueled By Births

Source: U.S. Census Bureau Interim Projections by race and Hispanic origin Release August 2008.

doing their part by contributing 131 births every *hour*, according to a calculation from Nielsen, based on census population projections. However, Hispanic and Asian birth rates have slowed down recently, which has been attributed largely to the lagging economy and a slow down in immigration.

In Figure 3.15 you can see that, even if immigration came to halt, the Latino population would continue to grow in the United States, thanks to our high birth rates, which account for one out of every four children born in the United States today.

HISPANIC HOUSEHOLD INCOMES

Historically, the Latino population has always been thought of as a "poor" population, but new studies show that, in fact, it is quickly climbing up the socioeconomic ladder. In spite of the fact that the Great Recession (2007–2009) has hit many hard, according to Steve Moya, a senior advisor at the Santiago Solutions Group, today 40 percent of Hispanic households earn $50,000 or more.[8] Figure 3.16 shows you how Hispanic median household incomes compare to other race groups categorized by the 2010 census.

Race or Ethnicity	Median Household Income
Hispanic	$40,200
White alone, non-Hispanic	54,200
Black alone, non-Hispanic	33,600
Asian alone, non-Hispanic	67,100
Other, non-Hispanic	50,700
ALL	50,000
Source: U.S. Census 2010 1 yr ACS	

Figure 3.16 Household Income by Race, 2010

The magic number, of course, is $40,000, which signifies entrance to the middle class. Remember, we are a very young population, so you can expect the number of middle-class Latinos to grow exponentially over the next few decades. When you compare Hispanic household incomes from 2000 to 2010 (see Figure 3.17), what you see is a dramatic *decrease* in the percentage of households earning under $35,000 a year and a dramatic *increase* in households earning $75,000 to $100,000.

In fact, when you look at the average household incomes in the top ten Hispanic DMAs, you can see that they are indeed very desirable, ranging from a low of $51,395 in Phoenix to a high of $81,846 in San Francisco.

And finally, in terms of disposable income, according to IHS Global Insight's 2011 Hispanic Market Monitor, Hispanic disposable income grew 52 percent over the past seven years, outpacing the U.S. disposable income growth by 21 percentage points (see Figure 3.19).

In its annual report on the Hispanic market, *Advertising Age* also includes some data on discretionary spending, which they define as "household spending on items such as education, reading, personal care, alcohol, tobacco, apparel, dining out, donations, household furniture, and numerous forms of entertainment." According to the 2012 edition

Hispanics Have Increased Wealth and Spending Power

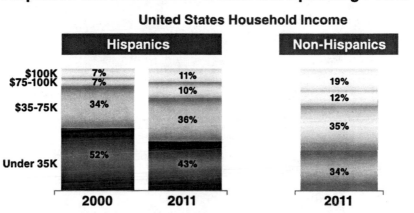

United States Household Income

Source: Nielsen PrimeLocation/Pop-Facts: 2011 Estimates, 2016 Projections

Figure 3.17 More Hispanics in the Middle Class

	Population (000)	Households (000)	Average Household Income
Los Angeles	7,818.8	1,883.9	$68,810
New York City	4,644.6	1,390.6	$64,528
Miami-Ft. Lauderdale	2,089.6	689.7	$68,048
Houston	2,194.3	599.1	$67,208
Chicago	1,975.7	507.5	$66,636
San Francisco-Oakland-San Jose	1,659.4	426.0	$81,846
Dallas-Ft. Worth	1,859.0	483.5	$58,557
San Antonio	1,360.5	396.2	$62,332
Phoenix	1,361.3	368.6	$51,395
San Diego	998.8	252.3	$69,085

Source: IHS Global Insight 2011 Hispanic Market Monitor

Figure 3.18 Hispanic Average Household Income by DMA in 2010

	2005	2012	% Change
U.S. Disposable Income (billions of dollars)	9,277.3	12,156.1	31%
Non-Hispanics Disposable Income	8,489.8	10,957.4	29%
Hispanic Disposable Income	787.6	1,198.7	52%
Source: IHS Global Insight 2011 Hispanic Market Monitor			

Figure 3.19 Projected Growth of Disposable Income 2005–2012

of the Hispanic Fact Pack, Hispanic discretionary spending represents 9.3 percent (up from 8.8 percent in 2011) or $1.52 trillion of total discretionary spending in the United States. But as you can see in Figure 3.20, in many of the top Hispanic DMAs the percentage of Hispanic spending is much higher than the national average, with San Antonio leading the pack at slightly over 50 percent of all spending in that market.

Rank	Selected DMA	Hispanic Spending (in billions)	% of DMA
1	Los Angeles	24	31.4
2	New York	12.3	11.1
3	Miami	10.8	42.5
4	San Antonio	6.2	50.8
5	Chicago	5.5	10.7
6	San Francisco	5.5	11.9
7	Dallas	4.9	14.6
8	Houston	4.3	14.8
9	Washington	1.3	3.1
Source: Hispanic Fact Pack 2012, *Advertising Age*			

Figure 3.20 Hispanic Share of Spending in Top U.S. DMAs

SHIFT FROM FOREIGN-BORN TO
U.S.-BORN LATINOS

The perception in the United States is that the majority of Hispanics are foreign born. While this was true between 1970 and 2000, the tortilla flipped in the middle of the 1990s when the U.S.-born Hispanic population became the majority for the first time. According to the 2010 update of the American Community Survey, 37 percent (almost 19 million) of Hispanics in the United States are foreign-born, down from 40.2 percent in 2002. Two-thirds of Latinos (67 percent) or about 32 million Hispanics are "native" born. Among the foreign-born Hispanic population in 2010, 35 percent entered the United States after 2000, 27.9 percent entered between 1990 and 1999 and another 19 percent came in the 1980s. Figure 3.21 shows you the breakdown of foreign-born vs. U.S.-born Latinos since 1950.

From a marketing perspective, the differences between foreign-born Latinos and U.S.-born Latinos are important to keep in mind. But country of origin is not the only factor to consider. Latino consumer behavior differences are also marked by other factors, like level of education, language usage, and whether they live in a traditional or emerging Hispanic area. I can be born in a foreign country and emigrate at a very young age and still be classified as foreign-born from a marketer's perspective, which would be a mistake since my consumer behavior will actually be closer to Latinos who are U.S.-born. So I recommend that you focus more on understanding exactly who your target market is in terms of age, gender, life stage, etc., and not focus so much on whether they were born here or not. Any good agency worth its salt will help you really understand *who* your target market is and where you can find them, when you are ready.

LANGUAGE PREFERENCE

Language usage and preference continues to be the most controversial of all the key factors to understand when addressing the Hispanic market since it goes to the core of how to speak to your consumer.

	Total Population	Non Hispanic	Total Hispanics	% Entry in Decade Total Hispanic
N/A (Born in the U.S.)	265,214,606	235,250,111	29,964,495	
Before 1950	562,718	437,653	125,065	0.6%
1950–1959	1,440,334	1,020,202	420,132	2.0%
1960–1969	2,766,749	1,619,409	1,147,340	5.5%
1970–1979	4,773,461	2,696,219	2,077,242	10.0%
1980–1989	8,089,636	4,144,238	3,945,398	19.0%
1990–1999	11,628,439	5,843,264	5,785,175	27.9%
2000 or later	14,873,746	7,609,023	7,264,723	35.0%
Year of Entry Total	44,135,083	23,370,008	20,765,075	
				% Native vs. Foreign Born
Native	269,432,814	237,520,349	31,912,465	63%
Foreign born	39,916,875	21,099,770	18,817,105	37%

Source: American Community Survey 2010 1 Year Estimates

Figure 3.21

Much debate goes on every day about language preference and usage, and the data runs the gamut. The problem is that there is no "universally agreed upon" definition for those terms, so it's hard to really know the truth, especially when language proficiency is self-reported. Here's an example. My cleaning lady, who is a Colombian immigrant and has lived in New York City for the past ten years, would answer yes to the question, "Do you consider yourself bilingual?" Granted, she *does* speak some, very limited, English—basically enough to converse with her clients and maybe her landlord and her kids' teachers—but she is *not really* bilingual. She really is more Spanish-dominant than bilingual.

It used to be that studies would classify people as being Spanish-dependent, meaning they *cannot* function properly in an English-only environment, which I think is a better way of measuring primary language. But with the increase of native-born Latinos dominating the demographics over the past two decades, the focus on language preference and usage has turned to how this larger, amorphous group called "bilinguals" behaves. I consider myself bilingual because I can function fully in either language. I can read, write properly, and conduct business in either language and often do, every day. That is not the case with most people who call themselves bilingual. All I am saying is, be careful when looking at data about language usage and preference.

One way to understand if your target is more Spanish dominant or English dominant is by looking into the language spoken at home, although that too can be inaccurate, especially for intermarried couples (where one is Hispanic and the other is non-Hispanic), of which there are more and more each day. In the end, the currency we all deal in as marketers is TV audiences and so Nielsen's definition (with all its flaws) continues to be the gold standard, in my opinion.

The Nielsen Company breaks down the language usage among Hispanic adults by tracking the language in which Hispanics consume media. Their 2012 report shows that a majority of Latinos, 56 percent, still consume media only or mostly in Spanish, but also acknowledges the emergence of English-language viewing amongst Latinos, with 44 percent watching mostly or only in English, as you can see in Figure 3.22. Bottom line, over 60 percent of all Latinos are bilingual and are consuming media in both languages. What makes them choose one language over another is the cultural relevance of the content, and that's why Spanish-language media still has the upper hand.

Perhaps what's even more interesting about the latest Nielsen report is the importance they see in the sustainability of the Spanish language

Language Usage among U.S. Hispanic Adults

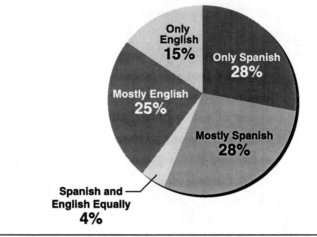

Source: State of the Hispanic Consumer. 2012 Copyright© 2012 The Nielsen Company

Figure 3.22

and Hispanic culture in the U.S. Using data collected by EthniFacts based on a 2011 national survey of Hispanic adults, Nielsen reported the following trends:[9]

- 37 percent of Hispanic adults who spoke English mostly when they were young children indicated that they learned enough Spanish to become bilingual at their present age. These bilingual Hispanics have high rates of wanting to read, watch, and explore more Spanish-language media channels in the next five years.
- Nine out of ten Hispanic parents and parents-to-be want their children to be able to speak Spanish, even though they also want them to become fluent in English.
- 51 percent of Hispanic adults say they speak to their closest friend in Spanish or in both English and Spanish (24 percent).

These findings are in line with other recent studies about the importance of culture, even among the younger, more bilingual millennials. According to *The Culture Connection, How Hispanic Identity Influ-*

ences Millennials, based on primary research conducted by Burke for Univision Communications, Inc. and published by *Advertising Age* in May 2012, Spanish is a social "glue" Hispanic millennials use to cement their social relationships, with 74 percent of "high culturally connected" Hispanic millennials saying "most of my friends can at least understand some Spanish," which was higher, in fact, than non-millennial Hispanics at 63 percent.[10]

ARE THERE SPANISH DIALECTS?

By Roberto Ruiz, SVP Strategy & Insights,
Univision Communications Inc.

A question that many clients ask frequently is what is our point of view on Spanish dialects, and specifically how to handle this issue in communicating with the U.S. Hispanic market. We all know that Hispanics in the United States are a heterogeneous mix of people from Mexican, Caribbean, and Central and South American origins. The issue arises when someone points out that different countries use different "dialects," and asks whether an ad should be written in that specific dialect. The idea of considering the Spanish spoken in Mexico as a "dialect" is shocking to me, as it is equivalent to saying that American English is a dialect. According to Webster's Dictionary, a dialect is "a regional or social variety of a language distinguished by pronunciation, grammar, or vocabulary, especially a variety of speech differing from the standard literary language or speech pattern of the culture in which it exists: Cockney is a dialect of English."

If we follow this definition it would be possible to have many dialects of Spanish. However, the definition is vague in terms of how much variation is needed to qualify for the term. As Webster's was of little help, I contacted other experts. Mila Ramos-Santacruz, who holds a doctorate in linguistics from Georgetown University, gave me some good advice. She explains that the word "dialect" has political connotations because it subordinates one language to another; hence, the term is seldom used. Also, from a linguistic perspective, the Spanish language is an absolute reference that nobody actually uses. What people use are local variations of the language. Thus Mexican Spanish, Argentine Spanish, etc., are all local variations of Spanish, as opposed to dialects of it. For example, in Mexico a bus is called camión, a word that in other Latin countries means "truck."

From a communications perspective we recommend using a variation-free Spanish when targeting the whole market. In those cases where marketers are trying to reach a specific segment—say, people of Mexican origin—using terms that are exclusive to this group can make the message stronger by striking a chord of familiarity and generating a more emotional bond. However, in those cases, one has to be careful in one's choice of words so as not to alienate or insult other groups by using words that may have different meanings or interpretations. In any case, we all have to be sensitive to using the Spanish language in a way that preserves its integrity but reaches our target consumer. After all, Spanish is one of the strongest links that unite this community, and if we damage it, we will weaken our cultural bond forever.

HISPANIC BUYING POWER

The Hispanic community's buying power is soaring. According to the Selig Center for Economic Growth, which publishes the "Multicultural Economy" report every couple of years, the Hispanic buying power surpassed the African American buying power in 2006. Demographics will continue to drive the brisk growth in Hispanic buying power over the next decade as proportionately more Hispanics enter the workforce for the first time or move up in their careers. Also census data show that Hispanic households are substantially larger than non-Hispanic households (3.2 persons per household vs. 2.4 persons for non-Hispanics), and have nearly twice as many children under eighteen. So, despite lower average incomes, Hispanics spend more than non-Hispanics in many categories including: dining out, housing, utilities, and transportation.

In fact, IBISWorld published a special report in August 2011 in which they forecast that in the United States over twenty industries in seven different sectors could benefit from the growing buying power of Hispanics, if they are able to capture a substantial share of this growing market. The seven sectors identified by IBISWorld are: food (grocery and restaurants), retail (especially clothing and electronics), education (higher education and technical schools), financial services, real estate, transportation (both automotive and airlines), entertainment (sports and movies), and media (TV, advertising, and magazines). These are all very important sectors of the American economy and yet not all of them are actively marketing to Hispanics.

"For more than two decades, Hispanic buying power growth has outstripped that of the general population. Despite difficulties during and following the recession of 2009, buying power of Hispanics continues to escalate steeply," writes Brian Bueno, author of the report "The Growing Hispanic Population Means Big Business for These 7 Sectors." "Over the next five years, the nation's buying power is projected to grow 27.5 percent to $14.7 trillion, while that of the Hispanic population is forecast to grow 48.1 percent to $1.6 trillion."

This Latino boom we are experiencing is very similar to the baby boom of the fifties, with a large and growing number of Americans entering the household formation stage. The Latino boom means that a majority of Latinos are transitioning from single, to married, to parents—three life stages where purchasing power is at its height. In fact, according to the founders of the Latinum Network, a think-tank-like network for companies that work in the Hispanic/multicultural space, "over the past decade, U.S. Hispanic spending has increased as much as $100 billion every few years."[11]

EDUCATION

The headline of June 13, 2012 in *U.S. News and World Report* is a bit misleading: GRADUATION RATE INCREASE PROPELLED BY LATINO ACHIEVEMENT. The fact is that while high school graduation rates for Latino students have increased steadily over the past couple of years—increasing a stunning 10 percent from 2008 to 2010 alone—only 73 percent of Latino students received a high school diploma in the graduating class of 2010, the latest for which statistics are available, compared to 79 percent of white students and 81 percent of Asian American students. The fact is that bridging the educational gap of Latino students is now seen as a demographic imperative for this country.

The Bureau of the Census predicts that by 2021, one in four students in the U.S. will be Hispanic. In key states like Texas and California, already half of the school-age population is Latino, so the future is already here. And the reality is this: as a country, we can not allow the fastest growing ethnic group to also be the least educated because our nation's future partly depends on us. So let's face the facts and work to close the educational gap among Latinos and other minorities.

"The future of America is in this question," said Stephen Klineberg of Rice University in Houston, a sociologist who has studied the economic and political implications of changing demographics, in an article written by Ronald Brownstein for the *National Journal*. "Will the Baby Boomers recognize that they have a responsibility and a personal stake in ensuring that this next generation of largely Latino and African American kids is prepared to succeed? This ethnic transformation could be the greatest asset this country will have, with a young, multilingual, well-educated workforce. Or it could tear us apart and become a major liability."[12]

The irony is that both young Latinos and their parents believe that education is very important for success in life. In fact, nine in ten (89 percent) Latinos believe that in order to get ahead in life these days, it is necessary to get a college degree. That is 15 percent higher than the general population (74 percent). However, in 2009, only 48 percent of Latinos planned to go to college versus 60 percent of the general population, according to a study published by the Pew Hispanic Center.[13] The good news is that more and more people in schools, government, and business are aware of the educational gaps and are starting to work on solutions to help Latino students and families overcome some very real obstacles they face when trying to accomplish this part of their American Dream.

According to Patricia Gándara, author of the article "The Latino Education Crisis" published in *Educational Leadership* in February 2010, "from their first day of kindergarten to their last day of school, Latinos, on average, perform far below most of their peers." Among the issues that Gándara identifies as hurting Latino academic achievement are: lack of access to preschool education and dual language immersion programs, overall lower parental education, and the need for stronger support systems for Latino students while they are in school.

The Pew Hispanic Center identified some other external issues that also negatively affect Latino educational achievement. According to them, nearly three-quarters (74 percent) of Hispanics between the ages of sixteen and twenty-five in a 2009 study said they had to cut short their education in order to help support their family, and 49 percent said their English skills were too limited to pursue a college education. Some of the other reasons why Latinos do not continue their schooling are listed in Figure 3.23.

I know from my colleague Mariela Dabbah, founder of Latinos in College, a not-for-profit organization whose goal is to help students and families find every resource available to succeed in higher education, that lack of knowledge of how to apply for college and pay for it is a huge obstacle for Latino families. This is why she conducts parent workshops in schools across the country to empower thousands of Latino families to support their children through college. So it's interesting to see the results of this Pew survey when Hispanics were asked why they thought

Why Not Continue Your Education?

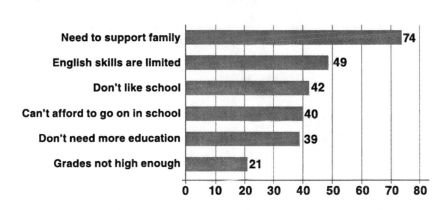

Source: Latinos and Education: Explaining the Attainment Gap, Pew Hispanic Center, October 7, 2009

Figure 3.23 Reasons Why Latinos Don't go to College

Latinos didn't do so well in school (See Figure 3.24). The top reasons mentioned were poor parenting or lack of parental involvement, poor English skills and different cultural backgrounds than their teachers.

But perhaps the most troubling statistic in the study was the notable increase in motherhood among young immigrant Latinas. "In 2007, 29 percent of all immigrant female Hispanics ages sixteen to twenty-five were mothers, compared to 17 percent of native-born female Hispanics and 12 percent of white females" (Fry 2009). The differences in educational achievement among foreign-born and native Hispanics are explored further and interesting to note here.

The good news is that native-born Latinos are faring much better than their immigrant counterparts, with 60 percent of native-born Hispanics eighteen to twenty-five saying they plan to get a college degree in 2009 versus only 29 percent of immigrant Latinos. More encouraging is the news from the Pew Hispanic Center's 2011 study on Hispanic College Enrollment, which reported a 24 percent spike in Latino college enrollments from 2009 to 2010, narrowing the gap significantly with other groups. Driven by a single-year surge of 24 percent in Hispanic enrollment, the number of eighteen- to twenty-four-year-olds attending college in the United States hit an all-time high of 12.2 million in

Major reasons why Hispanics don't do well in school	Latino Youth 16-25	Latino Adults 16 and older
Parents of Hispanic students don't play an active role	47%	61%
Hispanic students know less English	43%	58%
Too many teachers don't know how to work with Hispanic students	44%	47%
Hispanic students don't work as hard as others	31%	41%
Source: Latinos and Education: Explaining the Attainment Gap, Pew Hispanic Center		

Figure 3.24

October 2010, according to a Pew Hispanic Center analysis of recently released data from the U.S. Bureau of the Census.

"Much of this growth in college enrollment among young Hispanics has been at community colleges," writes Richard Fry, author of the 2011 Pew Hispanic report. "Of all young Hispanics who were attending college last October, some 46 percent were at a two-year college and 54 percent were at a four-year college. By contrast, among young white college students, 73 percent were enrolled in a four-year college, as were 78 percent of young Asian college students and 63 percent of young black college students."[14]

That is good news and I believe that efforts by large foundations and other corporations behind education achievement, such as the one the Gates Foundation does with Univision called *Es El Momento* or NBC/Telemundo's Education Nation/El Poder del Saber, do great work to elevate the conversation among Latinos about the importance of education and overcome perceived obstacles to getting a college education. According to Nielsen, the number of Hispanic college graduates is expected to double between 2000 and 2016 (Figure 3.25). Let's hope so. Our future as a nation literally depends on it, as you will see in the next section.

EMPLOYMENT

Critics and bigots argue that the constant flow of poorly educated, non-English-speaking immigrants undermines the U.S. economy when, in fact, it does just the opposite. The reality is that the influx of low-skilled workers in the United States not only keeps gardens and houses clean, these immigrants (regardless of whether they are Hispanic, Asian, or Eastern European) do the jobs nobody else wants to do—but everybody needs. When it comes to workforce participation, the truth is that Latinos will play an important role when it comes to replacing the tsunami of retiring Baby Boomers over the next two decades. According to "The Latino Labor Force at a Glance" report released by the Department of Labor's Bureau of Labor Statistics (BLS) in April 2012, 23 million

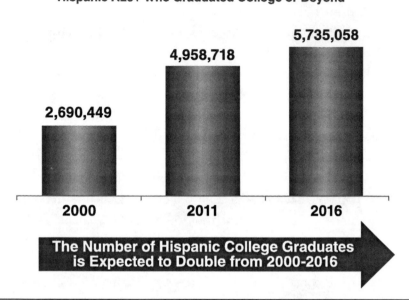

Hispanics Are Storming the College Campuses
Hispanic A25+ Who Graduated College or Beyond

Source: Nielsen PrimeLocation/Pop-Facts: 2000 Data, 2011 Estimates, 2016 Projections; Base: U.S. Hispanic A25+

Figure 3.25 Hispanic College Graduation Rates

Latinos were working in 2011, representing 15 percent of the U.S. labor force. By 2020, Hispanics are expected to comprise 19 percent of the U.S. labor force.

Hispanics already have the highest rate of labor force participation across any race or ethnicity with 67.5 percent in 2010, and according to the BLS, they will be the only ethnic or racial group whose workforce participation will go up by 2020. By comparison, the labor force participation of whites was 65.1 percent in 2010 and will be going down to 62.8 percent in 2020. For blacks it was 62.2 percent in 2010, also going down to 60.3 percent in 2020, and finally for Asians it was 64.7 percent in 2010 going down to 63.1 percent in 2020.

According to Rakesh Kochhar, who writes about social and demographic trends for the Pew Research Center, "from 2010 to 2020, His-

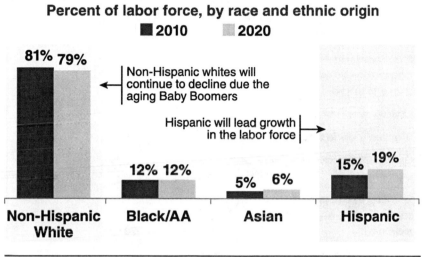

Hispanics will Help Replenish the Aging Workforce

Percent of labor force, by race and ethnic origin
■ 2010   2020

81% 79%

Non-Hispanic whites will
continue to decline due the
aging Baby Boomers

Hispanic will lead growth
in the labor force

12% 12%

5% 6%

15% 19%

Non-Hispanic   Black/AA   Asian   Hispanic
White

Source: BLS Division of Industry Employment Projections 2010-2020

Figure 3.26 Increased Hispanic Participation in the Labor Force

panics are expected to add 7.7 million workers to the labor force, while
the number of non-Hispanic whites in the labor force is projected to
decrease by 1.6 million. Consequently, Hispanics will account for the
vast majority—74 percent—of the 10.5 million workers added to the
labor force from 2010 to 2020. That share is higher than in the previous
two decades. Hispanics accounted for 36 percent of the total increase
in the labor force from 1990 to 2000 and for 54 percent from 2000 to
2010."[15]

In Figure 3.27 you can see how Latinos are more likely than whites
or African Americans to be employed in the private sector. Employed
Latinos are also much less likely to have a college degree than are either
whites or African Americans. This is partly due to the educational gap
we just talked about, which unfortunately had widened between 2000
and 2011. According to the BLS, the gap between employed whites
with a college education and employed Latinos with a college education

	Latinos (%)	Whites (%)	African Americans (%)
Characteristics of the employed			
Employed (employment-population ratio among those 16 and older)	58.9	59.4	51.7
Usually working part-time	18.9	19.9	18.0
Women (age 16 and over)	40.6	46.0	53.8
College graduates (age 25 and over)	16.7	36.1	26.0
Working in the private sector (wage and salary workers)	83.7	78.5	76.9
Working in the public sector	10.4	14.2	19.3
Self-employed (unincorporated)	5.8	7.2	3.8
Weekly earnings			
Total	$549	$775	$615
Men	$571	$856	$653
Women	$518	$703	$595
Characteristics of the unemployed			
Unemployment rate	11.5	7.9	15.8
Women (age 16 and over)	41.9	43.0	46.9
Median duration of unemployment (in weeks)	18.5	19.7	27.0
Long-term unemployed (27 weeks or more)	39.9	41.7	49.5

Source: Bureau of Labor Statistics, Current Population Survey
Note: Persons whose ethnicity is identified as Hispanic or Latino may be of any race. Those identified as White or Black includes those Latinos who selected White or Black when queried about their race.

Figure 3.27 Unemployment, Employment, and Earnings Characteristics by Race and Latino Ethnicity, 2011 Annual Averages

grew from 17.6 percentage points to 20.1 percentage points. However, according to the most recent estimates of college enrollment from the October Current Population Survey (CPS), Hispanic college enrollments jumped 24 percent between 2009 and 2010, which will hopefully help narrow that gap somewhat in the next couple of years.

And finally, the Latino entrepreneurial spirit is still alive and well, and probably one of the growing sources of employment for the future. According to the most recent Bureau of the Census Survey of Business Owners (2007), Latino-owned businesses were the fastest growing small-business sector prior to the recession; expanding at twice the rate of the national average between 2002 and 2007 (see Figure 3.28). "The number of Hispanic-owned businesses in the United States increased by 43.7 percent to 2.3 million, more than twice the national rate of 18.0 percent between 2002 and 2007," the U.S. Bureau of the Census announced in September 2010. "Hispanic-owned businesses generated $345.2 billion in sales in 2007, up 55.5 percent compared with 2002. The number of Hispanic-owned businesses with receipts of $1 million or more increased 51.6 percent—from 29,168 to 44,206 businesses between 2002 and 2007."

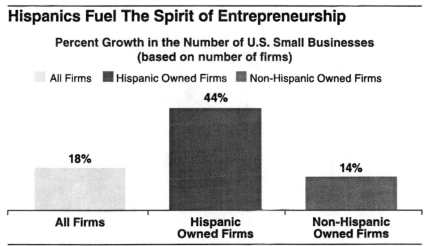

Hispanics Fuel The Spirit of Entrepreneurship

**Percent Growth in the Number of U.S. Small Businesses
(based on number of firms)**

All Firms ■ Hispanic Owned Firms ■ Non-Hispanic Owned Firms

44%

18%

14%

| All Firms | Hispanic Owned Firms | Non-Hispanic Owned Firms |

Source: U.S. Census Bureau Survey of Small Business Owners, 2002, 2007 Preliminary Statistis

Figure 3.28 Hispanic-Owned Businesses Growing Faster

According to the "Survey of Business Owners: Hispanic-Owned Businesses: 2007", nearly half of all Hispanic-owned businesses (45.8 percent) were owned by people of Mexican descent. Cubans were owners of 11.1 percent of all Hispanic-owned businesses, followed by Puerto Ricans at 6.9 percent. The other 34.5 percent of Hispanic-owned businesses were owned by people of "other" Hispanic origin. While the vast majority of these businesses had no paid employees, they still generated over $70 billion in receipts, an increase of 66.6 percent since 2002. Meanwhile, the number of Hispanic-owned businesses with one hundred or more employees increased by 26.4 percent and generated $74.2 billion in revenues, an increase of 76.6 percent from 2002. Figure 3.29 shows you a breakdown of the largest industry sectors of Hispanic-owned businesses, according to census data. For a look at the states where Hispanic businesses have been growing, see Figure 3.30.

Industries Accounting for the Highest Number of Hispanic-Owned Businesses: 2007

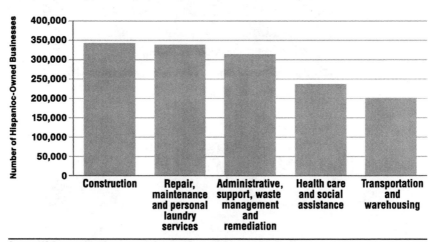

Source: US Bureau of the Census, 2007 Survey of Business Owners, Hispanic-Owned

Figure 3.29 Hispanic-Owned Business by Industry

Hispanic-Owned Firms

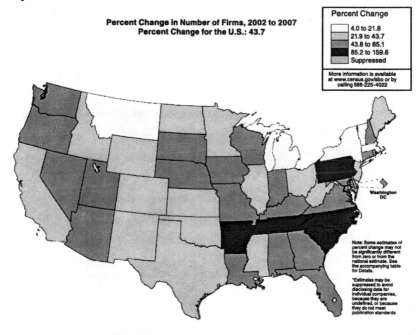

Percent Change in Number of Firms, 2002 to 2007
Percent Change for the U.S.: 43.7

Percent Change
- 4.0 to 21.8
- 21.9 to 43.7
- 43.8 to 85.1
- 85.2 to 159.6
- Suppressed

More information is available at www.census.gov/sbo or by calling 888-225-4022

Note: Some estimates of percent change may not be significantly different from zero or from the national estimate. See the accompanying table for Details.

*Estimates may be suppressed to avoid disclosing data for individual companies, because they are undefined, or because they do not meet publication standards

Source: U.S. Census Bureau, 2007 Survey fo Business Owners and 2002 Survey of Business Owners

Figure 3.30 Geographic Distribution of Hispanic-Owned Businesses

Key Takeaways:

- Latinos are fueling the population growth of the United States and are projected to reach 66 million by 2020.
- Mexicans account for 63 percent of all Latinos in the United States followed by "other" Latin Americans at 24 percent, 9 percent are Puerto Rican, and 4 percent are Cuban.
- California (14M), Texas (9.5M), Florida (4.2M), New York (3.4M), Illinois (2M), Arizona (1.9M), New Jersey (1.5M), and Colorado (1M) each have more than 1 million Latinos.
- 60 percent of Latinos are under the age of thirty-five and represent 20–25 percent of all age groups under thirty-five.

- 40 percent of Hispanic households earn $50,000 or more, and the average Hispanic household income in the top ten DMAs ranges from $51,000 to $81,000.
- Since 2000, U.S.-born Latinos have been fueling the growth of the Hispanic population with foreign-born Latinos accounting for only 37 percent.
- 56 percent of Latinos consume media mostly or only in Spanish while 44 percent consume media mostly or only in English.
- The Hispanic educational gap is a threat to America's future economic prosperity.
- Hispanics will account for the vast majority—74 percent—of the 10.5 million workers added to the labor force from 2010 to 2020.
- Hispanic-owned businesses grew by 44 percent between 2002–2007 and accounted for $345.2 billion in receipts in 2007.

NOTES

1. *Merriam-Webster Online.* Copyright © 2012 Merriam-Webster, Inc. www.Merriam-Webster.com.

2. U.S. Census Bureau, 2010 Census Briefs: The Hispanic Population: 2010. Issued May 2011. www.census.gov/prod/cen2010/briefs/c2010br-04.pdf.

3. Taylor, Paul, Mark Hugo Lopez, Jessica Hamar Martinez and Gabriel Velasco, "When Labels Don't Fit: Hispanics and Their Views of Identity," Copyright © 2012, The Pew Hispanic Center. www.pewhispanic.org/files/2012/04/PHC-Hispanic-Identity.pdf

4. Taylor, Paul, Mark Hugo Lopez, Jessica Hamar Martinez and Gabriel Velasco, "When Labels Don't Fit: Hispanics and Their Views of Identity," Copyright © 2012, The Pew Hispanic Center. www.pewhispanic.org/files/2012/04/PHC-Hispanic-Identity.pdf

5. Caldwell, Robin, "Bureau of the Census Apologies for 'Negro' Classification on Form," *Politic365.com*, March 30 2010. http://politic365.com/2010/03/30/census-bureau-apologizes-for-negro-classification-on-form.

6. *The State of the Hispanic Consumer: The Hispanic Market Imperative,* Quarter 2, 2012 Copyright © 2012 The Nielsen Company.

7. Yen, Hope, "Minority Birth Rate: Racial and Ethnic Minorities Surpass Whites in US Births for the First Time, Census Reports" *Huffington Post,* May 17, 2012. www.huffingtonpost.com/2012/05/17/census-minority-birth-rate_n_1523150.html.

8. Valdés, M. Isabel, *WIN! the Hispanic Market: Strategies for Business Growth*, Copyright © 2011. Published by Paramount Market Publishing, Inc., January, 2012.

9. *The State of the Hispanic Consumer: The Hispanic Market Imperative*, Quarter 2, 2012 Copyright © 2012 The Nielsen Company.

10. Kerwin, Ann Marie, "The Cultural Connection: How Hispanic Identity Influences Millennials," *Ad Age*, May 22, 2012. http://adage.com/article/hispanic-marketing/cultural-connection/234904.

11. Klein, Michael and David Wellisch, "Why Wall Street Will Look at Your Hispanic Strategy" in *WIN! the Hispanic Market: Strategies for Business Growth*, by M. Isabel Valdés, Copyright © 2011. Published by Paramount Market Publishing, Inc., January, 2012.

12. Brownstein, Ronald, "The Gray and the Brown: The Generational Mismatch," *National Journal*, July 24, 2010. www.nationaljournal.com/magazine/the-gray-and-the-brown-the-generational-mismatch-20100724.

13. Lopez, Mark Hugo, Latinos and Education: Explaining the Attainment Gap, Copyright © 2009. Published by the Pew Hispanic Center, October 7, 2009. www.pewhispanic.org/2009/10/07/latinos-and-education-explaining-the-attainment-gap.

14. Fry, Richard, The Changing Pathways of Hispanic Youths into Adulthood, Copyright © 2009. Published by the Pew Hispanic Center, October 7, 2009. www.pewhispanic.org/2009/10/07/the-changing-pathways-of-hispanic-youths-into-adulthood.

15. Kochhar, Rakesh, "Labor Force Growth Slows, Hispanic Share Grows," *All Things Census*, Pew Research Social & Demographic Trends, the Pew Research Center, February 13, 2012 http: www.pewsocialtrends.org/2012/02/13/labor-force-growth-slows-hispanic-share-grows-2.

4

HOW TO CAPITALIZE ON THE HISPANIC OPPORTUNITY

A s a group, Hispanics are a marketer's dream come true. Latinos are highly concentrated in a few urban areas, which makes them easy to reach. They are also approximately twelve years younger than their non-Hispanic counterparts (forty vs. twenty-eight median age), presenting marketers with new opportunities to build brand loyalty and generate domestic revenue growth for their brands long term. But the true economic clout of the Hispanic community comes from its larger households. Hispanics in the United States have an average of 3.4 persons per household versus 2.4 persons for non-Hispanic households. Add to that the fact that 54 percent of Hispanic households have children under the age of 18 at home vs. only 31 percent of Non-Hispanics and that 44 percent of Hispanic households have dual incomes vs. 35 percent of non-Hispanics[1] and it is easy to see why Hispanics are America's *über* consumers, buying more of everything from groceries to apparel, electronics, accessories, and cars.

Why aren't more companies capitalizing on their Hispanic opportunity today? Well, mainly because not many companies are marketing to the Latino community. And among those companies that do market their products and services, one of the biggest challenges they face is failing to understand that Hispanic consumers behave differently from their general market counterparts. The days of one-size-fits-all marketing plans are over. According to Nielsen, "Hispanic product con-

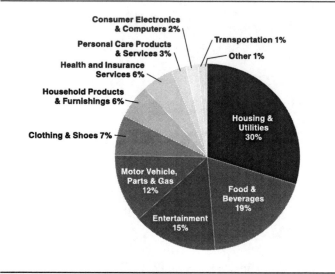

Source: IHS Global Insights Hispanic Monitor, 2011

Figure 4.1 Hispanic Consumer Spending 2010

sumption is indeed unique in many respects, and well differentiated in comparison to other U.S. consumers. Hispanics don't necessarily mirror consumption patterns of all consumers and, therefore, it is essential to understand their needs, wants, and shopping tendencies."[2] For example, an easy assumption to make is that, because Latinos cook from scratch at home more often than non-Hispanics, they would go to the grocery store more often or that they would spend more on promotional items. Although some research supports this assumption, according to Nielsen and other syndicated sources, this is actually not the case. "Across all retail channels, Hispanics tend to shop less often, but spend more per trip and are less likely to buy products at promotional prices," says Nielsen in its report "The State of the Hispanic Consumer: Hispanic Market Imperative." As you can see in Figure 4.2, this is true for both English-preferred and Spanish-preferred Hispanics.

With higher basket share overall, brands themselves, as well as their retailer partners, must do everything they can to attract Hispanics to products and stores. As the retail environment becomes more fragmented and more sophisticated in its product mix and offerings,

Shopping Trips and Dollars per Trip
Total Retail Channels

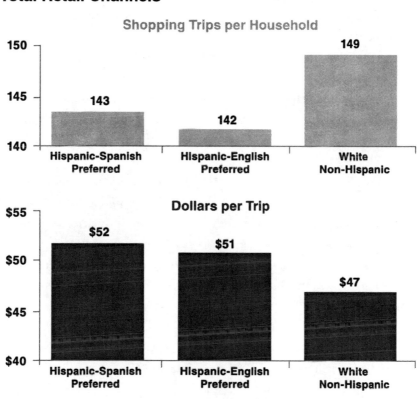

Source: Nielsen Homescan®, Total U.S.; 52 weeks ending 12/25/2011

Figure 4.2

retailers and marketers must do everything they can to develop stronger connections with the Hispanic consumer, especially since Hispanic families tend to be more brand loyal and often do shop in specific channels to fulfill specific needs.

According to the "Diverse and Distinct" report written in 2010 by Staci Covkin, Principal, Consumer & Shopper Insights for Symphony-IRI Group, now is the time to start focusing on how to capture the growing Latino consumer spending. "Hispanics spent more than $135 billion on consumer packaged goods. And projections indicate that this figure will rise 25 percent by 2020[3] ... On the whole, growth in average spend by Hispanic shoppers is outpacing that of non-Hispanic shoppers, with a 3 percent increase in spend for families versus less than 1 percent in the general population," says Covkin.

The Nielsen Company agrees with Covkin, and in Figure 4.3 you can see just how much more Hispanics over-index on certain product categories. Among the list of the Top 10 Hispanic Product Categories, according to Nielsen Homescan®, you will find certain food products, baby products, hair care and toiletries—all of which have cultural relevance for Latinos.

Clearly, in order to win share with this community, both manufacturers and retailers need to work together and better understand how Hispanic shoppers think and how they behave differently across channels. The SymphonyIRI report goes on to say that treating this population as a homogenous group would also be a huge mistake. "To protect and grow share across this powerful and growing demographic, it is critical to recognize and respond to the broad diversity within the Hispanic population," says SymphonyIRI.

SymphonyIRI Group joined forces recently with Synovate, the market research arm of Aegis Group, to create "Hispanic Link 2012," a

Top 10 Hispanic Product Catagories
Purchase Index: Share of Hispanic Dollar Sales Divided by U.S. Household Dollar Share X 100

Category	Hispanic Dollar Index to Total Households
Dried Vegetables and Grains	221
Hair Care	154
Shortening Oil	152
Baby Food	150
Women's Fragrances	149
Grooming Aids	144
Disposable Diapers	144
Family Planning	142
Photographic Supplies	142
Baby Needs	137

Source: Nielsen Homescan® 01/02/2011 – 12/31/2011

Figure 4.3

report that highlights a number of factors contributing to the shopping behavior of Hispanics. According to them, key segment differentiators include:

- Acculturation
- Economy
- Community
- Exposure to marketing/advertising
- Country of origin

As you can see, this is a complex consumer group, and while there certainly is a lot of syndicated research out there to help you better understand the Hispanic consumer, I always caution people to make sure that the research they work with has proper Hispanic panels that are truly reflective of the Hispanic population composition in terms of language usage, age, length of residency, and representation in key Hispanic markets. You can't just oversample for Hispanics online and think you're getting the real picture. Make sure you find out exactly what kinds of Hispanics were included in any syndicated research you may have access to before believing what the data says and jumping to conclusions about this consumer. Also, please note that if you are using Hispanic databases based on government statistics, like the Consumer Expenditure Survey (CES), the Hispanic samples in many of the counties included in these surveys are minimal and not projectable for the entire county. Nonetheless, there are many tools out there that can help you figure this out, and I have included a list of research companies with Hispanic offerings in the resource guide at the end of this book.

SNAPSHOTS OF THE SEVEN SECTORS FOR GROWTH

As mentioned in Chapter 3, in a special report on the Hispanic market published in August 2011, IBIS*World* identified seven business sectors that could potentially benefit most from the exploding demographic growth of the Hispanic community. Now, let's briefly go into each one to see why.

Food

All you need to do is to walk up and down store aisles across the country to witness how America's food preferences are changing. In addition to all the Goya products—which are synonymous with the Hispanic market and can be found in just about every American cupboard today—there are the *Dulce de Leche* Oreos, Flamin' Hot Cheetos and Nestle's *Aguas Frescas*. Our menus have been Latinized, too. There's the chipotle chicken wrap at McDonald's and Panera's Cuban chicken sandwich. That's the Latino effect I wrote about in Chapter 1. But why are these flavors/Latinized choices popping up now? Let's look at the numbers.

According to IBIS*World*, Hispanics spend 7.7 percent of their incomes eating at home compared to 6.0 percent for non-Hispanics. Regional supermarket chains, like Publix in the Southeast and H-E-B in Texas, have been capitalizing on specific food needs of Latino shoppers for decades, but now specialty food stores and Hispanic grocery stores are catching on by offering a much wider variety of foods and products that often include products that are appealing to the Latino consumer in that local area. That's right, it means store managers are digging deeper into their consumer research to find out the composition of their Latino consumers and stocking country-specific cooking ingredients and products. In fact, over the past five years, both Walmart and Publix have been testing new Latino store formats that specifically cater to Hispanics in high-density areas where Latinos represent a minority-majority, like Miami, Phoenix, and Houston.

The other side of the food category, of course, is eating out. To better understand the current landscape of the fast-food and quick-service restaurant category among Hispanics, especially millennials in the U.S., Univision partnered with Burke Inc. in Fall 2011 to conduct a proprietary research study. The results of the study revealed that Hispanic millennials actively frequent quick-service restaurants throughout the day, especially during breakfast, lunch, and afternoon snack times. (See Figure 4.4.) In fact, according to this study, Hispanic millennials are the most frequent users of quick-service restaurants with almost twelve visits in a typical month. This far exceeds

Hispanic Millennials Visit Fast Food Restaurants 12 times per month

In fact, more than half of all Hispanic Millennials are considered to be heavy fast food users, going more than 10 times per month. Hispanic non-Millennials and non-Hispanic Millennials are more likely to be Medium and Light QSR users.

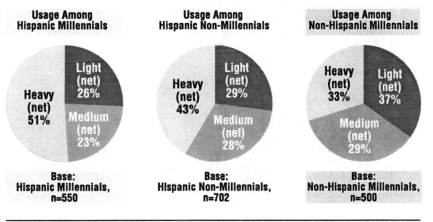

Usage Among Hispanic Millennials

Light (net) 26%
Heavy (net) 51%
Medium (net) 23%

Base: Hispanic Millennials, n=550

Usage Among Hispanic Non-Millennials

Light (net) 29%
Heavy (net) 43%
Medium (net) 28%

Base: Hispanic Non-Millennials, n=702

Usage Among Non-Hispanic Millennials

Heavy (net) 33%
Light (net) 37%
Medium (net) 29%

Base: Non-Hispanic Millennials, n=500

Source: Fast Food / Quick Service Restaurants Landscape Research, January 27, 2012.Conducted by Burke Inc.

Figure 4.4 Hispanic Millennials are Heavy Consumers of QSR

usage seen among their non-Hispanic counterparts, with only about eight visits per month.

The study goes on to explore reasons why Latinos visit fast-food restaurants. As for most Americans, the most common reason is a quick meal. However—and this is where the cultural behavior differs—Hispanics visit to spend time with family and to treat the children at more than twice the rate than non-Hispanic millennials.[4] (See Figure 4.5.)

These findings also support what IBIS*World*'s report said about Hispanic contribution to the fast-food restaurant industry. They project annualized growth rates of 4.3 percent over the next five years. (See Figure 4.6) Global Insights is even more bullish, projecting the average growth rate among Hispanics in spending on QSR from 2010–2015 at 8.2 percent vs. 4.5 percent for non-Hispanics. Finally, Hispanics also tend to dine out more frequently and when they do, they take the whole family with them, so the average amount of money spent per outing is also higher. According

Occasions		Hispanic Millennials *n=546*	Hispanic Non-Millennials *n=694*	Non-Hispanic Millennials *n=464*
Social Occasions	To spend time with family	44%	45%	21%
	To treat the children	24%	32%	11%
	To spend time with friends	21%	21%	17%
	For social occasion	7%	6%	10%
Conbenience/ Value Occasions	For a quick meal	57%	52%	79%
	When looking for value for money	13%	9%	28%
	For an indulgent treat	27%	38%	30%
Food Based Occasions	To satisfy a craving	26%	29%	52%
	For a better quality meal	18%	20%	27%
	For a quick meal	15%	16%	17%

Source: Fast Food / Quick Service Restaurants Landscape Research, January 27, 2012.Conducted by Burke Inc.

Figure 4.5 Reasons for Visiting a FFR/QSR Hispanic vs. Non-Hispanic

to "Latino Foodservice Trends in the U.S.," a new report from Packaged Facts (MarketResearch.com) released in 2011, "without the influence of Hispanic spending and population patterns, restaurant industry sales would have declined during 2008–2010." Again, according to IBIS*World*, Latinos and their families already account for a healthy 11.4 percent share of the single-location full-service restaurants[5] industry, and they project an annualized growth rate of 5.8 percent through 2016.

Retail

From Walmart to Kmart to Kohl's, some retailers have known the power of the Hispanic consumer and have been catering to them for many years now. Some of them are not only some of the largest advertisers on Spanish-language TV, they also are leading the pack in terms of developing product lines specifically targeted to Latinos, as was evidenced over the past few years when Kohl's announced partnerships with celebrity superstars like Sofia Vergara, as well as Jennifer Lopez

Food Industries				
Industry	Industry Size 2011 ($ mil.)	Hispanic Contribution		Annualized Growth (%)
		2011 ($ mil.)	2016 ($ mil.)	
Supermarkets and Grocery Stores	494,622	63,568	70,087	2.0
Fast Food Restaurants	165,409	18,831	23,251	4.3
Single Locations Full-Service Restaurants	91,400	10,406	13,765	5.8
Source IBIS*World*				

Figure 4.6 Hispanic Contribution to Food Industries 2011–2016

and Marc Anthony, in an effort to capitalize on the growing Latino youth market. And when it comes to children's clothes, well just forget about it! As you can imagine the Latino baby boom helps cash registers ring from coast to coast. In fact, according to IBIS*World*, Hispanics accounted for 19.2 percent of purchases for children's and infant's clothing in 2011 with a projected annualized growth rate of 4.5 percent.

"The Men's Clothing Stores industry is one of the more surprising industries extracting growth from the burgeoning Hispanic population," writes Brian Bueno from IBIS*World*. "Nevertheless, buying patterns that result largely from cultural differences among Hispanic males have long pointed toward this trend."[6] Citing the latest "Expenditure Survey" from the Bureau of Labor Statistics, Bueno says that Hispanic men spend 7 percent more on clothing than non-Hispanic men on a *per capita basis*—especially on shirts, coats, jackets, pants— and not surprisingly, uniforms. Our men like to look good, and personal care grooming products are also a big part of what they spend money on. Hispanics represent one out of five men between the ages of 18–49 according to the Census and a recent study revealed that in an average month, Latinos spend $32.31 on personal care products vs. $25.25 for

Retail Industries				
	Industry Size	Hispanic Contribution		
Industry	2011 ($ mil.)	2011 ($ mil.)	2016 ($ mil.)	Annualized Growth (%)
Department Stores	192,148	22,131	27,797	4.7
Consumer Electronic Stores	80,132	9,671	13,938	7.6
Children's and Infants' Clothing Stores	9,717	1,869	2,324	4.5
Men's Clothing Stores	9,030	1,168	1,532	5.6

Source IBIS*World*

Figure 4.7

non-Latinos.[7] That's 28 percent more on a monthly basis! In the Men's Clothing industry, IBIS*World* projects an annualized growth rate of 5.6 percent over the next four years. In Figure 4.7 you can see the main retail industries that will have most to gain from the predominantly younger Hispanic population, including of course, Consumer Electronics, which is projected to grow 7.6 percent.

Education

As we discussed at length in Chapter 3, over the past five years Hispanic graduation and college enrollment rates have soared, although they still lag behind all other racial groups in the United States. However, it is easy to see how important the contribution of Hispanics will be to the higher-education industry over the next five years, assuming there are no government cuts in financial aid assistance, especially Pell Grants. (See Figure 4.8.)

What is more interesting—and somewhat logical to me—is the contribution Hispanics will make in technical school enrollments. You see it is not uncommon for Latinos to work with their hands and master a trade or craft that perhaps has been in the family for years.

Financing with Pell Grants
Federal Pell Grant Taken Among Undergrads Enrolled at Proprietary Institutions

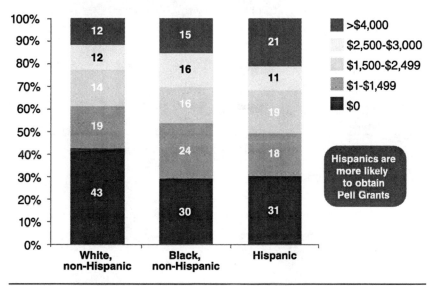

Source: U.S. Department of Education, National Center for Education Statistics, 2007-08 National Postsecondary Student Aid Study (NPSAS:08); Base: Enrolled at 2 or 4 year for-profit undergraduate schools

Figure 4.8 Breakdown of Pell Grants Taken by Race/Ethnicity

I recently read an article in the business section of *The New York Times* that bemoaned the loss of manufacturing jobs and the dilution of American craftsmanship in the United States. "Mass layoffs and plant closings have drawn plenty of headlines and public debate over the years . . . but the damage to skill and craftsmanship—what's needed to build a complex airliner or a tractor, or for a worker to move up from assembler to machinist to supervisor—went largely unnoticed," wrote Louis Uchitelle in the summer of 2012.[8] But that craftsmanship, which he describes as a birthright of our nation and "a vital ingredient of the American self-image as a can-do, inventive, we-can-make-anything people," is being kept alive by U.S. immigrants, many of whom are Latinos, according to sociologist Ruth Milkman of the City University of New York. "Pride in craft, it is alive in the immigrant world," Milkman told

	Education Industries			
	Industry Size	Hispanic Contribution		
Industry	**2011 ($ mil.)**	**2011 ($ mil.)**	**2016 ($ mil.)**	**Annualized Growth (%)**
Colleges and Universities	354,219	34,308	43,955	5.1
Trade and Technical Schools	16,608	2,059	2,819	6.5
Source IBIS*World*				

Figure 4.9. Hispanic Contribution to the Education Industry

Uchitelle. So to me it is not surprising that Hispanics will be attending vocational/trade schools in greater numbers over the next four years. (See Figure 4.9.)

Real Estate

For many Latinos, achieving their American Dream means buying a home. As more and more Hispanics join the workforce and enter the household formation stage, the residential real estate market obviously will see a big boom over the next five to ten years. As Alejandro Becerra writes in the "2011 State of Hispanic Homeownership" report published in March 2012 by the National Association of Hispanic Real Estate Professionals (NAHREP), "during the past decade and despite the substantial losses suffered during the foreclosure crisis, overall Hispanic homeownership increased from 45.7 percent to 47.3 percent, rising more sharply than overall minority homeownership, which rose from 47.4 to 48.0 percent, according to 2010 census figures. This is relative to the exponential effect that is beginning to take place as new buyers, who were largely unaffected by the housing crisis, enter the market and begin to offset the losses at a faster rate with their home purchases. In time, the real story of Hispanic homeownership will not be the community's overall rate of homeownership but the actual number of housing units it buys as the rate of household growth accelerates."[9] In terms of first-time homebuyers, NAHREP projects that over the next several decades, Latino and Asian homebuyers will be a big driving force of the housing market. "Hispanics are expected to account for 40 percent, or 4.8 million, of the estimated 12 million net new households within the next ten years. Both groups are expected to propel the demand for condominiums, smaller starter homes, and first trade-up homes over the next fifteen years," says the report.

This is in line with IBIS*World*'s special report, in which the Hispanic contribution to the housing market is expected to grow robustly through 2016, with a 17.6 percent annualized growth rate in the homebuilders industry and an 8 percent growth rate in the commercial leasing industry as you can see in Figure 4.10.

The commercial leasing increase can be partly attributed to the increase in Hispanic-owned or co-owned businesses, which in turn has been fueled by increased access to small-business loans over the last decade. As we saw in Chapter 3, according to the Survey of Small Business Owners by the U.S. Bureau of the Census, Hispanic-owned businesses increased nearly three times faster than those in the total population from 2002 to 2007. (See Figure 4.11)

According to NAHREP, "an estimated three million Hispanic businesses are generating $420 billion in sales annually and are expected to reach $539 billion by 2012. The Hispanic business sector has grown 114 percent over the last five years. Among all population groups, the

Real Estate Industries			
	Industry Size	Hispanic Contribution	
Industry	2011 ($ mil.)	2011 ($ mil.)	2016 ($ mil.)	Annualized Growth (%)
Home Builders	187,693	15,391	34,582	17.6
Commercial Leasing	145,468	4,400	6,465	8.0

Source IBIS*World*

Figure 4.10

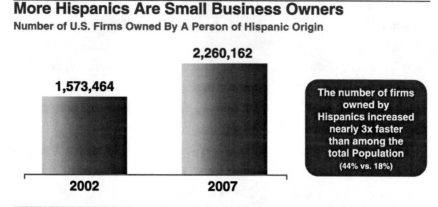

More Hispanics Are Small Business Owners
Number of U.S. Firms Owned By A Person of Hispanic Origin

Sources: U. S. Census Bureau Survey of Small Business Owners 2002 and 2007

Figure 4.11

entrepreneurial activity of Latinos increased the most between 2009 and 2010, with the growth rate of Latino businesses increasing from 46 percent to 56 percent. Today, one out of every 20 businesses in the U.S. is owned by Hispanics," says Becerra.[10]

Financial Services

If you have a housing boom, you must also expect to have a boom in financial services; after all, commercial banks will have to provide the mortgages for all those homes and new businesses. Although rather late to the Hispanic game, commercial banks are finally stepping up to create products that work for this community. But one of the challenges financial services companies are facing with the Hispanic community is their need for basic education and hand-holding when it comes to financial instruments such as credit cards, savings accounts, and checking accounts. With the exception of Wells Fargo, U.S.-based financial services companies have been laggards in capitalizing on the Hispanic opportunity. Recently, however, and in part thanks to partnerships with other banks from Spain and Latin America, large financial services companies are finally starting to dip their toes into the Hispanic market.

Financial Services Industries				
	Industry Size	Hispanic Contribution		
Industry	2011 ($ mil.)	2011 ($ mil.)	2016 ($ mil.)	Annualized Growth (%)
Commerical Banking	570,900	54,291	77,138	7.3
Credit Card Processing and Money Transferring	43,689	5,243	7,406	7.2

Source IBIS*World*

Figure 4.12 Hispanic Contribution to Financial Services Industry

Besides commercial banking, one of the big prizes in this sector is money-transfers, and I expect to see a lot of new players in this space over the next five years, which has traditionally been dominated by giants like Western Union. New technology and innovation will surely help smart companies capitalize on the 7 percent annualized growth rates projected by IBIS*World* in the financial services industries through 2016. (See Figure 4.12.)

Transportation
You can start seeing how all these industries are interconnected. As Latinos start new businesses and buy new homes, they will need more vehicles to move around in. As their families extend across the country or around the world, Latinos will also travel more domestically and internationally, so it's not surprising to see transportation on IBISWorld's list of industries that will benefit from the huge Hispanic growth that is coming our way. For the automotive industry, it's a no-brainer. Here are some facts: Hispanics represent 9.2 percent of new car buyers each year but they accounted for 13 percent of the growth in new car sales from 2010 to 2011. Hispanics, on average, spend $26,900 for a new vehicle (according to Polk), which is almost on par with the total U.S. average of $28,400 *and* they come back to market sooner. Ka-ching is right! But

Cultural Differences
Attitudes and Behaviors During the Auto Purchasing Process

Non-Hispanic	Hispanic
A hassle	An event
I expect service	How will I be treated
Knows the process	Fears the process
Pre-approval	Hope I get approved!
For me	For the family
My decision	Our decision
A transaction	An achievement
Deserved	Earned
Minimizes relationship with retailer	Values relationship with retailer
Satisfaction	A proud celebration!

Source: Univision M.A.S. More Auto Sales Focus Groups 2007. All rights reserved.

Figure 4.13 Hispanic vs. Non-Hispanic Differences in Auto Purchasing

this is an industry that really needs to understand the cultural differences of its Hispanic consumers in order to win market share. Figure 4.13 highlights some of the cultural differences that Hispanics have vs. non-Hispanics when purchasing a car, according to a 2011 study, which are rather eye-opening, if you ask me.

Smart marketers who adapt to the needs of this consumer, such as Toyota, Nissan, Honda, Chevrolet, and Ford—currently the top five car brands among Hispanics—will benefit the most from the projected 7.4 percent increase in Hispanic contribution to the auto industry. (See Figure 4.14.)

Entertainment and Media
And finally, a younger and faster-growing population should be an obvious source of growth for the entertainment and media businesses. Chris Dodd, the MPAA chief, has said it himself: "Hollywood needs

	Transportation Industries			
Industry	Industry Size 2011 ($ mil.)	Hispanic Contribution 2011 ($ mil.)	2016 ($ mil.)	Annualized Growth (%)
Car and Automobile Manufacturing	83,189	9,787	13,974	7.4
Domestic Airlines	147,178	13,178	16,876	5.1
Source IBIS*World*				

Figure 4.14

to do a better job attracting Hispanics, who already make up 25 percent of movie-going audiences." Hispanics are especially important for big movie openings, already accounting for 28 percent of opening night audiences.[11] According to an article in *Variety* about the worldwide box office for 2011, "Hispanic moviegoers represent the largest movie-going group relative to their population." But Hollywood is struggling to get their attention with the current slate of movies being produced. "I am confident we can do a better job of serving this growing population with themes that resonate strongly with them," Dodd said at CinemaCon in April 2012.

On television, Hollywood has yet to "crack the code" with Hispanic audiences, as demonstrated by the fact that even their top-rated shows only garner single-digit ratings with Latino viewers. According to an article in *The New York Times*, ABC's highly-rated *Modern Family* only had about 800,000 Hispanic viewers (out of a total of 12.9 million) in its 2012 season, CBS's *Two and a Half Men* averaged 611,000 Hispanic viewers out of an average of 14.6 million, and Fox's *Glee* averaged 518,000 Hispanics out of a total 8.7 million viewers last year.[12] "The numbers encapsulate the problem facing English-language television executives and advertisers: they desperately want to appeal to the more than 50 million Latinos in the United States (about three-quarters speak Spanish), especially those who are young, bilingual, and bicultural; but those viewers seem to want very little to do with American English-language television," wrote Tanzina Vega and Bill Carter in *The New York Times*. "They do, however, continue to watch Spanish-language networks in huge numbers. In May, on the final night of the most recent season of *Modern Family*, far more Hispanic viewers were watching the top Spanish-language show that week, the telenovela *La Que No Podía Amar* on Univision, which attracted 5.2 million viewers."

Beyond scripted dramas and comedy shows, the other area where you see huge audiences, of course, is sports—especially soccer. As we gear up for the 2014 World Cup in Brazil, it is interesting to note that a FIFA World Cup game held in 2010 between Mexico and Argentina drew 8.3 million Hispanic viewers, making it one of the most-watched programs in Spanish-language television history. By comparison, that year's Super Bowl XLIV between the New Orleans Saints and the Indiana Colts also attracted 8.3 million Hispanic viewers,[13] breaking the NFL's own record of Hispanic viewership, which was up 9 percent from the previous year. Think of it, a round of sixteen elimination match for the FIFA World Cup had as many Hispanic viewers as the mother of all football games. Get ready for the 2014 FIFA World Cup Brazil™.

In conclusion, as you can see in Figure 4.15 from IBIS*World*, you can expect significant contributions from Hispanics in various sectors of entertainment and media, from movies to TV, advertising, sports franchises, and magazines.

Are you stoked? I am! Okay, so now let's figure out how big your Hispanic opportunity is.

SIZING THE PRIZE

Whether you are thinking about marketing to Hispanics for the first time or if you are a veteran marketer who's "been there, done that," I strongly recommend that you seek the advice of Hispanic marketing experts who can help guide you through the right-sizing of your specific market opportunity. Too often the knee-jerk reaction to "selling" the Hispanic opportunity is to do a quick, back-of-the-envelope analysis of

Entertainment and Media Industries				
	Industry Size	Hispanic Contribution		
Industry	2011 ($ mil.)	2011 ($ mil.)	2016 ($ mil.)	Annualized Growth (%)
Advertising Agencies	29,215	2,979	4,277	7.5
Sports Franchises	24,098	1,862	2,688	7.6
Television Production	32,496	3,000	3,761	4.6
Movie Theaters	12,645	933	1,193	5.0
Magazine and Periodical Publishing	42,615	3,000	3,549	3.4
Source IBIS*World*				

Figure 4.15 Hispanic Contribution to Entertainment and Media Industries

what your "fair share" of the Hispanic market ought to be, based on your performance in the general market. Don't go there, you are doing yourself no favors.

All Spanish-language media companies know that they have an obligation to educate and train their new advertisers to properly market to Latinos. To do this, they have dedicated resources to help clients better understand their Hispanic target consumer and then offer solutions to help optimize their efforts to sell their products and services to the Latino community. Specialized marketing services companies like the Santiago Solutions Group (http://santiagosolutionsgroup.com/) or the Latinum Network (http://www.latinumnetwork.com/) can also help you clearly define the opportunity, and develop a strategic plan and specific tactics to execute against your Hispanic opportunity. Of course, this is what you get when you hire a Hispanic agency. If you are lucky enough to work in a big corporation that may already have a Hispanic advertising agency of record, well then, you are well ahead of the game. But if you are in the stage of not having an agency yet but trying to put together a plan for doing some Hispanic marketing, here's some advice from my good friend Carlos Santiago, chief strategist of the Santiago Solutions Group, a leading growth-strategy consultancy focused on aligning business strategy and marketing across multicultural, Hispanic, diversity, and generational segments.

In the chapter he authored for M. Isabel's Valdés's latest book, *WIN! The Hispanic Market, Strategies for Business Growth,* Mr. Santiago says, "business managers are hungry for making solid, well-informed, 'go or no-go' decisions, setting objectives that the organization can realistically undertake, and determining where and how much to invest for optimal growth and reasonable ROI."[14] He also bemoans the fact, as I do, that companies far too often don't do their homework before starting Hispanic marketing programs, which can lead to poorly conceived and executed initiatives that garner terrible results, if they are measured at all. This kind of "on again, off again" behavior, even by some of the largest, most savvy corporations—who should know better—is unfortunately still far too pervasive when it comes to Hispanic marketing. In fact, I would go as far as to say that this behavior has plagued Hispanic marketing (and multicultural marketing in general) for the past three decades, making a special appearance during the recent Great Recession. But if you are serious about winning with the Hispanic consumer, you must treat this market opportunity with consistency and plan for the long term in order to gain market share and generate consistent revenue growth.

According to a 2011 study also conducted by Santiago Solutions Group for the Association of Hispanic Advertising Agencies (AHAA), which analyzed 35,000 U.S. advertisers and their allocation trends to Hispanic media for the five years between 2006 and 2010, "a company allocating one quarter of its ad spend to Hispanic media over five years would generate annual revenue growth of 6.7 percent."[15] That is a very respectable growth rate and some best-in-class companies are already getting that much or more out of this market. "This research underscores that companies can't just pop in and out of the Hispanic market as a fad and see benefits. Real bottom-line benefits come from consistent, integrated approaches," says the AHAA report.

"By now, most companies have succeeded in communicating that this is an attractive opportunity to go after, but execution challenges often lead to unclear ROI, which in turn causes spotty commitment and an on-again, off-again approach to the market," warn Michael Klein and David Wellisch, co-founders and managing partners of Latinum Network, a business network that assists brands in taking advantage of the growing U.S. multicultural market through strategic analytics, cutting-edge research, and peer-to-peer collaboration. "Justifying incremental spending for 'just 17 percent of the U.S. population,' answering questions about general market backlash, and dealing with reflex responses like 'won't we just get them anyway?' typically distracts organizations from paying the right level of attention to the U.S. Hispanic market."[16]

To help you get started with right-sizing your opportunity, Santiago suggests you create a S-M-A-R-T plan. For more on how to develop that plan, make sure to buy *WIN! The Hispanic Market, Strategies for Business Growth*, but here's what a S-M-A-R-T plan requires, an approach to Hispanic marketing that is:

- Sustainable, because growth requires consistency
- Methodical, because your opportunity must be true and tested
- Aligned, because without alignment, it won't work
- Responsible, because you must have a goal set in order to reach it
- Timely, because timing is key for success

Each company and each brand will have different opportunities in terms of growth with the Hispanic market, so make sure you get help from the right experts to help you craft a right plan.

MULTICULTURAL ORGANIZATIONAL STRUCTURES

Corporate-wide alignment around *any* growth initiative is absolutely critical for success. So, one of the questions I often get asked is, how should companies set up their marketing operations to properly capitalize on their Hispanic opportunity? Over the past twenty-five years

Hispanic Marketing Structures

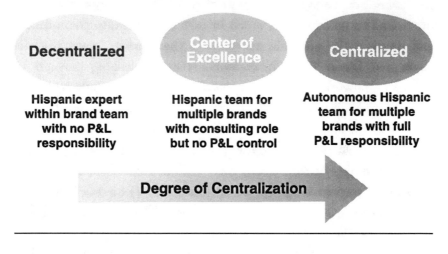

Figure 4.16 Hispanic Marketing Team Models

of working in the Hispanic market, I have been part of many different organizational structures. There are basically three models that I have seen most often. They vary by degree of centralization as well as bottom-line responsibility, but Figure 4.16 shows you the three most common organizational structures I have seen.

Decentralized

This model is usually formed with one or more director-level marketing executives who work within a brand team to help the team make decisions, analyze consumer data, and execute marketing plans for the Hispanic target. The Hispanic marketing director often helps brand managers determine how to create culturally appropriate executions for brand-centric plans. In this model, the Hispanic marketing executive generates business cases, tries to justify scale initiatives, shopper marketing, and research, but has *no* control over budget or P&L—that remains with the brand manager. More often than not, creative materials coming out of these teams are just translations of English brand campaigns.

The challenge: The Hispanic members of the brand team are constantly "selling into" brands for funding, and unless the brand managers have a bottom-line responsibility to bring in a certain amount of sales from the Hispanic market, usually it's the first place to cut when times get tough, and we all know they get tough every year.

Center of Excellence

This model usually entails the hiring of a seasoned VP-level marketing executive with some multicultural experience who reports to the CMO and often has several directors and managers to help coordinate efforts across enterprise. The center of excellence team works directly with agencies at both the national and local levels. Responsibilities include selecting Hispanic agency partners, approval of all creative for national marketing initiatives, overseeing research activities, collaborating with PR and community outreach teams, and local work. Hispanic marketing campaigns may feature creative executions that are more targeted and based on research-driven, brand-specific consumer insights.

The challenge: Although in this model the Hispanic VP manages and develops the Hispanic P&L, s/he must fight for an appropriate level of funding every year. Often—unless the CMO is a believer in the Hispanic opportunity—securing the necessary funding for long-term growth can be challenging. This may lead to inconsistent presence and results in the marketplace.

Centralized Team

This is the best-in-class model that is based on an integrated business unit, led by a general manager or equivalent title who reports directly to the president or CEO. This model includes a robust roster of marketing talent, including VPs, directors, brand managers, and assistant brand managers. This business unit is responsible for recommending strategies, setting budgets and plans, tracking results, and meeting sales goals. They oversee all agency partners and all execution. This is where best-in-class Hispanic creative usually comes from, as it is usually based on a Hispanic creative brief for each brand and allows for original, targeted creative that is focused on Hispanic consumer insights designed to move the needle in share of market.

The challenge: This model requires the company as a whole to put Hispanic marketing at the center of its long-term growth plans and make executives across the enterprise responsible for bottom-line results, even tying part of their bonuses to the year-over-year performance in the Hispanic market. Obviously this requires the ability to align departments across the enterprise and measure results, as well as a significant level of investment in talent and marketing budgets.

The only two models that really work, in my opinion, are the center of excellence and the centralized models. Unfortunately, the decentralized model is the most vulnerable to cuts and lack of consistency, so I would encourage you to not even consider it, but many companies do use this as a first step.

The best-in-class companies in the Hispanic market today are mainly using a center of excellence or centralized model, which was established first at P&G. Jim Stengel, the marketing guru of P&G for many years, put it best when he said, "This is not about Hispanic marketing. It's about marketing itself." He was a big believer in the Hispanic opportunity and helped P&G create a best-in-class organization. Here are ten steps you can take to make sure your marketing efforts in the Hispanic market are a success:

Ten Steps for Success:

1. Make Hispanic a top-down corporate priority. It must be led and encouraged by senior management and must drive accountability across the organization.
2. Make sure your efforts are driven by a solid business case, *not* by a drive for diversity among employees.
3. Hispanic marketing requires strategic focus and consistency over time. Your investment must be sustainable. Don't change your course, strategy, focus, or message every year. You must build brand equity, awareness, and trial over *time*. Remember, Hispanics are not a market within a market; we are part of the general market.

4. Make sure to invest appropriately in research to understand categories where you have "right to win."

5. Invest in appropriate metrics, but be sensitive to nuances. This is the hardest part, no doubt, but you must work with vendors to track sales, distribution, ROI, point-of-sale data, copy testing, etc.

6. Get organized to build expertise and continuity. You must provide institutional knowledge to keep the effort alive as business units change their people. Hispanic marketing efforts cannot be assigned to summer interns, assistant brand managers, or second-tier agency people.

7. Take a test-and-learn approach. Get your toe in the water. Test and learn, then expand. Always be testing something new, and above all, don't quit if you fail. Learn from your mistakes and move on.

8. Leverage all your agencies and vendor partners to fully integrate your Hispanic efforts and accountability into your general market efforts. Use Hispanic to extend your total reach, oftentimes at equal or lower cost.

9. Balance trial-and-equity building with retail programs. With Hispanic consumers, you need to need to overcome trial barriers by educating them and using in-store sampling to drive trial.

10. Make Hispanic an investment priority, not a budget item.

Key Takeaways:

- Hispanics provide marketers with new opportunities to build brand loyalty and generate revenue growth for their brands long term.
- Because of their relative youth and larger household size, Hispanics are America's *über* consumers, buying more of everything from groceries to apparel, electronics, accessories, and cars.
- The days of one-size-fits-all marketing plans are over.
- Seek the advice of marketing experts who can help guide you through the right-sizing of your specific market opportunity.

NOTES

1. Simmons NCS/NHCS Spring 2012 Adult 18+ Full Year Study. Copyright © 2012. www.experian.com/simmons-research/simmons-client-resource-center. html.

2. *The State of the Hispanic Consumer: The Hispanic Market Imperative*, Quarter 2, 2012, Copyright © 2012 The Nielsen Company.

3. Covkin, Staci, Diverse and Distinct: The Hispanic Population Deliver Numerous Segments and Opportunities—an Exceptionally Fast-Growing Market, Copyright © 2012 SymphonyIRI Group. www.symphonyiri.com/portals/0/ articlePdfs/Hispanic%20POV-May-2012.pdf.

4. "Hispanic Millennials" in Univision's Fast Food/Quick Service Restaurants Landscape Study, Univision and Burke Associates, January 27, 2012.

5. Bueno, Brian, The Growing Hispanic Population Means Big Business for These 7 Sectors, An IBISWorld Special Report. Copyright © 2011, IBISWorld, Inc. Published August 2011. www.ibisworld.com/Common/MediaCenter/ Growing%20Hispanic%20Population%20(2).pdf.

6. Bueno, Brian, The Growing Hispanic Population Means Big Business for These 7 Sectors, An IBISWorld Special Report. Copyright © 2011, IBISWorld, Inc. Published August 2011. www.ibisworld.com/Common/MediaCenter/ Growing%20Hispanic%20Population%20(2).pdf.

7. Univision/Experian Simmons, Male Grooming Study 2010, released April 2010.

8. Uchitelle, Louis, "A Nation That's Losing its Toolbox," *The New York Times*, July 22, 2012, Copyright © 2012 The New York Times Company. www.nytimes. com/2012/07/22/business/what-happened-to-the-craftsmanship-spirit-essay. html?pagewanted=all.

9. Becerra, Alejandro, NAHREP Report: The State of Hispanic Homeownership 2011. Published by the National Association of Hispanic Real Estate Professionals, March 2012. http://nahrep.org/state-of-hispanic-homeownership.

10. Becerra, Alejandro, NAHREP Report: The State of Hispanic Homeownership 2011. Published by the National Association of Hispanic Real Estate Professionals, March 2012. http://nahrep.org/state-of-hispanic-homeownership.

11. Nielsen Research Group, American Movie Goer Study Among Pop 12+. www. neilsen.com.

12. Vega, Tanzina and Bill Carter, "Networks Struggle to Appeal to Hispanics," *The New York Times*, August 5, 2012. Copyright © 2012 The New York Times Company. www.nytimes.com/2012/08/06/business/media/networks-struggle-to-appeal-to-hispanics-without-using-stereotypes.html?pagewanted=all&_r=0.

13. "Minority Viewership Drives Record-Breaking Super Bowl XLIV," *NielsenWire*, February 12, 2010 http://blog.nielsen.com/nielsenwire/media_entertainment/ super-bowl-xliv-minority-viewership.

14. Santiago, Carlos, "S-M-A-R-T Growth through Opportunity Right-Sizing," in *WIN! the Hispanic Market: Strategies for Business Growth* by M. Isabel Valdés, Copyright © 2011. Published by Paramount Market Publishing, Inc., January, 2012.

15. Advertising 2011 Budget Alignment: Maximizing Impact in the Hispanic Market. Published by the Association of Hispanic Advertising Agencies, www.ahaa.org.

16. Klein, Michael and David Wellisch, "Why Wall Street Will Look at Your Hispanic Strategy" in *WIN! the Hispanic Market: Strategies for Business Growth*, by M. Isabel Valdés, Copyright © 2011. Published by Paramount Market Publishing, Inc., January, 2012.

5

~~~~~~

THE TOP EIGHT
HISPANIC MARKETS

Now, to give you better insight into this rapidly changing market, let's take a closer look at each of the top Hispanic markets in the United States. I have culled data from several different sources to put together the "snapshots" of each market. The data are as current as possible, but will no doubt become outdated very quickly, so keep your eye out for the Latino Boom app, where we will update this data regularly and also include exclusive video interviews with top executives who are doing best-in-class Hispanic marketing. When I talk about "markets" in this chapter, I will be referring to Nielsen's proprietary Designated Market Areas (DMA®)[1] since DMA regions are more widely used inside and outside of the media industry.

For the media industry, of course, TV households is the currency in which everyone deals and, according to the latest Nielsen Universe estimates, there were 114.7 million TV households in 2012, of which 13.9 million were Hispanic. During the 2010–2011 season, 40 percent of new TV households were Hispanic[1] and in 2012, Hispanic households were projected to increase by 4.6 percent adding approximately 600,000 TV households to their share, narrowing the gap between Hispanic TV households and African American TV households significantly, according to the Nielsen Company.[2] Figure 5.1 shows you the impressive growth expected from ethnic TV households, reflecting a

	2010–2011 Season TV HHs	2011–2012 TV HHs	YOY Change
African American or Black	14,072,950	14,277,840	1.5%
Hispanic or Latino	13,348,190	13,957,750	4.6%
Asian	4,812,310	5,273,450	9.6%

Figure 5.1 Ethnic Breakdown of Nielsen TV Universe Estimates 2012

new shift in television viewing audiences as baby boomers age out of the key thirty-five to forty-nine demographic.

Before we get started on each individual market, let's first take a quick look at the top ten Hispanic DMA regions in Figure 5.2. The list

Rank			Households		
Hispanic	U.S.	Market	Hispanic	Total	% Hispanic
1	2	Los Angeles	1,876,110	5,569,780	33.7%
2	1	New York	1,345,140	7,387,810	18.2%
3	16	Miami-Ft. Lauderdale	730,160	1,583,800	46.1%
4	10	Houston	607,290	2,185,260	27.8%
5	3	Chicago	511,680	3,493,480	14.6%
6	5	Dallas-Ft. Worth	504,610	2,571,310	19.6%
7	36	San Antonio	422,860	880,690	48.0%
8	6	San Francisco-Oak-San Jose	414,730	2,506,510	16.5%
9	13	Phoenix (Prescott)	350,450	1,811,330	19.3%
10	87	Harlingen-Wslco-Brnsvl-McAllen	308,050	361,820	85.1%

Source: Nielsen Local Television Market Universe Estimates, January 1, 2012

Figure 5.2 Nielsen's Top Ten Hispanic DMA regions

of top ten Hispanic markets by DMA region varies slightly from the top Hispanic markets by population that you saw earlier because DMA regions are larger and measured in terms of households, which is not a constant as the average number of persons per household varies from market to market. However, please note that the percentages Hispanics make up of each market are above the national population average of 16 percent—in every market except Chicago. In fact, Latinos make up nearly half of the *total* TV audiences in Miami and San Antonio, and in the border town of Brownsville-McAllen, well, we rule!

LOS ANGELES, CALIFORNIA

DMA STATS

Hispanic ranking: 1
General market ranking: 2
Counties included: 9
Los Angeles, Orange, Ventura, Riverside, San Bernardino,
Kern–E, and Inyo in CA, and Esmeralda, NV

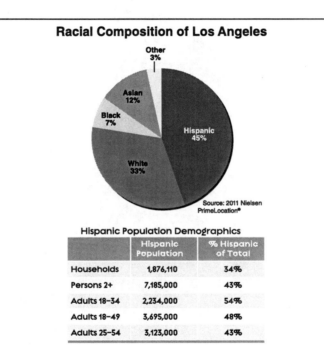

Racial Composition of Los Angeles

Other 3%
Asian 12%
Black 7%
Hispanic 45%
White 33%

Source: 2011 Nielsen PrimeLocation®

Hispanic Population Demographics

	Hispanic Population	% Hispanic of Total
Households	1,876,110	34%
Persons 2+	7,185,000	43%
Adults 18–34	2,234,000	54%
Adults 18–49	3,695,000	48%
Adults 25–54	3,123,000	43%

TV HOUSEHOLDS

Hispanic: 1,876,110
Total: 5,569,780
Percentage of HH with kids: 61 percent vs. 29 percent for non-Hispanics
Median age: 28.6 vs. 42.1
Any Spanish spoken: 89 percent
Average Hispanic HH income: $68,810

Source: Nielsen Universe Estimates 2012

HISPANIC CONSUMER SPENDING

$122.8 billion out of a total of $461.3 billion[3]

Contrary to the general market, where the New York DMA region is king, in the Hispanic market, Los Angeles is *número uno*. That's because more than 45 percent of the population in this DMA region is Latino. According to the 2010 census, eight states now have Hispanic populations of 1 million or more. California leads the list with more than 14 million Hispanics officially living in the state, which accounts for nearly one-third of the total Hispanic population in the United States. Hispanics in East Los Angeles make up 97 percent of the population in the area, making it the highest concentration of Hispanics excluding the commonwealth of Puerto Rico.[4] However, although Los Angeles is clearly a Mexican-dominant city, one must not think of L.A. as a monolithic market. First of all, the diversity of Mexicans is often overlooked, as people from Puebla are actually quite different from people from the capital (the Distrito Federal) or from Guadalajara. Secondly, the many generations of Mexican families are simply mind-boggling, with some families going back ten generations. Finally, Los Angeles has always been a magnet for newly arrived Latinos, especially Salvadorans and Guatemalans, making it home to many Spanish-dominant immigrants from Central America.

With 89 percent of Hispanics in this market speaking some Spanish, it is easy to see how L.A. is home to Univision's flagship station,

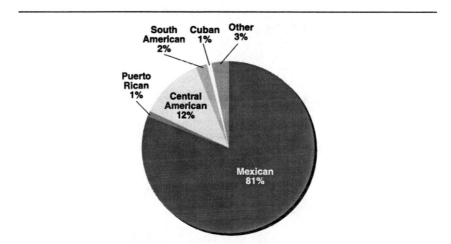

Source: Nielsen PrimeLocation®/Pop-Facts®: 2000 Data, 2012 Estimates

Figure 5.3 Country of Origin—Los Angeles

KMEX and to the largest Spanish-language newspaper, *La Opinion*. During the 2011–2012 television season, KMEX was the most watched television station in the country in total day viewing (Mon–Sun 6 a.m.– 2 a.m.) among adults 18–34, regardless of language.[5] This market is also home to fourteen Spanish-language radio stations and nine Spanish-language community papers. In terms of TV language usage, according to Nielsen, the breakdown is almost evenly split between Spanish dominant, bilingual and English dominant, as you can see in Figure 5.4. As Hispanic marketing evolves, L.A. is one of the cities I like to watch closely as mega-trends have emerged from it over the past couple of decades.

Finally, the Hispanic population in Los Angeles is expected to grow 37 percent from 2000 to 2016, accounting for 91 percent of the total population growth in this DMA region, according to PrimeLocation!

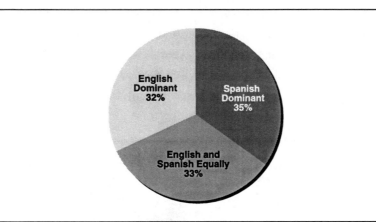

Source: Nielsen Media Research, 2012 Hispanic TV Households by Language Strata

Figure 5.4 Language Spoken at Home—Los Angeles

NEW YORK, NEW YORK

DMA STATS

Hispanic ranking: 2
General market ranking: 1
Counties included: 29
    Fairfield (CT), Bergen, Essex, Hudson, Hunterdon, Middlesex, Monmouth, Morris, Ocean, Passaic, Somerset, Sussex, Union, Warren (NJ), Bronx, Dutchess, Kings, Nassau, New York, Orange, Putnam, Queens, Richmond, Rockland, Suffolk, Sullivan, Ulster, Westchester (NY), Pike (PA)

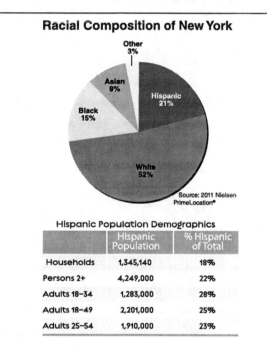

Racial Composition of New York

Other 3%
Asian 9%
Black 15%
Hispanic 21%
White 52%

Source: 2011 Nielsen PrimeLocation®

Hispanic Population Demographics

	Hispanic Population	% Hispanic of Total
Households	1,345,140	18%
Persons 2+	4,249,000	22%
Adults 18–34	1,283,000	28%
Adults 18–49	2,201,000	25%
Adults 25–54	1,910,000	23%

TV HOUSEHOLDS

Hispanic: 1,345,140
Total: 7,387,810
Percentage of HH with kids: 49.1 percent vs. 30 percent for non-Hispanics
Median age: 31.4 vs. 41.3
Any Spanish spoken: 93 percent
Average Hispanic HH income: $64,528
    Source: Nielsen Universe Estimates 2012

HISPANIC CONSUMER SPENDING

$87.3 billion out of a total of $679.6 billion[6]

As you can clearly see in Figure 5.5, New York is, by far, the most diverse Latino market in the United States. This DMA region is the largest in the general market, comprising twenty-nine counties from its four surrounding states. It is also one of the most expensive and difficult markets to enter. By its very nature, New York tends to attract immigrants from all over the world, and these tend to cluster not only as groups but also in certain areas. As a result, you can find large concentrations of Hispanics in different parts of the city. Dominicans, for example, concentrate in Manhattan's Washington Heights. Large communities of Colombians and Peruvians live in Queens, and Cubans still predominate in Union City, New Jersey. Although Puerto Ricans still make up the largest percentage of the Hispanics in New York, they are no longer concentrated in one area—a reflection of their higher level of education and economic power—although you can still find some of them living in Manhattan's famous Spanish Harlem. Because of these very distinct "pockets," certain areas like Brooklyn will have high concentrations of Jews in one neighborhood and Mexicans in the next. The changes in ethnic dominance can be felt almost block by block in New York City, which makes it a fun place to visit but a marketer's nightmare.

Because New York's economy is so strong, it attracts Latinos from all walks of life. Newly arrived, Spanish-dominant Mexicans can now be seen working as busboys in restaurants or as clerks in Korean grocery stores. Skilled Latino craftsmen can earn up to $30 an hour in construction. Many first- and second-generation Puerto Ricans or Dominicans can be found working white-collar jobs for the private sector or the government. And others set up single shingles as lawyers and doctors. Finally, many other Latino professionals can also be found working in the banking, telecommunications, and media industries that dominate the New York economic landscape. The ethnic pockets I referred to earlier which, by the way, exist in every Latino market, allow for Spanish-dominants to live comfortably without ever really "needing" to learn English. They can shop for all their needs in Spanish-speaking neighborhood stores, they can consume media in Spanish, and be informed

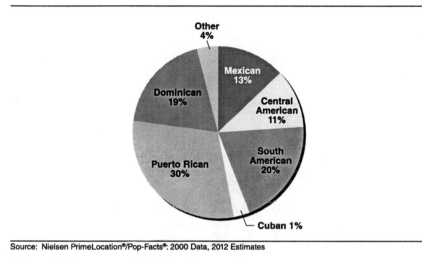

Source: Nielsen PrimeLocation®/Pop-Facts®: 2000 Data, 2012 Estimates

Figure 5.5 Country of Origin—New York

about what's going on in their local neighborhoods as well as back home, and they can even vote in Spanish.

With 93 percent of Hispanics in this market speaking some Spanish, and New York being the media epicenter of the country, it is not surprising that it is home to the corporate headquarters of both Univision Communications, Inc., and PBS's Spanish-language network V-me. You can also find sales and marketing offices for NBC's Telemundo, as well as Spanish-language cable networks MTV Tr3s, ESPN Deportes, Fox Hispanic Media, TV Azteca, and the bilingual network MUN2. New York is where the magazine *People en Español* was born, and since I wrote my last book, Meredith Hispanic Ventures was formed (I had the privilege to work with them for four years) and now publishes some of the most important women's magazines, including *Siempre Mujer* and *Ser Padres*. Other print media include the oldest Spanish-language newspaper of the country, *El Diario/La Prensa* along with four other community papers. In terms of radio, this DMA region has nine Spanish-language radio stations, and Spanish-language radio formats have for years been more popular in this market than their English-language counterparts.

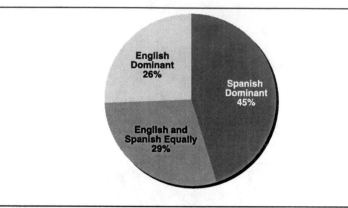

Source: Nielsen Media Research, 2012 Hispanic TV Households by Language Strata

Figure 5.6 Language Spoken at Home—New York

In terms of TV language usage, according to Nielsen, the New York DMA region is still Spanish dominant, with those consuming media equally in Spanish and English at 29 percent and English dominants making up one quarter of all viewers.

Finally, the Hispanic population is expected to grow 28 percent from 2000 to 2016, accounting for 87 percent of the total population growth, according to PrimeLocation.

MIAMI-FT. LAUDERDALE, FLORIDA

DMA STATS

Hispanic ranking: 3
General market ranking: 16
Counties included: 3
     Broward, Miami-Dade, and Monroe

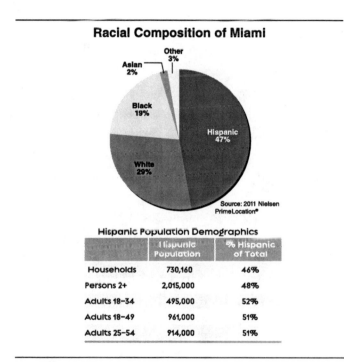

Racial Composition of Miami

Other 3%
Asian 2%
Black 19%
Hispanic 47%
White 29%

Source: 2011 Nielsen PrimeLocation®

Hispanic Population Demographics

	Hispanic Population	% Hispanic of Total
Households	730,160	46%
Persons 2+	2,015,000	48%
Adults 18–34	495,000	52%
Adults 18–49	961,000	51%
Adults 25–54	914,000	51%

TV HOUSEHOLDS

Hispanic: 730,160
Total: 1,583,800
Percentage of HH with kids: 39.2 percent vs. 27.9 percent for non-Hispanics
Median age: 39.2 vs. 39.7
Any Spanish spoken: 97 percent
Average Hispanic HH income: $68,048

Source: Nielsen Universe Estimates 2012

HISPANIC CONSUMER SPENDING

$44 billion out of a total of $103.4 billion[7]

Could Miami be a harbinger of America's future? I know that thought scares some people who see Miami as somehow un-American, dominated as it is by Latinos from all over the world who have come in droves over the past four decades to carve out a new future and who, along the way, built one of America's newest great cities. The Miami I left in 1989, when I got an offer to work in New York City, has grown up a lot. Miami today is home to global citizens who enjoy world-class performances at the Adrienne Arsht Center for Performing Arts, as well as professional sports in the three major leagues: baseball, basketball, and hockey.

From a business perspective, Miami became the financial center for Latin American banking in the late '90s and solidified its global role over the past decade. Today it is perhaps best known as a center for many middle-market companies, who use its ports as a distribution hub for products being sold in the U.S. or across the world, which is why Miami has also been called the "Hong Kong of the Americas." The young entrepreneurs who start businesses in Miami may speak with an accent, but they are still as American as apple pie, since their entrepreneurial spirit has been fueled by the same passion of all American immigrants who come to this country to fulfill their American Dream. Sometimes people tend to forget that the Latino immigrants' contributions to America have made our country richer and stronger over the past century.

Although the Cuban population is still dominant, the mix of Latinos in Miami has drastically changed since the '80s. In 1990, the Hispanic population of Miami was predominantly Cuban, after the huge influx of Cubans via the Mariel Boatlift in 1980. There were also a few Puerto Ricans for good measure. Today, however, Cubans comprise less than half of the total Hispanic population. The influx of Latin Americans fleeing their politically and economically unstable homelands (among them Brazil, Argentina, Colombia, and Venezuela) has brought many more South Americans to Miami. Miami is the only DMA region where Mexicans are actually a small minority, but because this town is also the production center for the largest Spanish-language television networks,

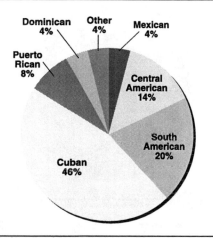

Source: Nielsen PrimeLocation®/Pop-Facts®: 2000 Data, 2012 Estimates

Figure 5.7 Country of Origin—Miami

the past decade has seen a steady flow of wealthy Mexicans. With all of them come many more Hispanics looking to fill the service needs of the newly arrived, wealthier Latin Americans

Miami is truly a unique place, as wave after wave of Latino immigrants who have come here have historically been more "well off." As a result, Miami's Latino exile communities—be they anti-Castro Cubans, anti-Sandinista Nicaraguans, or anti-Chavez Venezuelans—tend to be of the conservative bent. Nonetheless, the younger generations of Hispanics have helped move Florida from the red column (when they voted for George W. Bush) in 2004 to the blue column, as seen with Obama's victories both in 2008 and 2012.

One thing to note about the Miami DMA region is that it has the oldest median age of all the Hispanic markets, which is partly due to the older Cuban community and to the fact that the more recent arrivals also tend to be older. But the younger generations are growing fast and I wouldn't be surprised to see the median age go down over the next couple of decades since the Hispanic population is expected to grow 44 percent from 2000 to 2016, with minorities accounting for 100 percent of the total population growth, according to Nielsen PrimeLocation!

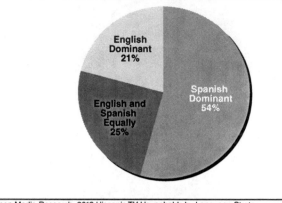

Source: Nielsen Media Research, 2012 Hispanic TV Households by Language Strata

Figure 5.8 Languge Spoken at Home—Miami

In terms of language, 93 percent of Hispanics in this DMA region speak some Spanish at home. Accordingly, there is a robust local Spanish-language media offering with fourteen radio stations and three very well-established Spanish-language newspapers: *El Miami Herald*, *El Sentinel* and *El Diario Las Americas*. In terms of TV language usage, according to Nielsen, the Miami DMA region is 54 percent Spanish dominant, with a quarter of viewers consuming equally in Spanish and English and English dominants making up another 20.9 percent.

HOUSTON, TEXAS

DMA STATS

Hispanic ranking: 4
General market ranking: 10
Counties included: 20
   Austin, Brazoria, Calhoun, Chambers, Colorado, Fort Bend, Galveston, Grimes, Harris, Jackson, Liberty, Matagorda, Montgomery, Polk, San Jacinto, Trinity, Walker, Waller, Washington, Wharton

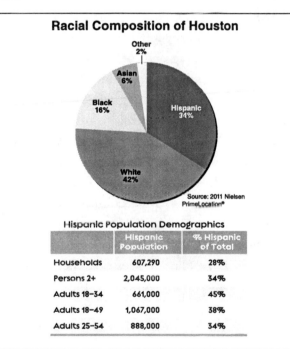

Racial Composition of Houston

Other 2%
Asian 6%
Black 16%
Hispanic 34%
White 42%

Source: 2011 Nielsen PrimeLocation®

Hispanic Population Demographics

	Hispanic Population	% Hispanic of Total
Households	607,290	28%
Persons 2+	2,045,000	34%
Adults 18–34	661,000	45%
Adults 18–49	1,067,000	38%
Adults 25–54	888,000	34%

TV HOUSEHOLDS

Hispanic: 607,290
Total: 2,185,260
Percentage of HH with kids: 57.9 percent vs. 33.1 percent for non-Hispanics
Median age: 27.8 vs. 39.2
Any Spanish spoken: 91 percent
Average Hispanic HH income: $67,208

Source: Nielsen Universe Estimates 2012

HISPANIC CONSUMER SPENDING

$38.6 billion out of a total of $186.6 billion[8]

Like Miami, Houston is another important hub for Latin America. But this port city has seen its share of ups and downs due to economic booms and busts. The most recent recession has hit this city hard and unfortunately has also negatively changed the tone of the conversation about the most recently arrived immigrants. According to the 2010 census, Latinos in Houston account for one-third of the total population and 62 percent of all students in the Houston Independent School System. In Harris County, Hispanics make up a whopping 45 percent of the population, making Houston one of the few major cities in the country with a Hispanic majority-minority. According to a study by Rice University's Stephen Klineberg and the Center for Houston's Future, "the growth of Harris County's population during the past quarter-century is thus primarily due to immigration from abroad, as well as to the birth of new babies, often the children of earlier immigrants and of U.S.-born Latinos." What you find in this market are two very distinct Hispanic groups: second- and third-generation bilingual *Tejanos* as well as newly arrived, Spanish-dominant immigrants. Because they are so completely integrated into Texas culture, you tend to almost take *Tejanos* for granted, but you shouldn't. They are loud and proud of their heritage and culture.

Although the city is 79 percent Mexican, there has been a growing number of new Latino immigrants (see Figure 5.9) from Central and South America—most recently from Honduras after Hurricane Katrina. According to the Rice University study, the newer immigrants from Cuba and South America are coming to Houston with higher levels of education than U.S.-born Hispanics, Mexicans, and other Central Americans, so be careful not to treat all Latinos in this market the same. Like Miami, Houston also has its share of Latino entrepreneurs; in fact, according to the Fiscal Policy Institute, 31 percent of small-business owners in Houston are foreign-born Hispanics.[9]

In terms of language, while 91 percent of Hispanics in this DMA region speak some Spanish at home, the younger U.S.-born Latinos are definitely more English-dominant. Nonetheless, keeping Hispanic culture alive and reaching Latinos with relevant content is one of the

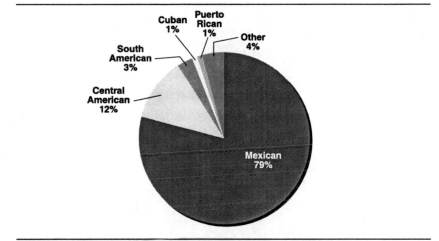

Source: Nielsen PrimeLocation®/Pop-Facts®: 2000 Data, 2012 Estimates

Figure 5.9 Country of Origin—Houston

reasons why there are fifteen Spanish-language radio stations in the DMA region and eight community newspapers. Figure 5.10 shows you language strata data from Nielsen that indicates that 45 percent of Hispanics in this DMA region are Spanish dominant, with a quarter consuming equally in Spanish and English while English dominants make

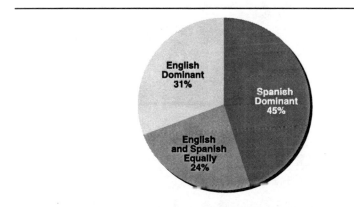

Source: Nielsen Media Research, 2012 Hispanic TV Households by Language Strata

Figure 5.10 Language Spoken at Home—Houston

up another 31 percent. And finally, in terms of population growth, Hispanics were expected to grow by 82 percent from 2000 through 2016, contributing about 60 percent of the total population growth of the DMA region. "There can be little doubt that the ways the lives of Houston's Latino immigrants and their children unfold will profoundly shape the region's future,"[10] concludes the Rice University study.

CHICAGO, ILLINOIS

DMA STATS

Hispanic ranking: 5
General market ranking: 3
Counties included: 16
   Cook, De Kalb, Du Page, Grundy, Kane, Kankakee, Kendall, Lake, La Salle, McHenry, Will (IL), Jasper, Lake, La Porte, Newton, Porter (IN)

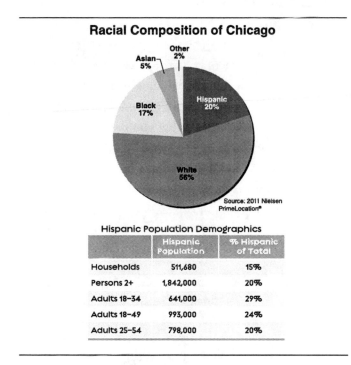

Racial Composition of Chicago

Other 2%
Asian 5%
Hispanic 20%
Black 17%
White 56%

Source: 2011 Nielsen PrimeLocation®

Hispanic Population Demographics

	Hispanic Population	% Hispanic of Total
Households	511,680	15%
Persons 2+	1,842,000	20%
Adults 18–34	641,000	29%
Adults 18–49	993,000	24%
Adults 25–54	798,000	20%

TV HOUSEHOLDS

Hispanic: 511,680
Total: 3,493,480
Percentage of HH with kids: 59.4 percent vs. 31.1 percent for non-Hispanics
Median age: 27 vs. 40
Any Spanish spoken: 90 percent
Average Hispanic HH income: $ 66,636
Source: Nielsen Universe Estimates 2012

HISPANIC CONSUMER SPENDING

$32.2 billion out of a total of $272.4 billion[11]

When you look at the dispersion of Latinos in the United States on a map it looks like a smiley face and Chicago is the winking eye. For me, Chicago has always been the heartbeat of the Midwest. Although it ranks number five in the Hispanic market, it is the third largest DMA region in the country and is home to one of America's greatest cities. When it comes to Hispanic marketing, Chicago is also home to some of the largest Hispanic agencies (Leo Burnett's Lapiz U.S.A, Draft/FCB, as well as Starcom MediaVest's Tapestry, the largest media buying agency in the Hispanic market) and veteran retailers like Kmart and Sears. Chicago has long been considered a good place to conduct focus groups or test market products geared toward the Latino community because you can easily recruit Hispanics of the various subgroups in order to match national averages (see Figure 5.11). Demography, however, is only one of the many criteria that you should use in determining appropriate test markets for your products.

The history of Latinos in Chicago dates back more than a century when one thousand Mexicans were counted in the 1910 census. The presence of the Latino community has been spreading from the city to the suburbs over the past fifty years. "The number of Latinos in

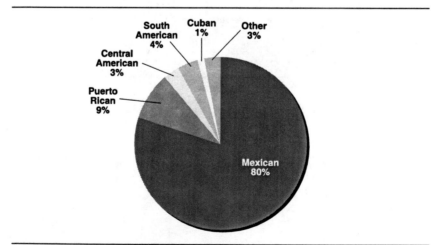

Source: Nielsen PrimeLocation®/Pop-Facts®: 2000 Data, 2012 Estimates

Figure 5.11 Country of Origin—Chicago

suburban Chicago grew from 291,053 in 1990 to 651,473 in 2000. Cicero, once an enclave of Italians and East Europeans, went from 37 percent Latino in 1990 to 77 percent ten years later," according to an article published by the Community Media Workshop.[12] In fact, Cicero was one of the cities featured in a recent exhibit from New York's Museum of Modern Art, "Foreclosure: Rehousing The American Dream," which I blogged about for Ad Age (http://adage.com/article/the-big-tent/hispanics-a-mega-buying-force/234056) in spring 2012 and is a fascinating view into what the future of urban and suburban housing in America could look like. But I digress.

Like Los Angeles, Chicago could be a bellwether for the country. Chicagoans seem keenly aware of the importance of the Latino community to its city and the future of the country. "Latinos are on the front line of a demographic revolution that in all likelihood will fundamentally transform the social and economic landscape of Chicago and the nation," writes John P. Koval, editor of a white paper titled "Latinos in Chicago: Reflections of an American Landscape," underwritten by the Chicago Community Trust Latino Research Collaborative and published in 2010

While the entrepreneurial spirit of Hispanics has revitalized many areas of Chicago, bringing new shops and restaurants from the Northwest to the Southwest side of the city, the biggest challenges facing Latinos in Chicago—and across the country, frankly—are the same challenges facing the African American community: bridging the gap in educational attainment and economic disparity. I will discuss at greater length the subject of the "graying and the browning of America" and its implications for the future of this country later on, but suffice it to say that I agree with the authors of this great white paper when they say, "Latinos and African Americans have long been marginalized educationally, economically, and politically. As they become a numeric majority, their educational, occupational, and political liabilities shift from important to critical for this country's future quality of life, prosperity, and global competitiveness. Clearly, Chicago and the nation cannot meet the challenges of a global world if the energy and creative poten-

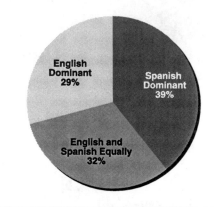

Source: Nielsen Media Research, 2012 Hispanic TV Households by Language Strata

Figure 5.12 Language Spoken at Home—Chicago

tial if over half of its population and labor force continue to be stifled educationally, occupationally, economically, and socially. The problem belongs to all of us. The solution is our shared responsibility."[13]

In terms of language, this is a market where language usage is evenly split among the three groups, according to Nielsen's language strata data (see Figure 5.12 above). Nonetheless, there is still a robust local Spanish-language media offering with seven radio stations and eight community newspapers, including the very well-established *La Raza*, which has been in existence since 1970. And finally, in terms of population growth, Hispanics were expected to grow by 44 percent from 2000 through 2016, contributing about 97 percent of the total population growth of the DMA region, according to Nielsen PrimeLocation.

DALLAS-FT. WORTH, TEXAS

DMA STATS

Hispanic ranking: 6
General market ranking: 5
Counties included: 32
> Anderson, Bosque, Collin, Comanche, Cooke, Dallas, Delta, Denton, Ellis, Erath, Fannin, Freestone, Hamilton, Henderson, Hill, Hood, Hopkins, Hunt, Jack, Johnson, Kaufman, Lamar, Navarro, Palo Pinto, Parker, Rains, Red River, Rockwall, Somervell, Tarrant, Van Zandt, Wise

Racial Composition of Dallas

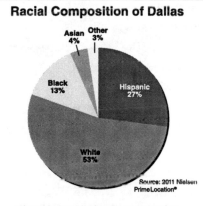

Asian 4%
Other 3%
Black 13%
Hispanic 27%
White 53%

Source: 2011 Nielsen PrimeLocation®

Hispanic Population Demographics

	Hispanic Population	% Hispanic of Total
Households	504,610	20%
Persons 2+	1,753,000	26%
Adults 18–34	610,000	36%
Adults 18–49	950,000	30%
Adults 25–54	771,000	26%

TV HOUSEHOLDS

Hispanic: 504,610
Total: 2,571,310
Percentage of HH with kids: 59.4 percent vs. 32.1 percent for non-Hispanics
Median age: 26.7 vs. 38.7
Any Spanish spoken: 89 percent
Average Hispanic HH income: $58,557
Source: Nielsen Universe Estimates 2012

HISPANIC CONSUMER SPENDING

$27.4 billion out of a total of $193.4 billion[14]

The Hispanic population in the Dallas–Fort Worth (DFW) area is projected to nearly double from the 27 percent it currently represents to 55 percent by 2040, according to the Texas State Data Center.[15] While Dallas will continue to attract newly arrived immigrants, the bulk of the growth in the Hispanic community will come from the children of immigrants who have settled here over the past several decades. The diversity of employment ranges widely from blue-collar work in the service sector, to white-collar work in the banking, telecommunications, energy, health care and computer technology sectors, which is why the city has been a magnet for the many Fortune 500 companies that have located their headquarters there. Dallas is also home to many Hispanic businesses, including Dieste, the largest Hispanic agency in the country with over $39 million in revenues, according to *Advertising Age*'s 2012 edition of the Hispanic Fact Pack.

With a median age that is twelve years younger than their non-Hispanic counterparts, it is easy to understand why the number of households with kids is almost double (59.4 percent) than those of non-Hispanic households (32.1 percent). Meanwhile, according to IHS Global Insight's Hispanic Market Monitor 2011, the average Hispanic household income in Dallas is $58,557, which makes it the third lowest of the top eight Hispanic markets. As in Chicago, this can partly be attributed to lower overall educational achievement levels of Hispanic students. But that trend could be about to change. According to a recent report by the Dallas Independent School District, the good news is that "over the past five years, Hispanic students have made significant progress narrowing the gap with their peers statewide on the four-year graduation rate, completion rate, and dropout rate." As a result, "the percentage of district Hispanic students graduating has risen to 88.7 percent, just a point and a half less than Hispanic students statewide. The percentage of Dallas ISD Hispanic students dropping out has been cut nearly in half since the class of 2007."[16]

Concentrated mainly in the DFW area, the Hispanic population is largely of Mexican ancestry, 86 percent (see Figure 5.13). But here's

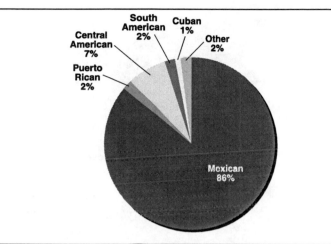

Source: Nielsen PrimeLocation®/Pop-Facts®: 2000 Data, 2012 Estimates

Figure 5.13 Country of Origin—Dallas

where generations make a difference. If you're watching the Dallas Cowboys or Mavericks play, look closely in the stands and you will see plenty of Latino fans. They are mainly second- and third-generation Mexicans who are bilingual and probably better educated than the average Latino in Dallas. Now, if you are watching a major league soccer game at the Dallas Stadium, chances are those fans are more used to cheering for the Mexican Soccer League favorites, the Pumas or the Chivas, than cheering for the Cowboys. But their money is just as green!

In terms of language, 89 percent of Hispanics in this DMA region speak some Spanish, although media consumption is evenly split, with 41 percent of TV viewers being Spanish dominant, according to Nielsen Language Strata, 24 percent consuming equally in Spanish and English, and English dominants making up another 35 percent, as you can see in Figure 5.14 on the next page. The local Spanish-language media offering includes fifteen radio stations, both AM and FM, running the gamut of formats, and a dozen and a half—that's right, eighteen—community newspapers.

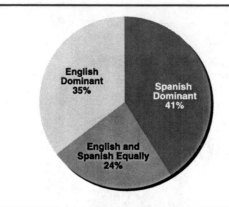

Source: Nielsen Media Research, 2012 Hispanic TV Households by Language Strata

Figure 5.14 Language Spoken at Home—Dallas

SAN ANTONIO, TEXAS

DMA STATS

Hispanic ranking: 7
General market ranking: 36
Counties included: 25
> Atascosa, Bandera, Bexar, Comal, De Witt, Dimmit, Edwards,
> Frio, Goliad, Gonzales, Guadalupe, Karnes, Kendall, Kerr,
> Kinney, La Salle, Lavaca, McMullen, Maverick, Medina, Real,
> Uvalde, Val Verde, Wilson, Zavala

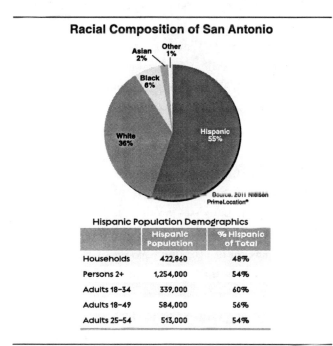

Racial Composition of San Antonio

Source: 2011 Nielsen
PrimeLocation®

Hispanic Population Demographics

	Hispanic Population	% Hispanic of Total
Households	422,860	48%
Persons 2+	1,254,000	54%
Adults 18–34	339,000	60%
Adults 18–49	584,000	56%
Adults 25–54	513,000	54%

TV HOUSEHOLDS

Hispanic: 422,860
Total: 880,690
Percentage of HH with kids: 48.7 percent vs. 29.4 percent for non-Hispanics
Median age: 31 vs. 40
Any Spanish spoken: 84 percent
Average Hispanic HH income: $62, 332
Source: Nielsen Universe Estimates 2012

HISPANIC CONSUMER SPENDING

$23.6 billion out of a total of $61.1 billion[17]

The home of the Alamo has seen many generations of Latinos establish roots there and, as a result, this is a DMA region where the majority of Latinos have been U.S. born for decades. In recent years, there has been an important influx of wealthy families from Monterrey, which could have a significant impact on the Hispanic business community. Already this bilingual and bicultural community has seen a strong movement toward retro-acculturation, the process by which one tries to reconnect with his or her roots by relearning the language and traditions of his or her cultural heritage. A testament to this trend is the various "meet-up" groups where Spanish is celebrated, spoken, and practiced. That's because Latino roots run deep here. According to history books, the first civilian settlement in Texas was San Antonio de Bexar, established in 1718 by the Spaniards, who also left a trail of eighteenth-century missions built along the San Antonio River that are part of the great colonial architectural attractions of the area, besides the famous Alamo.

According to the 2007 Survey of Hispanic-Owned Businesses published by the Bureau of the Census in 2010, San Antonio has the second-highest percentage of Hispanic-owned business (39.4 percent) among cities with populations of 500,000 or more. Only El Paso beats them with an impressive 59.8 percent of Hispanic-owned businesses based in that city. A look at the honorees for San Antonio's 2012 Hispanic Chamber of Commerce business awards dinner, is a veritable who's who of the Hispanic market, including Lionel and Kathy Sosa, living legends in the world of advertising; Lourdes Castro Ramirez, President and CEO of the San Antonio Housing Authority, described in the program as a Hispanic "rising star," as well as Ernest Bromley, co-founder and CEO of Bromley Communications, one of the top twenty Hispanic agencies in the country.

Because San Antonio is home to four U.S. Air Force bases and does not have a significant number of manufacturing or construction jobs that tend to attract more newly arrived immigrants, the Latino work force is predominately employed by the government. In terms of ancestry, a look at Figure 5.15 tells you it's Mexican, Mexican, Mexican with very little representation of Hispanics from other countries.

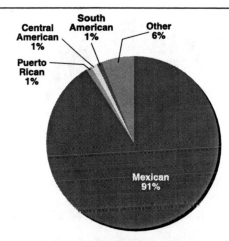

Source: Nielsen PrimeLocation®/Pop-Facts®: 2000 Data, 2012 Estimates

Figure 5.15 Country of Origin—San Antonio

Where you can tell this is not a "typical" Hispanic market is when you look at language usage and media consumption. In spite of the fact that the very first full-time Spanish-language TV station in America, KWEX-TV, was established in San Antonio, this DMA region has always ranked at the top of the list in terms of the percentage of Latinos who feel more comfortable speaking English. According to the 2011 Nielsen Language Strata, while 84 percent of Hispanics speak some Spanish at home, TV consumption in San Antonio is 59 percent English dominant, with 20 percent of viewers consuming equally in Spanish and English, and Spanish dominants making up another 21 percent, as you can see in Figure 5.16. And yet, this DMA region is home to seven Spanish-language radio stations and two bilingual community newspapers.

With an median age of thirty-one, San Antonio has the second-oldest Hispanic population of the top eight markets—behind Miami at thirty-nine—but it still beats the non-Hispanic median age of forty by nine years! Hispanics comprise 60 percent of kids age two to seventeen and 60 percent of adults eighteen to thirty-four, so this town is going to con-

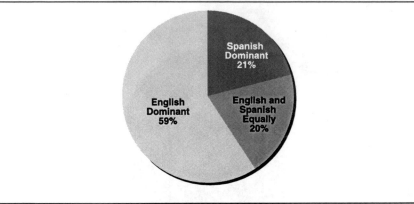

Source: Nielsen Media Research, 2012 Hispanic TV Households by Language Strata

Figure 5.16 Language Spoken at Home—San Antonio

tinue being predominantly Hispanic for years to come. In fact, in terms of population growth, Nielsen Population estimates that Hispanics will grow by 43 percent, accounting for 71 percent of the total population growth in the DMA region between 2000 and 2016!

SAN FRANCISCO, CALIFORNIA

DMA STATS

Hispanic ranking: 8
General market ranking: 6
Counties included: 11
    Alameda, Contra Costa, Lake, Marin, Mendocino, Napa, San
    Francisco, San Mateo, Santa Clara, Solano-W, Sonoma

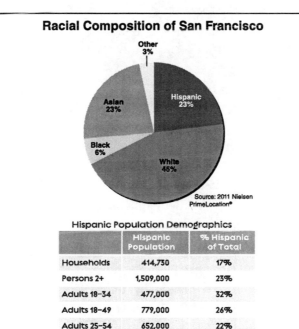

Racial Composition of San Francisco

Other 3%
Hispanic 23%
Asian 23%
Black 6%
White 45%

Source: 2011 Nielsen PrimeLocation®

Hispanic Population Demographics

	Hispanic Population	% Hispanic of Total
Households	414,730	17%
Persons 2+	1,509,000	23%
Adults 18–34	477,000	32%
Adults 18–49	779,000	26%
Adults 25–54	652,000	22%

TV HOUSEHOLDS

Hispanic: 414,730
Total: 2,506,510
Percentage of HH with kids: 53.1 percent vs. 27.7 percent for non-Hispanics
Median age: 29.1 vs. 42.4
Any Spanish spoken: 83 percent
Average Hispanic HH income: $81,846
    Source: Nielsen Universe Estimates 2012

HISPANIC CONSUMER SPENDING

$32.7 billion out of a total of $246.4 billion[18]

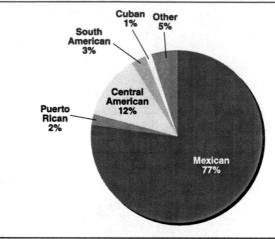

Source: Nielsen PrimeLocation®/Pop-Facts®: 2000 Data, 2012 Estimates

Figure 5.17 Country of Origin—San Francisco

This market is also made up of two very different kinds of Latino populations. The high-tech orientation of Silicon Valley makes San Francisco a magnet for sophisticated and well-educated Latinos. As a result, Hispanics in the Bay Area have the highest household income ($81,846) of all top Hispanic markets. On the other hand, the city of San Jose is dominated mainly by middle-class Mexican Americans who can be found working on assembly lines or in more skilled jobs, such as hospital technicians. There are also a growing number of Hispanics in the San Jose area who are small-business owners. Because the market comprises equally large segments of Latinos and Asians, this is a market that could also become a microcosm of what the future holds for very racially diverse cities, such as New York or Chicago.

The breakdown of Hispanics by country of origin (Figure 5.17) shows you that with 23 percent of Hispanics coming from countries other than Mexico, it's a fairly diverse group of Latinos, although naturally, Mexicans dominate.

While the Latino population in this area was projected to grow 39 percent between 2000 and 2016, it will account for 72 percent of the

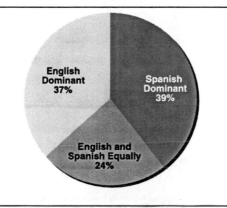

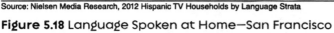

Source: Nielsen Media Research, 2012 Hispanic TV Households by Language Strata

Figure 5.18 Language Spoken at Home—San Francisco

total population growth. Hispanic birth rates are playing a key role in that growth. Even though recent studies show that U.S.-born Latinas are having fewer children than their foreign-born counterparts, 53.1 percent of Hispanic households in San Francisco have children versus only 27.7 percent of non-Hispanics. In terms of language, 83 percent of Hispanics in this DMA region speak some Spanish at home. Accordingly, there is a relatively robust local Spanish-language media presence, with eleven radio stations and nine community newspapers including *El Mensajero*, which has been serving Bay Area Spanish-language readers since 1987. In terms of TV viewing, according to Nielsen Language Strata, almost 40 percent are Spanish dominant, with a quarter of viewers consuming equally in Spanish and English, and English dominants making up another 37 percent, as you can see in Figure 5.18.

Key Takeaways:
- Expect impressive growth from Hispanic TV households, reflecting a new shift in television-viewing audiences as baby boomers age out of the key thirty-five to forty-nine demographic.
- Understand the market-to-market differences of the Hispanic community and keep them in mind as you develop local marketing initiatives.

NOTES

1. DMA is a registered service mark of The Nielsen Company. Used under license.

1. "40% of New U.S. TV Homes this Season Will Be Hispanic Households," *NielsenWire*, September 3 2010. http://blog.nielsen.com/nielsenwire/media_entertainment/40-of-new-u-s-tv-homes-this-season-will-be-hispanic-households.

2. "Number of Ethnic TV Households Grows: Asian TV Households Up Nearly 10 Percent," *NielsenWire*, September 26, 2011. http://blog.nielsen.com/nielsenwire/media_entertainment/number-of-ethnic-tv-households-grows-asian-tv-households-up-nearly-10-percent.

3. IHS Global Insight, Hispanic Market Monitor 2011. www.ihs.com/products/global-insight/index.aspx.

4. The U.S. Census Bureau, 2010 Census Briefs: The Hispanic Population: 2010. Issued May 2011. www.census.gov/prod/cen2010/briefs/c2010br-04.pdf.

5. Nielsen Station Index, (09/19/11—09/23/12). The Nielsen Company. Total Day is defined at Monday-Sunday 6 A.M.-2 A.M.. Rankings based on average impressions. Live+7.

6. IHS Global Insight, Hispanic Market Monitor 2011. www.ihs.com/products/global-insight/index.aspx.

7. IHS Global Insight, Hispanic Market Monitor 2011. www.ihs.com/products/global-insight/index.aspx.

8. IHS Global Insight, Hispanic Market Monitor 2011. www.ihs.com/products/global-insight/index.aspx.

9. My Fox Houston, "The Recipe for Foreign-born Entrepreneurship in Houston," *Fox News Latino*, June 21, 2012. http://latino.foxnews.com/latino/community/2012/06/21/recipe-for-foreign-born-entrepreneurship-in-houston.

10. Klineberg, Stephen L., Ph.D., An Historical Overview of Immigration in Houston, Based on the Houston Area Survey. Published June 2008. Rice University and the Center for Houston's Future. http://has.rice.edu/WorkArea/showcontent.aspx?id=250.

11. IHS Global Insight, Hispanic Market Monitor 2011. www.ihs.com/products/global-insight/index.aspx.

12. Community Workshop Staff, "Chicago's Latino Communities: Diverse, Growing," Community Media Workshop, May 2005. www.newstips.org/briefing-papers/chicagos-latino-communities-diverse-growing.

13. Korval, John P., Series Editor, Latinos in Chicago Reflections of an American Landscape, in the White Paper Series, published June 2010 by the Institute for Latino Studies, University of Notre Dame, with funding from The Chicago Community Trust Latino Research Collaborative and The Arthur Foundation

http://latinostudies.nd.edu/calendar/index.php?enum=1015.

14. IHS Global Insight, Hispanic Market Monitor 2011. www.ihs.com/products/global-insight/index.aspx.

15. Greater Dallas Hispanic Chamber of Commerce. www.gdhcc.com.

16. Texas Education Agency data cited by Dallas Independent School District. www.dallasisd.org/site/Default.aspx?PageType=3&DomainID=1&PageID=1&ViewID=047e6be3-6d87-4130-8424-d8e4e9ed6c2a&FlexDataID=14006.

17. IHS Global Insight, Hispanic Market Monitor 2011. www.ihs.com/products/global-insight/index.aspx.

18. IHS Global Insight Hispanic Market Monitor 2011. www.ihs.com/products/global-insight/index.aspx.

6

~~~~~

HISPANIC IDENTITY

As we discussed briefly in Chapter 3, the U.S. Bureau of the Census has been trying to improve the way it counts and classifies Americans by changing the way it asks questions about country of origin and race on the decennial census form. You may remember the brouhaha over adding the terms *Latino* and *some other race* to the 2000 census and allowing people to check more than one box when answering these questions. Contrary to what most people think, Hispanic is not a race; it is an ethnicity. So, as part of an ethnic community that has members of all races, answering the race question is sometimes difficult for Hispanics, and their responses (or lack thereof) to the 2010 census questions are a reflection of that. Clearly, the census is having a hard time properly counting and classifying Hispanics by race, mainly because Latinos do not see themselves reflected in these questions.

"Census forms through the decades have employed a changing list of race categories that reflect their times," writes D'Vera Cohn of the Pew Research Center. "But these categories do not always match people's ideas of who they are. Despite the Census Bureau's hopes that respondents would select from the offered race categories, 18.5 million people in the 2010 census chose a catch-all category: some other race. The number and share of the population choosing 'some other race' grew since the 2000 census. Most of those who chose 'some other race' were Hispanic," she adds.

Currently, the U.S. Bureau of the Census asks people to answer two questions about their race and origin. (Figure 3.4 in Chapter 3 shows you how the question appeared on most forms). In 2010, however, the U.S. Bureau of the Census tested some alternative questionnaire designs and wording in the hopes of improving responses to the race and origin questions, especially among Hispanics.

"Whenever you have people who can't find themselves in the question, it's a bad question," said Mary C. Waters, a sociology professor

8. What is Person 1's race or origin? *Mark* ⊠ *one or more boxes* **AND** *write in the specific race(s) or origin(s).*

☐ White — *Print origin(s), for example, German, Irish, Lebanese, Egyptian, and so on.* ↗

☐ Black, African Am., or Negro — *Print origin(s), for example, African American, Haitian, Nigerian, and so on.* ↗

☐ Mexican, Mexican Am., Chicano   ☐ Puerto Rican   ☐ Cuban
☐ Other Hispanic, Latino, or Spanish origin — *Print origin(s), for example, Argentinean, Colombian, Dominican, Nicaraguan, Salvadoran, Spaniard, and so on.* ↗

☐ American Indian or Alaska Native — *Print name of enrolled or principal tribe(s), for example, Navajo, Mayan, Tlingit, and so on.* ↗

☐ Asian Indian   ☐ Chinese   ☐ Filipino
☐ Japanese   ☐ Korean   ☐ Vietnamese
☐ Other Asian — *Print origin(s), for example, Hmong, Laotian, Thai, Pakistani, Cambodian, and so on.* ↗

☐ Native Hawaiian   ☐ Guamanian or Chamorro   ☐ Samoan
☐ Other Pacific Islander — *Print origin(s), for example, Fijian, Tongan, and so on.* ↗

☐ Some other race or origin — *Print race(s) or origin(s).* ↗

Figure 6.1a Some of the Alternate Race and Origin Questions Tested in 2010 (See also Figure 6.1b)

at Harvard who specializes in the challenges of measuring race and ethnicity, in "For Many Latinos, Racial Identity Is More Culture Than Color," an article for *The New York Times* written by Mireya Navarro.[1]

As Navarro notes, "the problem is more than academic—the census data on race serves many purposes, including determining the makeup of voting districts and monitoring discriminatory practices in hiring and racial disparities in education and health. When respondents do not choose a race, the Census Bureau assigns them one, based on factors like the racial makeup of their neighborhood, inevitably leading to a less accurate count." The Bureau of the Census assigns nonrespondents a race? Really? That is just plain scary! Given the problems the census has with nonresponses from certain communities, especially among Latinos, we have to come up with a better solution.

8. What is Person 1's race or origin? *Mark* X *one or more boxes.*

☐ White
☐ Black, African Am., or Negro
☐ Mexican, Mexican Am., Chicano
☐ Puerto Rican
☐ Cuban
☐ Other Hispanic, Latino, or Spanish origin — *Print origin, for example, Argentinean, Colombian, Dominican, Nicaraguan, Salvadoran, Spaniard, and so on.* ↘

☐ American Indian or Alaska Native — *Print name of enrolled or principal tribe.* ↘

☐ Asian Indian	☐ Japanese	☐ Native Hawaiian
☐ Chinese	☐ Korean	☐ Guamanian or Chamorro
☐ Filipino	☐ Vietnamese	☐ Samoan

☐ Other Asian — *Print race, for example, Hmong, Laotian, Thai, Pakistani, Cambodian, and so on.* ↘   ☐ Other Pacific Islander — *Print race, for example, Fijian, Tongan, and so on.* ↘

☐ Some other race or origin — *Print race or origin.* ↘

Figure 6.1b Some of the Alternate Race and Origin Questions Tested in 2010

One solution that I know the Bureau of the Census *is* working on already is the anticipated use of the Internet as a primary mode of self-response in the 2020 census, which could lead to increased response rates. The second, of course, is changing the way we ask the question, so it is easier to understand and to answer. "The U.S. Census Bureau is committed to improving the accuracy and the reliability of census results by expanding our understanding of how people identify their race and Hispanic origin," Director Robert Groves said in August 2012, when the results of the alternative questions tested in 2010 were released. The research conducted by the U.S. Bureau of the Census included the mailing of fifteen alternative types of census 2010 forms to 30,000 households, a follow-up telephone survey of a sample of those respondents, and almost seventy focus-group interviews across the United States and Puerto Rico on the general topic of self-identification. "Results from the 2010 Alternative Questionnaire Experiment reveal that the combination of the race and Hispanic origin question approach appears to be a promising strategy for collecting these data items," according to the Federal Register.[2] The Bureau of the Census follows the federal standards for collecting and presenting data on race and Hispanic origin established by the U.S. Office of Management and Budget (OMB) in October 1997.

Although the Office of Management and Budget acknowledged in 1997 that the race categories in the census "represent a social-political construct designed for collecting data on the race and ethnicity of broad population groups in this country, and are not anthropologically or scientifically based," it is important to get this right. Why? Because from 2020 to 2050, the Latino population is projected to add more people (66 million) to the United States every year than all other race/ethnic groups combined (31.1 million).[3] In January of 2013, *U.S.A Today* published an article that suggested that the Bureau of the Census was considering "eliminating the Hispanic origin question and combining it with the race question." Making Hispanics a race could facilitate their tracking by the census. But not everyone agrees. Former Census director Kenneth Prewitt, who is now a professor at Columbia University and is writing a book on the subject, says that the Census Bureau should just stop asking about race. "We ought to get rid of the race question and go to national origin," he told *U.S.A Today*. "That's what this country needs—not those 18th-century-old race groups," he adds. [4]

ARE YOU TALKING TO ME?

Researchers often try to quantify Hispanic "identity" by simply asking Latinos how they relate to certain terms or labels like "Latino" or "Hispanic" versus "American." I think this approach is fundamentally flawed. I am 100 percent American and 100 percent Latino, so when you ask me to choose between the two, you are not going to get a accurate answer.

All immigrants—not just Latinos—often have to straddle two worlds and cultures: the culture we come from (which, even for Latinos born in the U.S., is closely associated with our parents' country of origin) and the culture we have chosen to live in. The rich diversity that results from how people live and whom they choose as partners in life can often increase exponentially the number of cultures they are living in. For example, I have a friend who is half-black, half-Mexican, who had children with her white partner using sperm from a Peruvian friend, and their home is a true reflection of that cultural fusion. This is what *multicultural* really means. It is this rich cultural tapestry that we have been weaving in this country for hundreds of years. As the fastest-growing minority, Latinos are just the tip of the iceberg. Multiculturalism is not about understanding individual minority cultures in isolation, it is about understanding how the mix of cultures deeply transforms the way we live in the twenty-first century that goes way beyond race. It speaks of a duality that we all can relate to but often find hard to express.

One of my first assignments for Univision was to "bring to life" the 2010 census data in a video. As we worked on the script, we felt it was very important to try to capture this duality we experience everyday, as well as the overall invisibility of the Hispanic consumer in the eyes of the business community. By adding to the facts and figures some of our personal experiences as Latinos in the United States, we were able to do just that. In fact, when we posted this video on our YouTube channel, http://www.youtube.com/watch?v=pQnhuj11zgI, without a press release or any social media push of any kind, it immediately went viral. Why? Because it taps into that duality that is central to the Latino reality. The other reason this video was shared by so many across the country was because it tapped into our shared American experience, where *fútbol* and football both have a place in our hearts or where regaetton and rock and roll can safely coexist.

This shared American experience is forged by the everyday life of Latinos and their families. It doesn't really matter if they have been in this country for one year or for twenty years. It does not matter if they are enrolling their children in school for the first time, or if they are getting their first job out of college, or for that matter if they are starting a family or starting a business; as brown-skinned Latinos in this country who sometimes speak with an accent, Latinos get treated differently. Not that I would ever compare our experiences to those of the Black or Asian communities who have also suffered tremendous discrimination. I'm just saying that minorities in general have a common American experience of "otherness." What matters most, still, in this country is the color of your skin. This is an *old* American reality, but one that I think—I hope—is changing. I see it changing mostly in the younger generations. My nieces and nephews, for example, don't see people's color the way my parents' generation did. They are perhaps more accepting of different cultures because they have been exposed to so many more people of different cultures and religions right here, in the U.S., than they would ever have been in their home countries. They grew up in much more diverse environments—in school and in the neighborhood. They are able to watch TV from all over the world and travel to places like China or Russia that were not even accessible during my youth, which was not so long ago. Bottom line, they are much more open to trying new things from food to fashion and music and less quick to judge things from other cultures. In fact, culture has become the new currency of "cool," and for Latinos, our culture continues to be the connective tissue at the heart of who we are and how we identify in the United States.

THE IMPORTANCE OF CULTURE TO IDENTITY

Hispanics hail from twenty different countries, but the fact is that all those countries have some very important things in common: they share a common language, Spanish; a common religion, Catholicism; and they share a five-hundred-plus-year history as part of the American continent. Although each country has its own history and nuances, these three factors largely shape our Hispanic values and become a fundamental part of the Latino "culture" that we all share here in the United States.

According to the census, over 70 percent of all Hispanics living in the United States come from Mexico (63 percent) or other Central American countries (7.9 percent). People from Mexico and Central America have similar tastes in music (norteña, ranchera, cumbia, etc.) and in food (tamales, chilaquiles, tacos, and enchiladas, to name a few). The other 30 percent of Latinos in the United States come from the Caribbean or South American nations and tend to congregate in larger cities along the Eastern Seaboard of the United States. This "group" also has similar tastes in music (salsa, merengue, and bachata) and food, which is not as spicy (black beans, plantains, yucca, etc.). While these two "groups" are distinct from each other in many ways, both groups share many cultural and religious values. Once Hispanics come to the United States, however, they are all lumped together, by the census and everyone else, under this one giant "Latino" umbrella. In my opinion, this is probably one of the reasons why the country of origin continues to be the preferred way for Latinos to self-identify, even well into the second generation. According to the Pew Hispanic Center's study "Hispanics and Their Views of Identity," 62 percent of first-generation Latinos and 43 percent of second-generation Hispanics use their country of origin to describe themselves most often.[5]

A recent study, conducted by Mindshare for Yahoo as part of an Ethnodynamics series on marketing to ethnic minorities in the United States, confirms that "ethnicity is core to the identity of all minorities" and that 67 percent of Latinos strongly agreed that their ethnicity was "a significant part of my identity" while 78 percent were "proud of my ethnic identity."[6] When compared to other ethnic groups, Hispanics were more likely to "nurture" their ethnicity than were African Americans or Asians, according to this study. Figure 6.2 shows you how, on average, Latinos felt more strongly about their ethnicity and the influence it had on their identity than did Asians or African Americans in this study.

In fact, compared to other minorities, ethnicity had a greater influence on Latinos in a number of key areas from values and religion, to how they raise their kids or the neighborhoods they choose to live in. (See Figure 6.3.)

POLITICS, VALUES, AND RELIGION

These findings are in line with those outlined in the Pew Hispanic Center's report "When Labels Don't Fit: Hispanics and Their Views

	Hispanics	African/ Asian Americans
Expose my children to my ethnic background	60%	51%
Trying to get in touch with my ethnic identity	56	38
More comfortable with my ethnicity today	57	50
I like to be part of activities and traditions celebrating my ethnicity	66	60

Source: Marketing to Hispanics, Part 2 of the Ethnodynamics Series, Mindshare Added Value and Yahoo

Figure 6.2 Influence of Ethnicity on Identity, as Shown by Percentage Who "Strongly Agree" When It Comes To My Ethnicity.

How I feel	Hispanics	African/ Asian Americans
My individuality	61%	51%
My religion or faith	61	52
My values	60	53
My view on gender roles	55	37
Who I am with		
The neighborhood I live in	56	34
Raising my children	55	50
My close circle of friends	54	45
What I do		
Holiday events and celebrations	69	51
Eating habits and preferences	69	54
The vacations I take	47	27

Source: "Marketing to Hispanics," Part 2 of the Ethnodynamics series, Mindshare Added Value and Yahoo

Figure 6.3 Percentage Influence of Ethnicity Summary

of Identity." This Pew study says that Latinos are more religious than most Americans in the sense that more of them claim to have a religious affiliation. According to this Pew survey, 83 percent of Hispanics claimed to have a religious affiliation in 2011. This was slightly higher than the share seen in the general public, which was 80 percent. However, they are as likely as the general population to say that religion is important in their lives. "Overall, religiosity is highest among immigrant Latinos and lowest among those who are third generation," says the report. Not surprisingly, 62 percent of Latinos were Catholic; followed by 19 percent who were Protestant; and 14 percent who were unaffiliated (see Figure 6.4). However, Figure 6.5 shows you how the religious affiliation of Latinos varies

Religious Profile of Hispanics

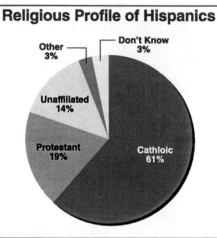

Source: Pew Hispanic Center, 2011 National Survey of Latinos; Pew Research Center for the People & the Press, aggregated January–December Surveys

Figure 6.4

from foreign born to native born, with each generation becoming more Protestant over time and skewing to more evangelical among second and third generation Latinos.

Based on their religious views, Hispanics sometimes are described as more conservative politically, but what's fascinating about the Latino community is that they are neither strictly conservative nor liberal. According to the Pew Hispanic Center's 2011 National Survey of Latinos, Hispanics are evenly split among conservative, moderate, and liberal political views. See Figure 6.6. This means that both Democrats

	Foreign Born %	Native Born %	Second Generation %	Third or Higher Generation %
Catholic	69	51	59	40
Protestant	16	22	18	30
Unaffiliated	9	20	18	24

Source: Pew Hispanic Center, 2011 National Survey of Latinos

Figure 6.5 Religious Affiliation by Generation among Hispanics

How Would You Describe Your Political Views?

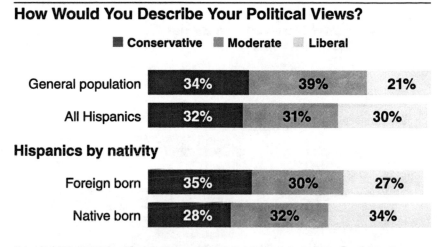

■ Conservative   ■ Moderate   ▒ Liberal

General population	34%	39%	21%
All Hispanics	32%	31%	30%

Hispanics by nativity

Foreign born	35%	30%	27%
Native born	28%	32%	34%

Notes: N=1,220, 2011 National Survey of Latinos; N=1,521, Pew Research Center for the People & the Press. Responses of "Don't Know" and "Refused" are not shown.

Source: Pew Hispanic Center, 2011 National Survey of Latinos; Pew Research Center for the People & the Press December 2011

Figure 6.6 Hispanic's Political Views

and Republicans have an opportunity to attract Latino voters in years to come and, not withstanding the 2012 election results, they both have their work cut out for them.

The big differences in Latino political views can be seen in terms of key social policy issues, such as size of government or more government investments in education, as well as issues like abortion. "When it comes to the size of government, Hispanics are more likely than the general public to say they would rather have a bigger government providing more services than a smaller government with fewer services," says the Pew Hispanic Center report. Figure 6.7 shows that a whopping 75 percent of Hispanics say they want bigger government with more services, while only 19 percent say they would rather have a smaller government with fewer services. I think this desire for bigger government partly comes from the larger role government plays in Latin American countries and a general belief that government should take care of its people. "By contrast, just 41 percent of the general U.S. public say they want a bigger government, while nearly half (48 percent) say they want

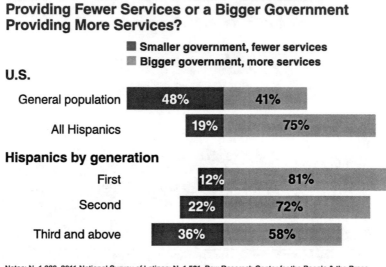

Figure 6.7 Hispanic Views on Size of Government

a smaller government," explains Pew. Again, the views of second- and third-generation Latinos tend to be more conservative. Ronald Brownstein encapsulated this struggle very well in 2010 when he wrote, "Over time, the major focus in this struggle is likely to be the tension between an aging white population that appears increasingly resistant to taxes and dubious of public spending, and a minority population that overwhelmingly views government education, health, and social-welfare programs as the best ladder of opportunity for its children."[7]

When it comes to abortion, first generation and older Hispanics still hold a more conservative view than the general public, but my-oh-my, how quickly have these views changed. In 2002, when the Pew Hispanic Center released its first National Latino Survey, 77 percent of Latinos found abortion "not acceptable." According to this most recent report, just 58 percent of first-generation Latinos and 63 percent of Latinos who are sixty-five years old or older, find abortion "illegal in

Do You Think Abortion Should Be Legal or Illegal?

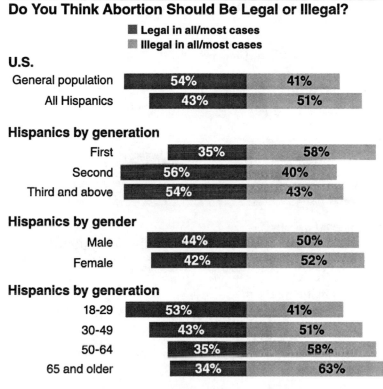

Legal in all/most cases
Illegal in all/most cases

U.S.

	Legal	Illegal
General population	54%	41%
All Hispanics	43%	51%

Hispanics by generation

	Legal	Illegal
First	35%	58%
Second	56%	40%
Third and above	54%	43%

Hispanics by gender

	Legal	Illegal
Male	44%	50%
Female	42%	52%

Hispanics by generation

	Legal	Illegal
18-29	53%	41%
30-49	43%	51%
50-64	35%	58%
65 and older	34%	63%

Notes: N=1,220, 2011 National Survey of Latinos; N=1,521, Pew Reserach Center for the People & the Press. Responses of "Don't Know" and "Refused" are not shown.

Source: Pew Hispanic Center, 2011 National Survey of Latinos; Pew Research Center for the People & the Press December 2011

Figure 6.8 Hispanic Views on Abortion

all/most cases." But when you look at the results for both second- and third-generation Latinos, you can see that they are more in line with the general population in the U.S. on this issue, with more than half of Latinos saying that abortion should be legal in all/most cases.

With regard to homosexuality, the pendulum has really swung the other way. Whereas the majority of Latinos (72 percent) found gay sex "unacceptable" according to the 2002 National Survey of Latinos, in 2011 almost two thirds of Hispanics (59 percent) said that homosexuality should be accepted by society. Obviously, the way the questions were asked was different in each survey, so it's hard to compare results.

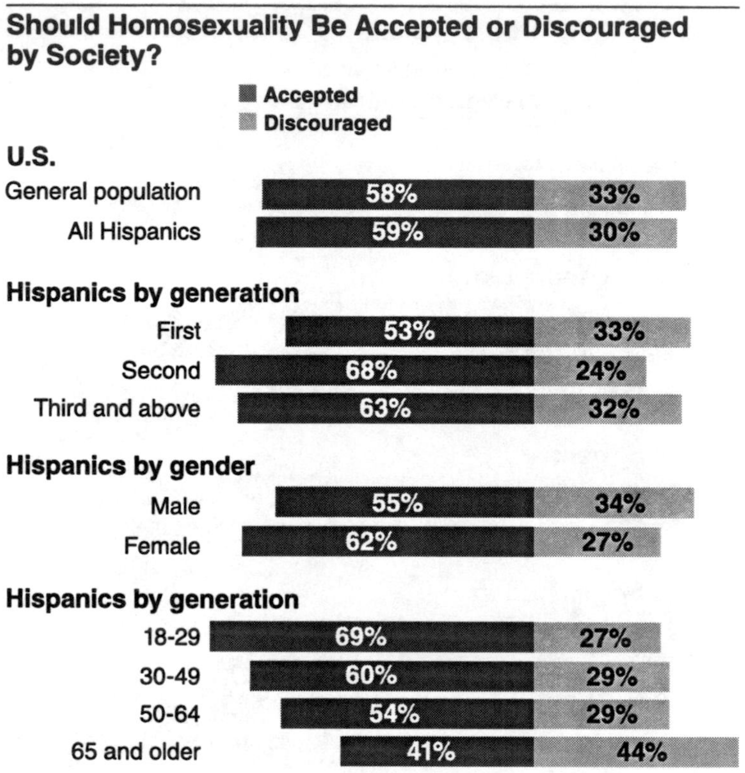

Should Homosexuality Be Accepted or Discouraged by Society?

■ Accepted
▨ Discouraged

U.S.

	Accepted	Discouraged
General population	58%	33%
All Hispanics	59%	30%

Hispanics by generation

	Accepted	Discouraged
First	53%	33%
Second	68%	24%
Third and above	63%	32%

Hispanics by gender

	Accepted	Discouraged
Male	55%	34%
Female	62%	27%

Hispanics by generation

	Accepted	Discouraged
18-29	69%	27%
30-49	60%	29%
50-64	54%	29%
65 and older	41%	44%

Notes: N=1,220, 2011 National Survey of Latinos; N=1,521, Pew Reserach Center for the People & the Press. Responses of "Don't Know" and "Refused" are not shown.

Source: Pew Hispanic Center, 2011 National Survey of Latinos; Pew Research Center for the People & the Press December 2011

Figure 6.9 Hispanic Views on Homosexuality

Nonetheless, the only group of Hispanics who think that homosexuality should be discouraged by society are older Hispanics (sixty-five years old or older) although they too are almost evenly split.

And finally, let's look at interracial or interethnic marriages, which I addressed earlier when talking about multiculturalism in America. According to another study by the Pew Hispanic Center, 8 percent of all marriages in the United States and 15 percent of all *new* marriages in 2010 were ones in which the bride and the groom were not of the same race or ethnicity. That is more than double the share of interracial or interethnic marriages that occurred in 1980.[8] Wendy Wang of the Pew

Research Center analyzed data from the U.S. Bureau of the Census's American Community Survey (ACS) from 2008 to 2010, and findings from three of Pew's own nationwide telephone surveys that explored public attitudes toward intermarriage. She found that more than one-third of Americans (35 percent) say that a member of their immediate family or a close relative is currently married to someone of a different race. What's more, 63 percent of Americans say it's okay to marry outside their ethnic or racial group. For Hispanics, that number goes up to 84 percent. This is huge and, by the way, may be the "secret" behind the success of some TV shows like ABC's *Modern Family*.

According to "The Rise of Intermarriage," the study mentioned above from Pew, nearly one-third (28 percent) of Asians and one-quarter (26 percent) of Hispanic newlyweds in 2010 married outside of their race compared to 17 percent of blacks and 9 percent of whites. "When it comes to educational characteristics, more than half of white newlyweds who marry Asians have a college degree, compared with roughly a third of white newlyweds who married whites. Among Hispanics and blacks, newlyweds who married whites tend to have higher educational attainment than do those who married within their own racial or ethnic group," writes Wang.

When asked if intermarriage was good for society, one in four Americans (43 percent) said that more people of different races marrying each other has been a change for the better in our society, while 11 percent said it has been a change for the worse and 44 percent felt it has made no difference.

THE INFLUENCE OF CULTURE IN HISPANIC IDENTITY

"Instead of assimilating into U.S. culture, Hispanics are adding American ways to their traditional heritage and culture. Culture, for many U.S. Latinos, is tied to their self-identity," writes Beth Snyder Bulik in "The Cultural Connection, How Hispanic Identity Influences Millennials," a Trend Report published by *Advertising Age* in May 2012. Based on data from a comprehensive study fielded by Burke on behalf of Univision Consumer Insights Research, this report explores in-depth the cultural connections of Hispanic Americans and how culture influences their consumer behavior. The research was particularly focused on understanding and, more important, *quantifying* the connection Latinos have to their culture and how that may or may not differ between Hispanic millennials (defined as persons between the ages of eighteen and thirty-four) and Hispanic non-millennials (defined as Hispanics ages thirty-five or above) given the fact that younger Hispanics are more bicultural and bilingual than their non-millennial counterparts. As a result of this research, a new quantitative metric was created, the Cultural Connection Index or CCI. CCI "identifies the relative importance of cultural influences on three specific dimensions that best explain what influences Hispanic behaviors. Those dimensions are family, heritage, and community. The higher the ratings are for attributes associated with these dimensions by respondents, the higher the resulting scores are for cultural connection," says the report.

At 85 million strong,[9] millennials are the new baby boomers. Defined broadly as adults between the ages of sixteen and thirty-five, millennials are a very attractive target for any company in this economically challenged environment. This is why the U.S. millennial consumer has been the focus of numerous studies over the past five years. "On average, U.S. millennials already shell out and influence the expenditure of hundreds of billions of dollars annually—an amount that will only increase as they mature into their peak earning and spending years," writes the Boston Consulting Group in their special report "The Millennial Consumer, Debunking Stereotypes" published in April 2012. "Millennials' expectations are different from previous generations, and companies need to rethink their brands, business models, and marketing accordingly," they add.

However, none of the major studies on millennials published to date have delved into Hispanics in particular, which is surprising given that at 17 million strong, Hispanic millennials already account for 21 percent of the total U.S. millennial population. By 2020, Hispanics will

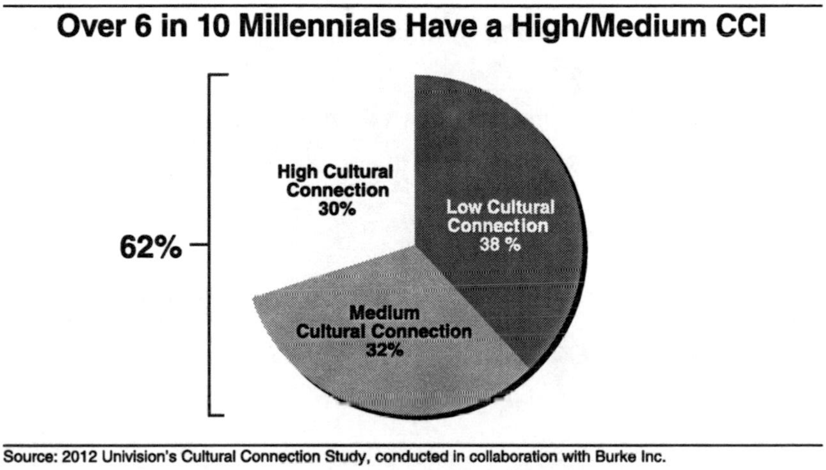

Over 6 in 10 Millennials Have a High/Medium CCI

Source: 2012 Univision's Cultural Connection Study, conducted in collaboration with Burke Inc.

Figure 6.10 Hispanic Connection to Their Culture

account for one in four millennials in the United States and given the fact that among this group, Hispanics are considered "trend-setters" in technology adoption and social media, it is frankly surprising that Hispanics are only mentioned in passing in terms of their relative size and their impact on the diversity of the so-called "next generation."

So let's delve a bit more into the study published by *Advertising Age*, "The Cultural Connection, How Hispanic Identity Influences Millennials." Contrary to the popular belief that younger Hispanics are distancing themselves from their culture and language, this study found that close to two-thirds (62 percent) of Hispanic millennials have a high or medium cultural connection.

More important, cultural connection seems to grow stronger the longer Latinos live in this country. Even after a decade of living here and being exposed to American traditions, entertainment choices, food options, etc., four in ten Hispanic millennials reported having a high cultural connection.

Like the Mindshare study I cited earlier, this study also found that a majority of Hispanic millennials (61 percent) and almost all of the high-CCI millennials (97 percent) like to pass Latino customs and traditions

Culture Important Among Millennials
Who Immigrated 10+ Years Ago

How long have they been living in the U.S.?

	Total Millennials	High CCI Millennials	
Less than 5 years	26%	16%	
5-10 years	33%	39%	Nearly 1 out of 2 culturally connected Millennials have lived in the U.S. for more than 10 years.
10+ years	36%	40%	
Did not say	5%	6%	

Source: 2012 Univision's Cultural Connection Study, conducted in collaboration with Burke Inc.

Figure 6.11 Hispanic Cultural Connection Grows Stronger Over Time

on to their children. Similarly, over half (51 percent) of all Hispanic millennials and 93 percent of high-CCI millennials like to observe family traditions, customs, and holidays through frequent parties, events, and celebrations.

Millennial Hispanics also agree that it's important to socialize with others within the Hispanic community. In general, millennial Hispanics with high CCIs are more social by nature and much more likely to agree with the statement "I have a large circle of friends" than those with a low CCI—62 percent vs. 19 percent, respectively. This culturally connected group is also more likely to have close friends who are *Hispanic*, with 90 percent of high-CCI millennials saying that "it is important to socialize with others within my Hispanic community." This suggests that our community is close-knit and helps explain the power and influence of Latinos in social media, which we will discuss in greater detail in the next chapter. But let me just share a few eye-opening data points from this study on technology adoption and social media.

"The distinctive combination of relative youth, community, culture, and language preference positions Hispanics to become pioneers in new media trends and further accelerate technology uptake," says the

Nielsen Company in its report "The State of the Hispanic Consumer: The Hispanic Market Imperative." This is clearly substantiated by the Burke study as well, which showed that 72 percent of Hispanic millennials own a smart phone and 24 percent own a tablet. But look at Figure 6.12 and you will see that high-CCI Latinos are even more technologically connected, with 81 percent owning a smart phone—more than double the rate for Hispanic non-millenials—and 27 percent owning a tablet computer.

So, what do you think they are doing on these devices? That's right, talking to friends and family, sharing stuff on social media, and looking for things to buy or relevant content to consume. According to this study, 86 percent of Hispanic millennials have a Facebook account and 40 percent have a Twitter account (see Figure 6.14). In fact, according to Nielsen, Hispanics are more likely to follow a brand or a celebrity online than average U.S. adults and are more likely to post links to articles, videos, etc. (See Figure 6.13.)

It's no wonder that Hispanics are the fastest-growing ethnic group on Facebook and wordpress.com. The *über*-social nature of Latinos provides a great opportunity for marketers to engage them in dialogue and solicit their opinions—in either English or Spanish. That's the thing people often don't get about culture: it can be expressed in different languages. Culture transcends language, although as you will see, Spanish is still a very important piece of the puzzle, even for younger Latinos. Spanish is an expression of our culture, but not the only one. My abil-

More Culturally Connected = More Tech Connected

	Smartphones	Tablet Computer
Total Millennials	72%	24%
High CCI Millenials	81%	27%
Non Millennials	34%	25%

Source: 2012 Univision's Cultural Connection Study, conducted in collaboration with Burke, Inc.

Figure 6.12 Hispanic Millennials Are Technology Geeks

Hispanics Adult Online Engagement

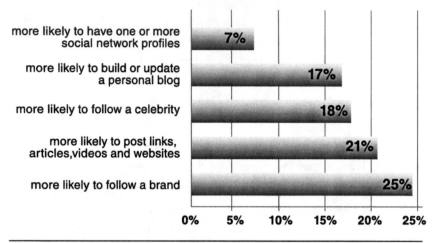

Source: Nielsen State of the Hispanic Consumer Report: The Hispanic Imperative Quarter 2, 2012

Figure 6.13 Hispanic Online Engagement

ity to speak Spanish is *part* of who I am, but *does not define* who I am. Get it? It's like being redheaded or left-handed or of Irish or German descent.

The reason Hispanics are such avid users of technology is because it helps them stay connected to their people, their news, and their culture. The story is strongest for high-CCI millennials. We know a substantial

Active Users of Social Media

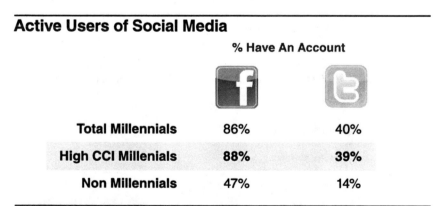

	% Have An Account	
	f	t
Total Millennials	86%	40%
High CCI Millenials	88%	39%
Non Millennials	47%	14%

Source: 2012 Univision's Cultural Connection Study, conducted in collaboration with Burke Inc.

Figure 6.14 Hispanics and Social Media

Spanish is Used with Friends and Family

Even More so for High CCI Millennials

	"I often use Spanish to commect and make friends"	"Spanish is the tprimary language we speak in home"
Total Millennials	35%	49%
High CCI Millenials	66%	79%
Non Millennials	42%	61%

Source: 2012 Univision's Cultural Connection Study, conducted in collaboration with Burke Inc.

Figure 6.15

portion of those culturally connected Hispanics have family outside the U.S., so it makes sense that:

- 89 percent say technology makes it easier to connect with friends and family,
- 84 percent say it helps them follow the latest events in their country of origin through online news and other sources.
- And 65 percent say technology has made it easier for them to connect with their culture and heritage.

Finally, let's talk about language. While it is true that the majority of Hispanic millennials are bilingual (61 percent), one of the ways Hispanics stay connected to their culture is by speaking Spanish or watching Spanish-language TV. By the way, according to this study, 49 percent of Hispanic millennials said they speak Spanish *at home*, which goes up to 79 percent for high-culturally connected millennials. But you really realize just how important Spanish is to the younger generations when it is the language that over one-third of Hispanic millennials say they *often use* to connect and make friends. For high-CCI millennials, that percentage nearly doubles to 66 percent. (See Figure 6.15.)

For more information on how the Cultural Connection Index affects Hispanics shopping and brand behavior, technology adoption, or even media and entertainment preferences, you can download the study for FREE online by visiting adage.com at http://adage.com/trend-reports/report.php?id=65.

Now let's go to a review of the Hispanic media landscape, so you can figure out where best to connect with this highly engaged and desirable Latino consumer.

Key Takeaways:

- Latino identity is complex, because Hispanic is not a race, it is an ethnicity. Therefore, Latinos can be of all races.
- The census is having a hard time properly counting and classifying Hispanics mainly because Latinos do not see themselves reflected in the race and origin questions. As a result, of the 50.5 million Hispanics counted by the 2010 census, 18.5 million Hispanics said they were "some other race" not white or black or Asian.
- Proper racial classification, however, is critical because the census data on race serves many purposes, including determining the makeup of voting districts, distribution of government funding of programs and services, and proper tracking of racial disparities in education and health.
- Getting the race and origin question right is key because from 2020 to 2050, the Latino population is projected to add twice as many people to the United States every year than all other race/ethnic groups combined.
- When compared to other ethnic groups, Hispanics are more likely to "nurture" their ethnicity than are African Americans or Asians.
- Politically, Hispanics are evenly split among conservative, moderate, and liberal views.
- Cultural fusion is becoming the norm in America, with more than one-third of Americans (35 percent) saying that a member of their immediate family or a close relative is currently married to someone of a different race and 63 percent of Americans saying it's okay to marry outside their ethnic or racial group. For Hispanics, that number goes up to 84 percent.

NOTES

1. Navarro, Mireya, "For Many Latinos, Racial Identity Is More Culture Than Color," *The New York Times*, January 13, 2012. Copyright © 2012 The New York Times Company. www.nytimes.com/2012/01/14/us/for-many-latinos-race-is-more-culture-than-color.html?pagewanted=all&_r=0.

2. "Notices," *Federal Register*, Vol. 77, No. 88, 26737, Monday, May 7, 2012. Published by the GPO. www.gpo.gov/fdsys/pkg/FR-2012-05-07/pdf/2012-10953.pdf.

3. U.S. Census Bureau Interim Projection by Race and Hispanic Origin, released in 2008. www.census.gov.

4. El Nasser, Haya, "Census Rethinks Hispanic on Questionnaire," *USA Today*, January 4, 2013. Copyright © 2013 Gannett. www.usatoday.com/story/news/nation/2013/01/13/hispanics-may-be-added-to-census-race-category/1808087.

5. Taylor, Paul, Mark Hugo Lopez, Jessica Hamar Martinez and Gabriel Velasco, "When Labels Don't Fit: Hispanics and Their Views of Identity," Copyright © 2012. Published by the Pew Hispanic Center, April 2012. www.pewhispanic.org/files/2012/04/PHC-Hispanic-Identity.pdf.

6. "Marketing to Hispanics," Part 2 of the Ethnodynamics series from Mindshare, Added Value and Yahoo!, 2011.

7. Brownstein, Ronald, "The Gray and the Brown: The Generational Mismatch," *National Journal*, June 24, 2010. www.nationaljournal.com/magazine/the-gray-and-the-brown-the-generational-mismatch-20100724.

8. Wang, Wendy, The Rise of Intermarriage: Rates, Characteristics Vary by Race and Gender, Copyright © 2012, The Pew Research Center, released February 16, 2012 by Pew Research Social & Demographic Trends. www.pewsocialtrends.org/files/2012/02/SDT-Intermarriage-II.pdf.

9. U.S. Census Bureau, Report based on the most recent population estimates released May 17, 2012. www.census.gov/newsroom/releases/archives/population/cb12-90.html.

7

THE CHANGING MEDIA LANDSCAPE

"Due to sheer numbers, Hispanics have wielded significant influence on the media landscape, shaping programming content, dedicated channels and vehicle offerings."

Nielsen Company

In today's world, media no longer just means television, radio, and print. Although the vast majority of advertising dollars are still dedicated to those traditional media platforms, the onset of digital/video innovation and emerging media technologies have affected the media landscape so significantly that the industry now routinely offers "second" and "third" screen experiences, and we spend most of our time discussing how consumer behavior and media consumption are changing the media game altogether.

With advances in technology, especially smart phones and tablets, media proliferation has also grown exponentially and with it, a new kind of media fragmentation that is singularly controlled by savvy consumers who demand the ability to enjoy their favorite content on the platform of their choice, whenever they want. And at the leading edge of that consumer base is the Hispanic community. "Hispanics access media from every platform available and often lead the general market as early adopters of emerging technologies," says Nielsen. Already nearly 60 percent of Hispanic households have at least one video and Internet-enabled cell phone, compared to only 43 percent of the so-called general market.[1]

In fact, I'd say that Hispanic audiences are at the center of a "perfect storm" that is brewing in the media world. With a median age of twenty-nine versus forty-one for non-Hispanic whites, Latinos are smack in the middle of the bull's-eye for companies that are interested in reaching young adults, especially those who are heading into the family-formation years and who are *influencers* when it comes to brand preferences. And yet, some very established media companies are just now waking up to the huge opportunity these consumers represent. In his 2012 cover story for *Forbes* magazine, "The Next Media Jackpot: The Fight for the $1 Trillion Hispanic Market," Jack Bercovici talks about how FOX, Comcast, and ABC/Disney are finally getting into the Hispanic game, fifty years after Univision began broadcasting.

"There's a misconception that this is an easy-to-reach segment because they have fewer and more contained options to them," Monica Gadsby, CEO of SMG Multicultural, which incudes the two largest media-buying agencies in the Hispanic marketplace (Tapestry Partners and 42 Degrees), told *Forbes* magazine. "You almost need to think of it as the opposite. The reality is that Hispanic Americans have more options than any other consumer. They have options that make any consumer's head spin, and what happens at that point is good TV just becomes good TV."

And good TV means ratings and viewers, something marketers are willing to pay a premium for, especially in the sweet spot of adults 18–34, regardless of what language they speak. Remember that duality I was talking about in the last chapter? Our viewing choices are doubled because of our ability to watch anything we want either in Spanish *or in English*. This could be one of the reasons Hispanics are also leading in terms of media consumption. According to Nielsen, Hispanics spend 68 percent more time watching video on the Internet and 20 percent more time watching video on their mobile phones compared to non-Hispanic whites. And from 2011 to 2012, Hispanics increased home broadband usage by 14 percent, which is more than double the 6 percent growth of broadband use in the general market.[2] Furthermore, in a world where live television viewing is still king, Spanish-language TV is proving to be almost DVR proof, with live viewing during prime time at 94 percent on Univision versus 72 percent for ABC or 76 percent for FOX.[3] While only 31 percent of Hispanic households own a DVR player versus 41 percent of the general market, according to Nielsen, "Hispanic DVR households are two to three times more likely to timeshift English than Spanish-language programming."

Finally, although it was once feared that the pull of the digital world would compete against television's share of consumer attention, studies are finding that consumers are, in fact, using both platforms— simultaneously. Recently reported data indicates spikes in tablet and mobile usage *during* prime time TV viewing hours, as consumers react to and engage with others while they are viewing their favorite TV shows. The bottom line is that Hispanics are more engaged with Spanish-language media and are leading other groups in terms of media consumption and usage of emerging technologies, which can be partly attributed to their relative youth vis-à-vis the general market consumer. I will delve more into the behavior of Hispanics with digital media later on, but now let's see how much things have changed in the Hispanic media landscape.

A BRIEF HISTORY OF HISPANIC MEDIA IN THE U.S.

As have all immigrant groups, over the past one hundred years, Hispanics in the United States created media outlets to communicate important information in their own language to their people. The Spanish-language newspaper of Los Angeles, *La Opinion*, and its New York counterpart, *El Diario/La Prensa*, have each been serving the Spanish-speaking populations of those cities for more than eighty years now. The first Spanish-language radio station, KCOR in San Antonio, began transmitting in Spanish in 1945. Unlike other "ethnic media" that have disappeared over time, as the decades have passed, the Spanish-language media landscape has grown even stronger. By covering news and transmitting programs from back home, Spanish-language media have been able to establish a direct line of communication that keeps Hispanic culture and the Spanish language alive in this country. Research studies indicate that the usage of English in Latino households was at an all-time high in the late sixties and early seventies. That trend toward English language usage should have continued in the Hispanic market, but it did not. In fact, it has gone in reverse. Why? Several reasons: An awakening of the Hispanic identity has made Latinos more proud of their heritage. Second, the United States experienced a constant and significant influx of Hispanic immigrants since the 1980s. This phenomenon coincided with the development of a national (as opposed to only local) Spanish-language media footprint, which, in turn, spurred the growth of the Hispanic advertising industry in the United States. As a result, the use of Spanish at home and at work has been steadily increasing over the past twenty years. When Nielsen Media Research started tracking Spanish-language media in 1992, only seven of the top twenty-five programs viewed by Hispanics in the U.S. were in Spanish. Today, twenty-two of the top twenty-five ranked programs among Hispanic adults 18–34 are in Spanish as are fifteen of the twenty-five top ranked programs among *bilingual* Hispanic adults 18–34.[4]

Since its launch in 1956, Spanish-language television has become the largest and most profitable segment of Hispanic media. For thirty years, Univision was the only choice for Spanish-speaking television viewers in the United States. A second Spanish-language broadcast network, Telemundo Group, was launched in 1984 (although the Telemundo brand existed as a single station in Puerto Rico since 1954). The first Spanish-language cable network, Galavision, was launched in 1979 following the boom of cable television in the United States. However, it would take almost twenty years for Galavision to have any competition at all in the cable market. It wasn't until the early '90s, when cable channels were expanding their footprints in Latin America, that a second Spanish-language cable network, GEMSTV, was created. The third Spanish-language cable network, FOX Sports en Español, was launched in 1996, when the News Corp. joined forces with Liberty Media to further diversify Hispanic cable-television offerings. However, the true explosion of Spanish- and English-language programming geared toward U.S.

Hispanics started in the year 2000. Since then, the number of Spanish-language broadcasters in the United States has more than doubled: Univision and Telemundo now share airwaves with UniMÁS, Azteca América, EstrellaTV, and Mega TV, while the number of Spanish-language cable networks has increased exponentially, from fifteen in 1999 to the more than seventy channels available today.

On the English-language front, the number of Hispanic-oriented television shows on network and cable TV is just a short list of relative hits and misses. Most recently the biggest hits were *The George Lopez* show, a sitcom which ran from 2002 to 2007 and ABC's dramedy *Ugly Betty*, which ran from 2006 to 2010. The list of misses is much longer and includes PBS's *American Family* in 2002, CBS's *Cane* in 2007, NBC's *Outlaw* in 2010, and last year's FOX's *Q'Viva*—a bilingual talent competition hosted by Jennifer Lopez and Marc Anthony, who were in the middle of getting a divorce. *Q'Viva*, a search for the most talented acts in Latin America, aired first on Univision to decent ratings but then tanked on FOX a few months later. After much speculation, George Lopez did get a new gig, this time as the host of a late night talk show on TNT, but that too was cancelled after just two seasons in 2011.

Clearly, Hollywood has not able to "crack the code" with Latino viewers. In response to a recent *New York Times* article, "Networks Struggle to Appeal to Hispanics," my fellow blogger on *Ad Age*, Luis Miguel Messianu, says networks don't attract Latino viewers because they are still caught up in stereotypes. "We went from Carmen Miranda and Charo to Sofia's character Gloria Delgado-Pritchett, a spicy but low-IQ trophy wife (ironic since Sofia is considered to be very smart and a sharp businesswoman)," wrote Messianu, who is also the president of one of the leading Hispanic agencies, Alma. According to *The New York Times* article, during the 2012 season, ABC's hit show *Modern Family* had an overall viewership of almost 13 million, but only 6 percent of them were Latinos. Anemic Latino viewership is also the case with all the other Hollywood hits, like *Two and a Half Men*, *Grey's Anatomy*, and *Glee*. "The discrepancy between English- and Spanish-language shows is most acute among shows that are scripted in English.

The issue, many viewers and critics argue, is that there still hasn't been the Hispanic equivalent of *The Cosby Show*, meaning a show that deals with Latino culture in a way that doesn't offend viewers with crude stereotypes," write Tanzina Vega and Bill Carter in their article for *The New York Times*.[5] Not offending us with stereotypes is one part of the truth; another simple truth is that Spanish-language TV continues to have more relevant content. Big events or shows, like the Latin Grammys or Premios Juventud, often beat all other English-language networks on the night they air. The same is true for important soccer matches. We are two years away from the next World Cup in Brazil, and yet the recent "friendly match" between Mexico and the U.S.A.'s Men's national teams on August 21, 2012, drew 8.1 million viewers, making Univision's coverage of the match the number one broadcast program in prime time among Adults 18–34, Men 18–49, and Men 18–34, regardless of language according to Nielsen.[6]

CHRONOLOGY OF SPANISH-LANGUAGE MEDIA IN THE UNITED STATES

1955 In response to the growing number of Mexican workers living in the southwestern United States (and almost ten years after the first Spanish-language radio stations appeared in the United States), Hispanic media pioneer Raoul A. Cortéz inaugurates the first Spanish-language TV station in San Antonio, Texas. KCOR-TV, Channel 41, broadcast seven hours of live programming a day, supplemented with Mexican programming supplied by Emilio Azcárraga Vidaurreta, then chairman of Grupo Televisa, the largest Spanish-language media company in Mexico. Shortly after the launch of KCOR-TV, Cortéz launched KMEX, Channel 34, in Los Angeles, this time in partnership with Azcárraga Vidaurreta. In 1961, KCOR was acquired and changed its call letters to KWEX, when the son of Azcárraga Vidaurreta, "El Tigre," Emilio Azcárraga Milmo, joined forces with Emilio Nicolas, Sr., and two other media pioneers, René Anselmo and Frank Fouce, to form the first group of Spanish-language TV stations in the United States. Together these men would play a critical role in the development of Spanish-language TV in the United States.

1961 "El Tigre" Azcárraga Milmo, Anselmo, and Fouce create Spanish International Network (SIN), the precursor to Univision, with the launch of New York's WXTV, Channel 41, and two other TV stations. Over the next decade SIN would continue to acquire television stations and station affiliates in key Hispanic markets in order to create a national footprint, but until then, by and large the stations acted independently from one another.

1962 McHenry Tichenor, who had been broadcasting Spanish-language programing on his English radio stations near the border of Texas since 1949, converts KGBS into a full-time Spanish-language radio station. His radio empire, Hispanic Broadcasting Corporation would become the largest network of Spanish-language radio stations. This year was also important for the advertising industry as Luis Diaz Albertini opened the first Hispanic advertising agency, Interamericas which was the Hispanic agency for Goya Foods. Thanks to Albertini's persistence his agency, which would become famous under the moniker SAMS (Spanish Advertising and Marketing Services), would soon count among its clients Columbia Pictures, Azteca Films, and Kent cigarettes.

1976 In an attempt to centralize its network of station affiliates, SIN starts distributing its television programming via domestic satellite, thus creating, for the first time, a national Spanish-language television footprint.

1979 Emilio Azcárraga Milmo's Grupo Televisa launches Galavision as the first Spanish-language cable network in the United States. They also open an editorial office in Miami to exploit their hugely successful magazine group in Mexico, looking for ways to expand the circulation of their most profitable magazines in the United States.

1983 Raul Alarcon, Sr., launches Spanish Broadcasting Systems, Inc., which today owns and/or operates twenty FM stations located in seven of the largest Hispanic markets in the United States. The company is now run by his son, Raul Alarcon, Jr.

1986 The FCC forces SIN to sell its network and station affiliates after an investigation concludes that a majority of the company is controlled by foreign investors. Hallmark steps in and buys SIN, and one year later changes the network's name to Univision.

1987 Seeing an opportunity to enter the Spanish-language broadcast market in the United States, several former Univision executives create Telemundo Group by combining the strongest television station in Puerto Rico, WKAQ-TV, Channel 2, with the oldest Spanish-language station in New York, WNJU, Channel 47, and launching WSCV, Channel 51, in Miami. Picking up affiliates and buying stations whenever it could, Telemundo quickly challenged the leadership of Univision by pioneering a slate of Hispanic programming that was "made in the U.S.A."

1992 Hallmark sells Univision for $550 million to a group of investors led by boxing promoter Jerrold Perenchio. Perenchio's acquisition of Univision is supported by "El Tigre" Emilio Azcárraga Milmo's Grupo Televisa and Venezuelan media mogul Gustavo Cisnero's Venevision (the two media powerhouses of Latin America, which today still account for a large percentage of all Spanish-language TV production in the world). The deal is seen as a coup because Univision got first right of refusal to all of Televisa's and Venevision's television programming in exchange for 15 percent of Univision's advertising revenue. This year, Nielsen Media Research also introduces the Nielsen Hispanic Television Index, NHTI, which becomes the first truly comprehensive view of how Hispanics consume major media in the United States as part of their ongoing syndicated research system. Finally, in 1992, Azcárraga Milmo buys the largest Spanish-language magazine group in the United States, with fifteen titles, Miami-based Grupo de Armas for $130 million. With the acquisition of the Grupo de Armas, Editorial Televisa becomes the largest Spanish-language publisher in the U.S.

1993 Former Telemundo executive Gary McBride creates GEMS TV, the first Spanish-language cable network for women in the United States. A secondary strategy for this new cable network was to sell its programming to the growing Latin American cable market.

1996 In order to consolidate Univision's Spanish-language offerings so that advertisers could buy across both broadcast and cable platforms, Univision acquires Galavision, the largest Spanish-language cable network, from its partner Grupo Televisa. This same year, News Corp. and Liberty Media acquire Prime Deportiva and convert it into FOX Sports en Español, the first regional cable network dedicated to Latin sports in the United States. In the print sector, Christy Haubegger, a twenty-eight-year-old Stanford Law School graduate launches *Latina* magazine, seeing a void in service magazines for Latina women *in English*. Later on that year, *People en Español* launches as a quarterly magazine and quickly becomes the most successful magazine launch in Spanish-language history. This year was also the year Fernando Espuelas and Jack Chen launch Starmedia, the first pan-regional Internet portal for Spanish and Portuguese speaking audiences. And finally, in 1996 the leaders of the largest Hispanic agencies got together and formed AHAA, the Association of Hispanic Advertising Agencies, to help champion corporate investments in Hispanic marketing in the United States.

1997 The merger of Tichenor Media Systems and Heftel Broadcasting creates Hispanic Broadcasting Corporation, a radio station group that for the first time has a presence in all of the top ten U.S. Hispanic markets.

1998 Sony Corporation and Liberty Media lead a small consortium of investors in the acquisition of the Telemundo network for $539 million. Yahoo en español launches.

2001 TV Azteca, Grupo Televisa's biggest rival in Mexico, decides to enter the U.S. broadcast market by launching Azteca América in partnership with Pappas Telecasting, which owned a series of independent stations in key Hispanic markets across the United States. After being acquired by Sony, Telemundo begins heavily betting on the growing Hispanic youth segment (eighteen- to twenty-five-year-olds); as a result, it rebrands its women-oriented channel GEMS TV to create MUN2, a new cable channel with programming geared toward younger, bilingual Hispanics.

2002 The FCC approves the acquisition of Telemundo and MUN2 by NBC for $1.89 billion, becoming the first major U.S. network to add a Spanish-language broadcast channel to its fold. In order to prevent TV Azteca from acquiring a ready-made, full-power distribution network throughout the United States, Univision creates a second broadcast network using the thirteen TV stations it acquired from Barry Diller in 2000 and launches a second broadcast network, Telefutura (which changed its name to UniMÁS in December of 2012). The effort is aimed at combating the gains made by Telemundo and MUN2 in the younger Hispanic demographic.

2003 AOL launches AOL Latino. On the cable front, a 24-hour soccer channel called GOLTV launches.

2004 ESPN Deportes launches in January into a relatively crowded Spanish-language sports space dominated by Univision, Galavision, Telemundo, and FOX Sports en Español. This year also saw the birth of SiTV, the first English-language channel for Latinos in the United States. On the print side, Impremedia, LLC, was fighting off launches in the Spanish-language newspaper space from Mexiamerica, which launched four *Rumbo* newspapers in Texas and the Chicago Tribune's *Hoy* with papers in New York, Chicago, and Los Angeles. Utlimately Impremedia would establish itself as the largest Spanish-language national newspaper "chain." Born out of a merger between the two largest Spanish-language newspapers, *La Opinion* and *El Diario/La Prensa*, co-founded by John Paton, a maverick newspaper man, and current CEO Monica Lozano, Impremedia now owns nine print publications and numerous online websites.

2005 Shortly after going public, Spanish Broadcasting Systems, which up until then had only been in the radio business, acquired a small Key West UHF station to launch a new Spanish-language TV network, Mega TV. Although the new venture struggled initially to build a network, by March 2010, the company had eleven affiliates around the U.S. and a channel on the Spanish-language DirecTV Más satellite service.

2006 Univision and Telemundo join the Nielsen Television Index, which provides television ratings for all the major U.S. Networks such as ABC, CBS, NBC, and FOX, in a move to be on equal footing for advertising dollars after the 2000 census again showed huge gains in the Hispanic population. The move, however, ignites a heated debate on the National People Meter samples and whether they accurately reflect Hispanic audiences. In July, after a rocky auction that involved a bid by an investor group led by Israeli-American billionaire Haim Saban, Mexican broadcaster Grupo Televisa SA, a part owner of Univision and key supplier of Univision's programming, sues Univision over royalties and the right to distribute its programming in the United States over the Internet. In September, MTV *Tr3s* was launched when it became available on all cable and satellite systems that previously carried MTV en Español. Although it mainly broadcasts Spanish-language programs, the channel set out to compete with MUN2 to be a bicultural entertainment destination with lifestyle shows, customized music video playlists, and news documentaries, as well as English-subtitled programming in Spanish imported from their sister channels in Spain and Latin America. The channel is targeted toward younger, bilingual Latinos, and non-Latino Americans ages twelve to thirty-four.

2007 The FCC approves the deal to sell Univision Communications Inc., the nation's largest Spanish-language broadcaster, for $13.7 billion to a consortium of investors led by Haim Saban. In March, V-me, a twenty-four-hour digital broadcast service, was launched. Because it is a public television service in the United States, V-me is available free over the air and on basic cable through its association with PBS member stations, making it the fourth largest Spanish network in the U.S. Its programming "works to pursue a single goal—serving the Latino community and our partners with incomparable programming and community projects that make an impact in our communities and our world," said V-me's General Manager, Alvaro Garnica, at their 2012–2013 upfront presentation. The lineup of shows runs the gamut from entertainment to news and children's programming. This year, MySpace launches a service for it Spanish-language users called MySpace en Español.

2009 In June, Univision and Televisa settle their lawsuit over royalties and Internet use. In September, Liberman Broadcasting, an established player in Spanish-language radio since the 1970s and television since the 1980s, launches *Estrella TV*. Best known for its twenty-one major-market Hispanic radio stations, this Los Angeles-based broadcast company launched Estrella TV to expand its TV offerings and to give Univision and Telemundo a run for their money in five of the top ten Hispanic markets. The network's target demo is Hispanics between the ages of eighteen and forty-nine, with original programming that consists of news, musical variety, dramas, comedy, and talk.

2010 Univision Communications, Inc. and Grupo Televisa, SAB announce an agreement to expand and extend the long-term programming license agreement (PLA) to 2020 and, upon satisfying certain conditions, to at least 2025. Televisa also agrees to make a $1.2 billion investment and contribute its 50 percent interest in TuTV Networks in exchange for a 5 percent equity stake and debentures convertible into an additional 30 percent equity stake of Univision in the future, subject to existing laws and regulations. In addition, Televisa has the option to acquire an additional five percent equity stake in Univision in the future.

2011 Latino-focused English-language cable channel formally known as SiTV changes its name to Nuvo TV. "SiTV was confusing," CEO Michael Schwimmer told Laurel Wentz of *Advertising Age*. "People would ask if that was 'sea' like the ocean or 'see' like you can see television. You can imagine what's it's been like dealing with that sort of confusion." After being launched in 2004 to great expectations by Jeff Valdez—a Hollywood insider who was behind some of the early English-language Latino-themed shows on cable TV like the *Latino Laugh Festival* for Showtime and *The Brothers Garcia* for Nickelodeon—the channel struggled to find an audience, although it did have a breakout hit in *Model Latina* which is now in its sixth season. Their programming sweet spot seems to be reality TV shows aimed at the young, bicultural audiences, but distribution seems to be its biggest challenge.

2012 saw a new flurry of activity with the announcement of five new TV network launches by the biggest players in the media world. Interestingly, all but one were in Spanish. In April, Univision launched two new cable networks: a sports channel, Univision Deportes, and a *telenovela* channel, TLNovelas. It also announced a joint venture with Disney's ABC News to develop a twenty-four-hour cable news and lifestyle network *in English,* called Fusion, which is expected to launch in 2013. Comcast announced a deal with Hollywood media maven Roberto Rodriguez to launch a general entertainment channel called El Rey. Inspired by MTV, El Rey "hopes to follow in the tracks of successes like AMC and FX, starting out with one or two signature original shows and gradually ramping up from there," writes Jeff Bercovici in *Forbes* magazine.

In fall 2012 the newest entrant to the Hispanic television space, MundoFOX, launched with high hopes of chipping away at the Spanish-language network share of viewing that Univision (with a 73 percent) and Telemundo (with a 21 percent) have in primetime among Hispanics (adults 18–49)[7] in the U.S. Their strategy is to counterprogram the two leading networks with anything but *novelas*, which are a mainstay of Spanish-language TV. Instead, MundoFOX and its primary production partner, Colombian studio RCN, are betting on teleseries, which are basically weekly scripted dramas, to attract new viewers and advertisers. The new network does have support and the deep pockets of Rupert Murdoch, who has a reputation for disrupting the TV status quo. "FOX has a history of making breakthrough television. We've done it in English, and we're going to do it in Spanish," Hernán López, president of MundoFOX, told *Forbes*.

In the digital space, it is important to note that both FOX and NBC launched Spanish-language websites and Univision launched UVideos, the first bilingual digital video network that allows viewers access to the best Univision content.

OVERVIEW OF MEDIA LANDSCAPE BY INDUSTRY

Like their English-language counterparts, in Hispanic media, television is king, with network, spot and cable TV garnering 69.2 percent of the total advertising spend in 2011, according to *Advertising Age* (Figure 7.1). Although the Internet, spot radio, and cable TV were the fastest-growing Hispanic media sectors, according to *Ad Age*'s 2012 edition of the Hispanic Fact Pack, they still only captured less than one-fifth of the $7.14 billion spent in Hispanic media in 2011. Hispanic print media have been able to hold onto 16 percent of the advertising spend, in spite of steady year-over-year growth in the Internet sector, which for the first time captured more total advertising dollars ($420 million in 2011) than magazines ($365 million).[8] Overall, Hispanic media spend increased 4.6 percent from 2010 to 2011, which is a rather healthy growth rate compared to the anemic growth rate of 0.8 percent reported by Kantar Media for U.S. advertising spend in 2011.[9]

Spanish-Language Television

According to the Nielsen Company, the share of Hispanic adults 18–49 watching Spanish-language television during broadcast prime has steadily increased from 36 percent during the 1992–1993 season, when they started tracking it, to 47 percent during the 2011–2012 season (Figure 7.2).

Hispanic Media Ad Spending in 2011

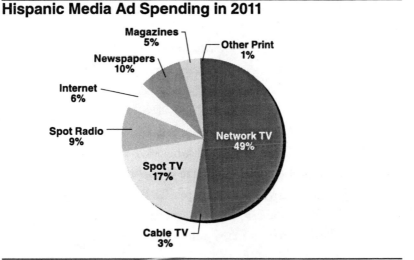

Source: Hispanic Fact Pack 2012: Annual Guide to Hispanic Marketing and Media
© 2012 Crain Communications Inc.

Figure 7.1

Spanish-language TV vs. English-language TV
Percent Share of Hispanic Adults 18-49 Viewing in Prime Time

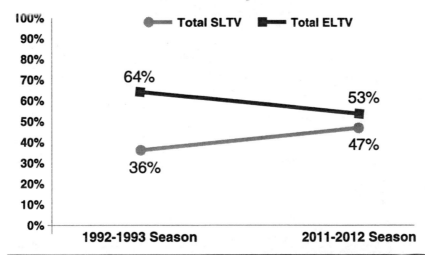

Source: The Nielsen Company, NHPM Live data, 1992-1993 Season (10/26/1992-09/19/1993) and NPM-H
Live+7 data, 2011-2012 Season (09/19/2011-09/23/2012), Broadcast Prime Mon-Sat 8pm-11pm, Sun 7pm-11pm.
Based on time period (viewing source) averages. Spanish-language TV based on Spanish Broadcast, Spanish
Cable and Spanish Independents; English-language TV based on English Broadcast, English Ad-Supported
Cable, English Other Cable and English Independents

Figure 7.2

The company that has been driving much of the increase of Spanish-language TV viewership for the past fifty years has been Univision Communications, Inc. Its media portfolio consists of two broadcast networks, Univision and UniMÁS (formerly known as Telefutura), and it also owns the largest cable channel, Galavision. On an average week in May 2012, those three networks reached 20.5 million Hispanics ages twelve and above.[10] Over the past two years, Univision has added nine more niche cable channels to its vast array of TV offerings. Univision also owns the largest Spanish-language radio network, which in an average week reaches 16.4 million Hispanics listeners ages twelve and above.[11] Finally, Univision also leads on the digital front, with an average of 15.6 million visits to its many online sites and 33.7 million mobile visits every month.[12]

Under the leadership of Randy Falco, Univision has also taken new steps in distributing its content everywhere, forging new partnerships with distribution platforms like Hulu and Microsoft's Xbox. It is connecting with Hispanic consumers via social media or enhanced mobile offerings that include a new digital video service as well as a series of popular apps—many of which easily shot up to the number one spot in the iTunes App Store when they launched.

Univision network regularly leads all Spanish-language television demos and day parts, delivering more Hispanic eyeballs than anyone else. In fact, if you look at Nielsen's list of the top ten Spanish-language shows watched in prime time by Hispanic adults eighteen to forty-nine during the 2011–2012 season (Figure 7.3), all of them were on Univision, averaging between four and six million viewers a night. That's about four to five times more than the number of Latinos watching any the top-rated English-language shows, such as *The Voice, American Idol, X Factor* or *Dancing with the Stars* (Figure 7.4). Add to that the fact that 72 percent of Univision's prime-time audience is unduplicated,[13] which refers to the percentage of an audience who only watches one particular network, and you'll start to understand why *Fast Company* named Univision one of the fifty most innovative companies in 2011, declaring that it was "threatening the TV establishment."

Rank	Programs (Days)	Net Work	Hispanic Household % Rtg	Hispanic Household Aa(000)	Hispanic Viewers 2+ Aa(000)
1	Teresa Mon	Uni	27.0	3,769	6,488
2	Teresa Thu	Uni	23.2	3,239	5,205
3	Teresa Tue	Uni	23.0	3,216	5,094
4	Teresa Fri	Uni	22.4	3,132	5,108
5	Teresa Wed	Uni	22.1	3,087	5,069
6	Fuerza Del Destino Tue	Uni	20.3	2,835	4,722
7	Fuerza Del Destino Thu	Uni	20.2	2,826	4,789
8	Fuerza Del Destino Mon	Uni	20.2	2,817	4,862
9	Fuerza Del Destino Wed	Uni	20.0	2,786	4,757
10	Que No Podia Amar Thu	Uni	19.1	2,660	4,553

Source: Nielsen Company, NPM-H (09/19/2011-09/02/2012) Broadcast Prime Mon-Sat 8:00pm-11:00pm, Sun 7:00pm-11:00pm. Excludes breakouts, specials, and sports airings. Most current data.

Figure 7.3 Top Ranked Programs on Spanish-Language Television

Rank	Program	Net work	HH Mc Us Aa%	HH Mc Aa(000)	P2+ Mc Aa(000)
1	American Idol—Wed	FOX	6.5	902	1,303
2	Fred 2: The Movie	NICK	6.4	888	1,430
3	Dancing With The Stars	ABC	6.3	877	1,203
4	Voice	NBC	6.2	866	1,340
5	Dancing W/Stars Results	ABC	6	843	1,166
6	American Idol—Thu	FOX	5.9	825	1,201
7	X-Factor—Wed	FOX	4.9	688	1,046
8	X-Factor—Thu	FOX	4.9	681	1,022
9	Big Time Movie	NICK	4.7	662	1,023
10	Voice: Results Show	NBC	4.7	659	958

Source: Nielsen Company, NPM-H (09/19/2011-09/02/2012) Broadcast Prime Mon-Sat 8:00pm-11:00pm, Sun 7:00pm-11:00pm. Excludes breakouts, specials, and sports airings. Ad-supported networks. Most current data.

Figure 7.4 Ranker Includes English-language Broadcast and Cable TV; 09/19/2011–09/02/2012

Univision's main rival is Telemundo, which—along with its sister cable network MUN2—was acquired by NBC Universal in 2002. Telemundo owns or operates fifteen stations in major cities in the U.S. and can be found on forty-seven affiliates across the country. In January 2011, Comcast took control of NBC Universal via a merger with General Electric. Shortly thereafter, the new company's executives put Lauren Zalaznick in charge of their Hispanic networks and said they saw opportunities to produce more revenue for the company through Telemundo. Zalaznick is seen as a strong programmer and marketer who is famous for, among other things, building the Bravo channel into a hit with its reality programming.

During the past ten years, Telemundo's strategy has been to try to counterprogram Univision by investing in original productions that they hope will have more appeal to U.S. Hispanic audiences than programs made in Mexico or Venezuela and broadcast here in the United States. The strategy has yet to pay off, however, as their share of the market has remained at 21 percent of the total audience over the past ten years. They did strike gold in 2011 with the telenovela *La Reina del Sur.* Based on a novel of the same name written by the critically acclaimed Spanish author Arturo Perez-Reverete and produced in conjunction with Spain's Antena 3 and Colombia's RTI Producciones, *La Reina del Sur* became Telemundo's highest rated program in the network's twenty-year history, averaging 4.2 million (persons 2+) viewers in its final episode.[14] During its sixty-three-episode run, *La Reina del Sur* averaged about 2.0 million viewers (adults 18–49), which is great for any channel. *La Reina del Sur* did break another record: the most expensive telenovela ever produced by Telemundo, with a $10 million price tag. Nonetheless, drug cartel storylines seem to be doing well for Telemundo, which in July 2012 debuted a Colombian television series from Caracol TV, *Pablo Escobar: El Patron Del Mal* (*Boss of Evil*) which also did very well with Hispanic audiences. According to TVbythenumbers.com, in its premiere week *El Patron del Mal* "averaged nearly 2.1 million total viewers (persons 2+) and nearly 1.2 million adults (adults 18–49), according to Nielsen."

To the surprise of many in the television industry, the *telenovela* format has turned into an incredibly successful, multibillion-dollar industry, with Mexico's Grupo Televisa leading the way in terms of global sales. Because of their universal storylines, telenovelas "travel well" and have become popular all over the world, from Russia to the Ivory Coast in Africa. Some people think that since the majority of Hispanics in the United States are Mexican, they remain faithful to shows from their homeland, and while that is partly true, it is not the only reason telenovelas garner such great ratings. Unlike American soaps, telenovelas do not go on forever; on average they last 120 episodes which means they are on air between four and six months. The ones on Univision air first in Mexico and Puerto Rico, so if they are good, there will be a built-in buzz about them even before they air here in the United States. The ones on Telemundo may have also aired previously in Latin America, as they too have production partnerships with producers in Latin America and Spain. But as mentioned earlier, their programming strategy has been to create original productions which, as we in the TV business know, is always riskier and requires more investment in promotion and tune-in advertising.

While they are not well known or understood by the English-speaking world, telenovelas are Hispanic America's version of Must-See TV, so let me share with you some insights on telenovelas that my colleagues Cynthia Ashworth, SVP of Advertising Sales and Jessica Rodriguez, EVP Progam Scheduling and Promotions for Univision, put together based on insights from former Univision COO Ray Rodriguez, to explain how *telenovelas* compare to the English-language TV formats with which you may be more familiar.

THE TELENOVELA PHENOMENON

Let's start with the stars of telenovelas: They are the A-list of the A-list. I know this can seem backward to some people, because in English, TV stars go on to Hollywood movies. But in the Hispanic world, it's the other way around: if you are an actor, movies are good, but when you land the lead in a telenovela, you know you've hit the big time. That's right, novela stars are the biggest stars in Spanish entertainment.

Then you've got the storylines. It's like taking a chapter of a bestselling book that everyone, of all ages, is wrapped up in—*Harry Potter* or *Twilight* or a classic like *Gone with the Wind*—and bringing it directly to primetime TV. But what's different from a Hollywood blockbuster is that you see these characters—and get wrapped up in their stories—night after night. Think of *Grey's Anatomy*, or *24*. You can't wait for the next episode. You need your nightly fix.

Furthermore, these are stars that all Latinos know and love. They are household names in Hispanic America. The best actors from all over Latin America try to land key roles in telenovelas and when they do, they are revered all over the U.S. and in Latin America. That's why you can see them everywhere gracing red carpets and magazine covers, and their careers often span decades.

William Levy, of *Dancing with the Stars* fame, who became a Hispanic superstar in 2011 with the hit telenovela *Triunfo del Amor*, was on the cover of last year's *People en Español*'s "50 Most Beautiful" issue. And of the fifty honored by *People en Español*, twenty-three of them were telenovela stars! By the way, Levy is also in the pages of English-language *People*, too—there was tons of coverage of his rumored affair with J. Lo after he appeared in her "I'm Into You" video.

Latina magazine, which is an English language publication, chronicled their "Top 10 Telenovelas of all time" in a 2012 issue. And *TV y Novelas* magazine—America's equivalent would be *Us Weekly*—is dedicated to going behind the scenes to get the inside scoop and juicy tidbits on the private lives of novela stars.

Because of their serialized nature and over-the-top storylines and characters, many people think of our novelas as Spanish soap operas, but the similarities are few. How else can you explain the fact that while daytime soaps are an endangered species—with the recent demise of *All My Children* and *One Life to Live*—telenovelas are hotter than ever? Novelas feature the Hispanic world's very best writers, producers, and actors; lavish production values, well-defined characters, and a powerful story arc that always builds to a satisfying ending. There are so many great plot twists that viewers are loath to miss a single episode.

Tapping into familiar themes: good versus evil, star-crossed love, and sibling rivalry; and brimming with passion, heartbreak, and family rivalries, these programs, often with strong female leads, reflect not just the Latin temperament but the universal desire for success and happiness. For Hispanics around the world, these are aspirational, but relatable, contemporary stories; the characters provide a nightly escape from their everyday lives, and the next day's water-cooler gossip. And they always end Happily Ever After.

But don't be fooled into thinking that novelas are just one format. There are genres within the genre. There are kid novelas, which are U.S. Hispanics' version of *High School Musical*, or blockbusters that are our version of *Grey's Anatomy* or the *CSI* series. There are also young adult novelas like *Gossip Girl* and *90210*. Epic novela productions can rival U.S. audience favorites such as *The Tudors* or *Boardwalk Empire*, and of course, the timeless classics are our versions of *The Wizard of Oz* and *Gone with the Wind*.

Part of the reason for their broad appeal—including men, teens, and the eighteen to thirty-four age group—is that novela-watching is a tradition that's passed down from one generation to the next. Many Hispanic families gather together in front of the TV every night to find out what has happened to the characters in their favorite novela. The nightly ritual of dinner/homework/bed often gets reworked to accommodate novela-watching, and many Hispanics do not take calls during that hour. As with popular English-language TV shows and movies, many popular catch phrases—as universally known as "You had me at hello" or "I'll have what she's having" for English speakers—enter the Hispanic lexicon through novelas.

On both Univision and Telemundo, novelas air Monday through Friday. But unlike American soaps, which used to dominate daytime

Hispanic TV network viewership

By broadcast TV coverage as a percent of all Hispanic TV households. May 2012 ratings.

RANK	NETWORK (PARENT)	HOUSEHOLD RATING	HOUSEHOLDS IN THOUSANDS	HOUSEHOLD SHARE	P 2+ HISPANIC VIEWERS
1	Univision (Broadcasting Media Partners)	15.0	2,092	25	3,487
2	Telemundo (Comcast Corp. [NBC Universal])	5.5	764	9	1,156
3	ABC (Walt Disney Co.)	3.0	414	5	558
4	Fox (News Corp.)	2.7	382	5	538
5	TeleFutura (Broadcasting Media Partners)	2.6	364	4	608
6	CBS (CBS Corp.)	2.1	294	3	398
7	NBC (Comcast Corp. [NBC Universal])	2.0	276	3	385
8	Estrella TV (Liberman Broadcasting)	0.9	131	2	202
9	CW (CBS Corp./Time Warner)	0.8	118	1	144
10	Azteca America (TV Azteca)	0.6	82	1	125
10	PBS (Public Broadcasting Service)	0.6	82	1	100
12	Ion Television (Ion Media Networks)	0.5	74	1	97

Source: Nielsen National People Meter Hispanic Sub Sample (www.nielsen.com) based on Hispanic prime-time viewership from 7 p.m. to 11 p.m., Monday through Sunday (4/30/2012-5/27/2012). Rating is % of Hispanic TV households; share is % of those households with TV sets in use and watching the network. P 2+ counts total Hispanic viewing persons in thousands tuned in to the network. Viewing estimates include 7 days of DVR.

Source: Hispanic Fact Pack 2012: Annual Guide to Hispanic Marketing and Media © 2012 Crain Communications Inc.

Figure 7.5

programming, telenovelas remain on Spanish-language television's prime-time schedule because they are ratings juggernauts. Their cliff-hangers and plot twists make novelas virtually DVR-proof, with 96 percent of Univision's prime-time novelas viewed live by a highly engaged audience who tune in every weeknight for an average of four to six months. Few other programming genres earn this type of viewer commitment. In an industry where sure things are few and far between, telenovelas are about as close as you can get.

Figure 7.5 shows you a ranking of network viewership among all Hispanic TV households according to Nielsen's National People Meters, based on the May 2012 ratings, where you can see how Univision and Telemundo lead in terms of Hispanic viewers *and also how they stack up* against all the other broadcast networks. This top-ten list shows Univision's second broadcast network Telefutura (which was recently rebranded as UniMÁS) in fifth place, ahead of CBS and NBC, followed by newcomer Estrella TV, which beat the CW; and Azteca America coming in at number ten, neck and neck with PBS.

CABLE TV

With the exception of Galavision, the development of Spanish-language cable channels did not occur until the 1990s, when the cable industry first developed Spanish-language networks for the growing cable markets of Latin America. After an initial relatively successful run, Spanish-language cable channels stopped growing due to the limitations of the existing Latin American cable distribution and a volatile advertising market. As a result, these cable channels had to look for more stable markets for growth, and it was only natural for them to focus on the growing U.S. Hispanic market over the past two decades.

"Cable is playing an increasingly important role within Hispanic households, as more and more viewing shifts toward the more targeted offerings of cable," says the *Hispanic Marketer's Guide To Cable: 2011 Upfront Edition*, published by the Cable Advertising Bureau. "Today, the vast majority of Hispanic households—85 percent—have cable or satellite. DVR households have more than doubled in the last three years. And households with at least four TV sets are growing fast, now representing a third of Hispanic homes," adds the report.

In order to compete with the Spanish-language broadcasters, Hispanic cable television is touting its ability to target specific segments of the Hispanic market that may be underserved by the broadcasters. With the advances in digital technology, the bandwidth available for new channels has grown exponentially, so cable providers can now offer consumers hundreds more channels in their packages. For Hispanic channels, however, the biggest challenge continues to be whether they are located in English- or Spanish-language tiers and how those channels are being bundled by different providers.

Industry insiders are watching to see what Comcast does after having acquired NBC Universal in 2011, especially after the spectacular failure that was the mega-merger between AOL and Time Warner, which ended in 2009. According to the *Washington Post*, "the deal marries the nation's biggest cable and Internet service provider with NBC Universal's library of entertainment—which includes *30 Rock* and Bravo's *Top Chef*—and marks the first time a cable company has owned a major network."[15] The biggest concerns, of course, revolve around three key issues: killing or chilling the emerging online video market; unfairly raising prices for NBCU's content for other cable distributors; and potential "net neutrality" challenges by other Internet providers. Each one of these issues is—on its own—huge and has the potential to transform the future media landscape. We will have to stay tuned and see what happens.

What interests me most, as a Hispanic marketer, is to see what—if anything—they do that's innovative in the multicultural space, since Comcast now owns Hispanic-focused (Telemundo and MUN2) and black-focused media properties (TV One). My sense is that they are too busy with the larger issues of the merger to care about how to optimize their opportunity to innovate with the fastest-growing and most influential populations in the United States, but I hope I am wrong.

Univision's President of News, Isaac Lee, once said, "If content is king, distribution is King Kong." And for Spanish-language cable channels, carriage continues to be one of the biggest challenges. In terms of household penetration, Galavision is the clear leader with 71 percent coverage of all Hispanic TV households, followed by MUN2, with 51 percent coverage, and MTV's *Tr3s* with 46.8 percent. Figure 7.6 shows you the list of the top ten Hispanic cable channels according to *Ad Age*'s 2012 edition of the Hispanic Fact Pack.

In terms of ratings, the leader again in the Spanish-language cable market is Galavision, delivering more Hispanic adults viewers ages eighteen to forty-nine every season than any other Hispanic cable channel. In fact, during the 2011–2012 season Galavision even beat the two other Spanish-language *broadcasters*, Estrella TV and Azteca America, delivering an average of 77,000 total viewers (adults 18–49) a day according to Nielsen.[16] The secret behind their success? A heavy dose of Mexican soccer combined with edgy new programs (like *Los Heroes de Norte*) and old Mexican classics (like *El Chavo del Ocho*). Of course sports in general, and soccer in particular, is a passion point for Hispanic viewers and that passion has helped fuel the success of Galavision and other cable channels like ESPN Deportes and FOX Deportes, which have enjoyed tremendous growth over the past decade. Another passion point for Latinos is music, which clearly MTV's *Tr3s* has also been capitalizing on for quite some time.

Of the other Latin American channels that have successfully broken into the Hispanic market, there are several worth mentioning. With the help of its parent company, Discovery en Español has done very well over the past ten years, coming in at number six in the May 2012 rankings, offering a wide variety of family-oriented shows that Discovery Channel is well known for. But one that is not on the list and also deserves mentioning is CNN en Español, the 24-hour cable news spin-off of CNN, which was a pioneer in Spanish-language news when it first launched in the late 1990s. CNN has recently revamped under the leadership of Cynthia Hudson, who in 2011 launched three new shows, *Café CNN*, *CNN Dinero*, and *Conclusiones*, in an effort to mix up the repetitive headline news format that

Spanish-language cable networks

By cable TV coverage as a percent of all Hispanic TV households. May 2012 ratings.

RANK	CABLE NETWORK (PARENT)	CABLE COVERAGE AS A PERCENT OF ALL HISPANIC TV HH	SHARE AS PERCENT OF HISPANIC CABLE HH
1	Galavisión (Broadcasting Media Partners [Univision])	71.4%	84.5%
2	Mun2 (Comcast Corp. [NBC Universal's Telemundo])	51.6	61.0
3	Tr3s (Viacom's MTV)	46.8	55.4
4	Fox Deportes (News Corp.)	45.9	54.4
5	ESPN Deportes (Walt Disney Co.)	37.8	44.7
6	Discovery en Español (Discovery Communications)	30.9	36.6
7	Nuvo TV (Nuvo TV)	30.6	36.2
8	Discovery Familia (Discovery Communications)	25.1	29.7
9	Gol TV (Gol TV)	24.6	29.1
10	Utilisima (News Corp.)	20.3	24.1

Source: Nielsen National People Meter Hispanic Sub Sample for May 2012 (www.nielsen.com). There are 11.83 million Hispanic cable households out of 13.96 million Hispanic TV households (up from 12.95 million TV households in 2010). Networks are those with coverage of 20% or more. These are monthly averages of homes able to receive cable.

Source: Hispanic Fact Pack 2012: Annual Guide to Hispanic Marketing and Media © 2012 Crain Communications Inc.

Figure 7.6

these channels feed off. In December of 2012, a week after Jeff Zucker was named president of CNN, CNN en Español announced they were launching a new Spanish-language syndicated programming block targeting U.S. Hispanics called *CNN Latino*. The eight-hour block promises to deliver a "broad spectrum of programming that will include news, lifestyle, documentary, talk, and debate as an alternative to traditional Hispanic networks." This was the sixth new launch announcement for U.S. Hispanic media in 2012. As Margo Channing famously said in *All About Eve*, "Fasten your seatbelts. It's going to be a bumpy night."

DIGITAL CABLE TV

And finally, as the proliferation of niche channels continues, whether they are traditional cable channels or newer broadband Internet channels, the one development that has everyone talking is over-the-top TV, a general term used to describe a service you use in order to get access to TV content that is not available to you through your cable service provider. Over-the-top-TV has the potential to disrupt the traditional TV business model and is being fueled by both emerging technologies and consumers' desire to control what they watch, which may lead to à la carte TV channel/program offerings to satisfy individual viewing needs instead of traditional platform bundles.

Consider this from the Hispanic millennials study from Burke and Univision. Twenty-three percent of high-CCI Hispanic millennials said they had watched their favorite TV shows by downloading them to their smart phone and 20 percent watched on their tablet computer. And when it comes to movies, across the board Hispanic millennials are more likely to stream. Hispanic millennials with a high cultural connection index averaged 10.8 streams over the past three months, which was two more streams a month than the total Hispanic millennial population.

In the Hispanic market in 2009, Telemundo was the first to provide Hispanic consumers with a vast array of Spanish-language digital video content that had never been made available online before, when they launched a "video bar" allowing Hispanic viewers access to their prime-time shows through Telemundo.com. "With the launch of this innovative video bar, viewers can easily access episodes whenever they want from wherever they are," said Peter Blacker, Executive Vice President of Digital Media and Emerging Businesses, at the time of the launch. Since then innovative digital video services like Hulu and HBO GO have changed the game, especially in terms of monetization of TV video content, as well as cool social media sharing tools that allow brands to tap into the passions of their TV show fans.

Now Univision promises to "change the game" for Hispanic viewers with its new digital video network called UVideos which launched in fall 2012. UVideos includes thousands of hours of on-demand content where viewers can interact with their favorite current shows from Univision's portfolio of television networks. It is broadly accessible via multiple devices and platforms for a multi-screen experience, including game consoles, smartphones, tablets, and Internet-enabled TVs. UVideos allows viewers to watch, discuss, and share content across any device and will be fully optimized for both English- and Spanish-speaking audiences. It also features second-screen companion experiences such as TV check-ins, social streams, alerts, and bonus content for viewers to connect with each other and with Univision talent. Get ready for a TV *revolución*.

SPANISH-LANGUAGE RADIO

Radio is the pioneer format of Spanish-language media. It predates Spanish-language television by ten to fifteen years, and like Spanish-language broadcast television, is growing faster today than general-market radio. When talking about pioneers in the Spanish-language radio industry, one must talk about the legacy of the Tichenor family from Texas. The Tichenors were the first to broadcast Spanish-language programming on their English-language stations—as early as 1949. McHenry Tichenor was a radio entrepreneur who had acquired the license to KGBS in Harlingen, Texas. Shortly after buying this station, he realized that the ratings were very low. So, in order to improve his ratings, Tichenor started broad-casting Spanish-language programs at night, figuring that the proximity to Mexico would help attract new listeners. The strategy worked, and the Tichenor family continued to acquire radio stations in Texas. Prompted by the success of his nighttime programs, Tichenor converted KGBS into a full-time Spanish-language radio station in 1962. After that the Tichenor radio empire was literally built on the power of Spanish-language formats, and the rest, as they say, is history.

Another pioneer in Spanish-language radio is Eduardo Caballero, who, in 1973, started the first and largest rep firm for Spanish-language radio, Caballero Spanish Media, which he sold to Interep in 1995. Leg-endary for his advocacy of Hispanic media, Caballero was inducted into the Advertising Hall of Fame in spring 2011 not only for his work in Spanish-language radio and TV early on, but also for continuing to set the pace for many in the Hispanic media world.

According to Arbitron, in 1980 there were sixty-seven Spanish-lan-guage radio stations. In fall 2012, there were 1,009 Spanish-language stations. Although that sounds like a lot, keep in mind that that fig-ure represents only 7.5 percent of all commercial radio stations in the United States.[17] The number of Spanish commercial radio stations has increased 30 percent in the last ten years. Most of the growth in Span-ish-language radio, however, has occurred via consolidation. Up until the late '90s, Spanish-language radio industry was growing organically. Small independents started buying up more and more stations and converting them to Spanish-language formats, but there was no real national presence until 1997. The 1997 merger of Tichenor Media Sys-tems and Heftel Broadcasting created Hispanic Broadcasting Corpora-tion, a radio station group which for the first time had a presence in all of the top ten U.S. Hispanic markets, changing the Spanish-language radio landscape forever. In 2002 Univision bought HBC and changed its name to Univision Radio.

Spanish-language radio ownership in the United States is concen-trated in the hands of six companies: Univision, again, is the leader with sixty-nine radio stations across the United States, followed by Entravision Communications Group with forty-three stations, Liberman Broadcasting with nineteen, Spanish Broadcasting Systems with eighteen stations, Clear Channel with sixteen, and CBS Spanish with four stations.

According to Arbitron's *Hispanic Radio Today 2011*, radio's reach among both English-dominant and Spanish-dominant Hispanic listeners sits between 95 percent and 96 percent—a slight uptick from 2010. "Radio continues to be a 'weekend warrior' with Hispanic men and women, attracting an average 85 percent of men twenty-five to fifty-four and 84 percent of women twenty-five to fifty-four—higher than any weekday time period," says the report.

Arbitron tracks ten Spanish-language formats and six English-language formats that reflect the listening choices of Hispanics in the United States. (Figure 7.7)

Clearly you can see that with a 19 percent share and a cume of 11.5 million listeners,[18] Mexican regional music leads in terms of Hispanic audience share. The Mexican regional format has grown into a ratings giant over the past twenty years, especially in southwestern markets where Hispanics of Mexican origin also concentrate. What's interesting about this format is that it is no longer only followed by Spanish dominant listeners. "Among Hispanics 25 years of age and older, Spanish-dominant listeners drove the format. However, a significant percentage of the 12–24 year-old audience was English-dominant, reflecting the format's popularity with younger bicultural and bilingual Hispanics," says Arbitron.

The same is true with the number two format, Spanish contemporary, which enjoyed its strongest performance since Spring 2006, attracting 10 percent of Hispanic radio listeners with a cume of 9.6 million listeners.[19] Interestingly, "Like Mexican regional, Spanish contemporary's younger audience is in decline, with adults 25–44 representing nearly half of the format's listeners. Still, a significant percentage of English dominant listeners are teens and young adults, a reflection of this audience segment's desire to retain their cultural connectivity," says Arbitron, adding that in 2010 "at-work listening contributed to the ratings climb for the format."

Format	Share
Mexican regional	19.9%
Spanish contemporary	10.0%
Pop contemporary hit radio	8.3%
Spanish adult hits	7.8%
Rhythmic contemporary hit radio	7.6%
AC and soft AC	7.1%
Classic hits	3.6%
Spanish tropical	3.2%
News/talk/information and talk/personality	3.1%
Country and new country	2.8%
Spanish news/talk	2.1%
Spanish religious	0.9%
Spanish variety	0.9%
Tejano	0.7%
Spanish oldies	0.3%
Spanish sports	0.2%

Source: Format definitions are supplied to Arbitron by the radio stations. Data comes from TAP-SCAN™ Web National Regional Database, Fall 2010

Source: Hispanic Radio Today 2011, *How America Listens to Radio*, Arbitron

Figure 7.7 Most Poular Radio Format Among Hispanics; Mon–Sun, 6a–12a, AQH persons 12+, Fall 2010

In 2005, when I wrote my first book, the second most favored format was English-language Top Forty, but at the time Arbitron did not factor in language preference in its market reports. In an effort to improve the accuracy of its ratings Arbitron rolled out a new Portable People Meter (PPM) system starting in 2007. The PPM is a wearable portable device much like a pager or cell phone that electronically gathers inaudible codes that identify the source of a broadcast, such as a radio station. Arbitron recruits and compensates a cross section of consumers to wear these meters for an average of one year and up to two years and tracks their results to produce its radio ratings. They first launched the PPM in two markets (Philadelphia and Houston) and rolled out the next forty-six markets in 2008–2010. The remainder of Arbitron's 150+ markets still use the diary.

The new PPM system was met with major resistance from media companies that service ethnic communities via radio in the United States. In 2007 they formed a coalition and filed suit against Arbitron. The PPM Coalition ("PPMC") consists of National Association of Black-Owned Broadcasters, Spanish Radio Association, Minority Media and Telecommunications Council, Association of Hispanic Advertising Agencies, Border Media Partners, Entravision, ICBC Broadcast Holdings, Spanish Broadcasting System, and Univision. In 2008, the PPMC asked the Federal Communications Commission to open an inquiry, under Section 403 of the Communications Act, into Arbitron's use of Portable People Meters. PPMC argued that the new PPM methodology undercounted minority radio listeners and would seriously harm minority broadcasting. In 2010, after several meetings between members of Arbitron and the PPMC, a resolution was reached whereby Arbitron agreed to implement a "methodology enhancement plan" that addressed the concerns of the coalition. Reached for comment on the progress of the resolution, Horacio Gavilán, Executive Director of AHAA, the Voice of Hispanic Marketing (formerly known as the Association of Hispanic Advertising Agencies), which took a leading role in this dispute, said, "I'm happy to tell you that we have been working closely with Arbitron and the rest of the coalition members to solve all the issues around PPM as it relates to the methodology and in person recruitment."

According to *Ad Age*'s 2012 edition of the Hispanic Fact Pack, about 9 percent of all Hispanic advertising budgets go to spot radio, which in 2011 was worth roughly $666 million, an increase of 11.3 percent over 2010. Figure 7.8 shows you the top ten Hispanic radio stations in the country by weekly cume, according to Arbitron.

While Spanish-language television is clearly the dominant player in terms of Hispanic advertising share, Spanish-language radio often comes in second because it delivers both *reach and frequency*. Usu-

Top Spanish-formatted radio stations

By fall 2011 weekly cume persons.

RANK	STATION (MARKET)/FORMAT	OWNER	WEEKLY CUME PERSONS [1]	AVERAGE LISTENERS [2]	TIME SPENT LISTENING [3]
1	KLVE-FM (Los Angeles) Spanish contemporary	Univision Communications	1,792,800	37,700	2:30
2	WSKQ-FM (New York) Spanish tropical	Spanish Broadcasting System	1,718,500	49,000	3:30
3	WXNY-FM (New York) Spanish contemporary	Univision Communications	1,718,000	41,600	3:00
4	KSCA-FM (Los Angeles) Mexican regional	Univision Communications	1,618,000	33,000	2:30
5	KLAX-FM (Los Angeles) Mexican regional	Spanish Broadcasting System	1,340,800	26,500	2:30
6	WPAT-FM (New York) Spanish contemporary	Spanish Broadcasting System	1,290,400	26,700	2:30
7	KRCD-FM (Inglewood, Calif.) Spanish adult hits	Univision Communications	1,163,200	19,600	2:00
8	KBUE-FM (Los Angeles) Mexican regional	Liberman Broadcasting	1,084,200	22,500	2:45
9	KLYY-FM (Riverside, Calif.) Spanish adult hits	Entravision Communications Corp.	1,055,800	25,600	3:00
10	KLTN-FM (Houston) Mexican regional	Univision Communications	766,400	24,700	4:00

Source: Arbitron (www.arbitron.com), Fall 2011, persons 12+, Monday through Sunday, 6 a.m. to midnight. Stations qualify to be reported if they have received five or more minutes of listening in a single quarter-hour in at least 1 in-tab diary in the market, Monday through Sunday midnight to midnight (total week), during the survey period. Encoded stations qualify to be reported if they have received credit for five or more minutes of listening within a quarter-hour from at least one PPM Panelist during the Monday through Friday, 6 a.m. to midnight daypart for the survey period. 1. Stations ranked by weekly cume persons, or the number of unique consumers per week. 2. Average number of listeners per quarter-hour. 3. Weekly time spent listening in hours and minutes.

Source: Hispanic Fact Pack 2012: Annual Guide to Hispanic Marketing and Media © 2012 Crain Communications Inc.

Figure 7.8 Top Ten Hispanic Radio Stations by Fall 2011 Weekly Cume Persons.

ally radio is considered only a frequency vehicle, because it delivers the same message to the same audience over and over. But as you have already seen, Spanish-language radio is different, mainly because music formats are more popular than talk radio and because of the nature of Spanish-language television programming. Remember, telenovelas fill the primetime schedules of the two largest Spanish-language networks, and since they are on at the same time every day, they tend to draw the same people at the same time night after night. So, smart media buyers use Hispanic radio as a cost-effective "reach" vehicle because of Spanish radio's ability to offer different music programming in different markets at the same time. Since the various music formats that exist today in Spanish-language radio also closely reflect different segments of the Latino population across the United States (regional Mexican = Mexicans; tropical = Puerto Ricans, Cubans, and Dominicans; Spanish contemporary and pop contemporary = Latino youth), media buyers can specifically target those segments of the Hispanic community they are most interested in reaching. Finally, another very important thing to note about the Spanish-language radio industry is that unlike the Spanish-language television networks, radio networks have been much more flexible with advertisers about what language to run spots in. So it is not uncommon to be listening to a Spanish-language radio station with bilingual radio hosts that not only use both languages on air, but also mix in English-language spots in their commercial lineup.

SPANISH-LANGUAGE PRINT

Another common myth about the Latino market is that Hispanics don't read. Nothing gets my goat more than this misconception because it denies the historical love affair Hispanics have always had with the written word. I am happy to report that the Spanish-language publishing industry is alive and well all over the world. All you have to do is go to Mexico City or Buenos Aires or Barcelona, and you will find people everywhere you look, young and old, consuming all sorts of print products, especially books, newspapers, and magazines. I grew up in Spain—a country that is the size of Texas—and I vividly remember that everybody in Madrid read at least three newspapers a day. (There are about half a dozen national newspapers in Spain.) In fact, going to the corner kiosk to buy your newspapers or magazines was, and still is, a sacrosanct tradition, a way of communing with your neighbors and partaking of life in your neighborhood.

I'm not even sure how this myth came about here in the United States, but I can tell you that it is definitely not true. Perhaps the misconception began because it is hard as hell to find a good bookstore that sells modern Spanish-language literature. What you usually find in bookstores are classic works of Spanish literature or books that are "required reading" at the local university. In New York City, for crying out loud, there are only a handful of Spanish-language bookstores. I buy most of my Spanish-language literature when I'm traveling abroad, as do most of my friends. Thankfully, that has been changing over the past decade now that the book publishing and book-selling giants (HarperCollins, Lerner, Penguin, and Simon & Schuster) have launched Spanish-language imprints realizing there is a huge untapped market of Hispanic readers in the United States.

In terms of newspapers and magazines, it wasn't until very recently that some of the major newsstand chains started carrying Spanish-language newspapers and magazines. As long as I've been in this country, which is more than twenty years now, the place to get your Spanish-language newspapers or magazines was at the local bodega, or grocery store. In the barrio, of course, there always were one or two independent newsstand owners who carried Spanish-language materials, but you have to know where to go.

NEWSPAPERS AND MAGAZINES AD REVENUE

Print media are a bellwether for the economy, so when the Great Recession hit, newspapers and magazine were the first to feel it. After five very tough years, however, print media seem to be bouncing back. According to the Media Economics Group's Hispanic Magazine Monitor, the largest Hispanic magazines saw a 7.4 percent increase in gross ad revenues from 2010 to 2011.[20] The size of the total pie remained about the same, however, which for magazines meant 5 percent of total advertising spend or $365 million dollars in 2011. Newspapers still have a larger percentage of the pie (9 percent), which totaled $702 million dollars in gross ad revenue in 2011, but they have been hit the hardest in these past five years, with year-over-year declines in both revenue and circulation since 2007.[21]

Like their English-language counterparts, Hispanic newspapers have seen declines in circulation partly due to readers migrating to online plat-

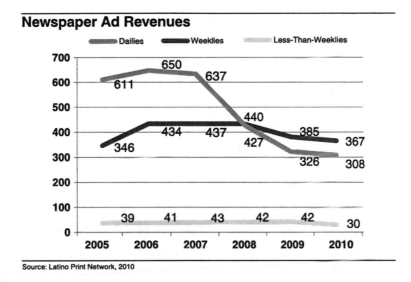

Newspaper Ad Revenues

Source: Latino Print Network, 2010

Figure 7.9

forms. Impremedia's CEO, Monica Lozano has said, "We know that the Hispanic consumer is diverse and wants to receive their content on the platform of choice." As a result, Impremedia has been producing more digital content and has struck several important content-sharing partnerships with other media companies, like Univision, Critical Media's Syndicaster, and McClatchy.

Although Impremedia is the largest player in the newspaper sector, smaller, regional players also exist and some of them seem to be thriving. The Tribune Company owns the daily *Hoy Chicago* and several other Spanish-language weeklies that have been doing quite well. According to the report from the Pew Research Center's report on the State of News Media 2011, *Hoy Chicago* increased its circulation by 40 percent in September 2010 and its readership by 27 percent over the three years prior while *Hoy Los Angeles*, a weekly, had been able to hold onto a weekly circulation of 142,470 for the twenty-six weeks ending in March 2011. In Florida, Tribune also owns two weeklies that are distributed for free. Both weeklies are named *El Senteniel*, one is located in Fort Lauderdale and the other in Orlando. Both weeklies saw increases in distribution from 2010 to 2011. In Fort Lauderdale, *El Senteniel* grew a whopping 23 percent for the period ending March 2011 to 126,150, while the Orlando edition saw a more modest increase of 3 percent to 100,878. Figure 7.10 shows you the list of the top Hispanic weeklies by circulation.[22]

According to the National Association of Hispanic Print publications, in aggregate the number of Hispanic newspapers has not changed significantly over the past five years, with weeklies and less-than-weeklies accounting for 90 percent of the total number of publications, although dailies play an very important role in larger markets. The good news is that Hispanic newspaper readership is highly concentrated where Latinos live, making those consumers easier to reach for media buyers. Eighty-six percent of Hispanic newspaper readers reported reading a newspaper at least once a week in 2011 and they are much younger, with 57 percent of Hispanic newspaper readers being between the ages of eighteen and thirty-four versus only 19 percent of Anglo daily newspaper readers.[23]

Hispanic Weekly Newspaper Circulations

Newspapers	Circulation	City
La Raza	152,300	Chicago
Vida en Valle	151,933	Sacramento
Hoy	142,470	Los Angeles
El Sentinel	125,150	Ft. Lauderdale
La Prensa Riverside	107,500	Riverside, Calif.
El Mensajero	104,000	San Francisco
El Sentinel	100,878	Orlando
Al Dia	96,836	Dallas
RUMBO	50,500	Houston
La Prensa	35,000	Orlando

Source: impreMedia (El Mensajero, La Raza, La Prensa, RUMBO, Vide en Valle). Portada (La Prensa Riverside). Audit Bureau of Circulations (Al Dia Wed. Circ only. Sat. circ is 120,405). Tribune (Hoy Los Angeles, El Sentinel Fort Lauderdale, El Sentinel Orlando).

Source: Pew Research Center's Project for Excellence in Journalism Report on the State of News Media 2011

Figure 7.10

PROFILE OF THE HISPANIC MAGAZINE READER

According to the Hispanic Market Profile report published in 2007 by the Magazine Publishers of America (MPA), more than 75 percent of all adult Hispanics actually read magazines—about eleven issues per month. That is about the same number of magazines read on average in the United States. So why don't Hispanic magazines explode? I think the answer to that question is complex. First, Latinos come from countries where mail subscriptions are not customary. General market magazines usually get 70 percent of their circulation from subscriptions so Hispanic magazines have an uphill battle on this front. Another culprit in the low circulation figures is the lack of representation on the newsstands—or, better said, the lack of a national magazine distribution system for Spanish-language publications, although digital subscriptions may help overcome this problem in the long run. Finally, the lack of Spanish-language magazines with large circulations means that advertisers often have to pay premium prices to place ads in these magazines. When advertising budgets are small and clients are trying to reach a broad audience, you can see why Spanish-language magazines are a hard sell. It's the classic chicken-and-egg story. In order to compete with TV or radio, where CPMs (cost per thousand) are in the $8–$24 range, Spanish-language print publications need to grow their circulation and bring down their CPMs from $20–$50 to something more competitive. But do not be mistaken. Latinos love to read magazines.

Hispanic magazine readers are also very desirable consumers for brands to reach. For starters they are younger, with a median age of 33.6 versus 43.7 for total magazine readers in the United States, according to the latest MPA Hispanic Market study (2007), with 53 percent of Hispanic magazine readers between the ages of eighteen and thirty-four vs. 32.3 percent of total magazine readers. Hispanic magazine readers are also squarely in the middle class, with a median household income of $45,192 and although less than half (49.4 percent) are married, over 61 percent have at least one child under the age of 18 living at home, versus 41.7 percent of total magazine readers, making them prime targets for national advertisers. Figure 7.11 gives you a snapshot of the Hispanic magazine reader today.

	Total Adults	Hispanic/ Latino Adults
Read Magazines	84.3%	75.4%
Average Number of Issues Read in a Month	11.2	11.6
Age		
18–34	32.3%	53.1%
35–49	30.6%	29.4%
50+	37.1%	17.5%
Median Age	43.7	33.6
Household Income		
Median Household Income	$56,728	$45,192
Education		
Graduated High School or More	87.9%	67.3%
Attended College or More	56.6%	37.2%
Employment		
Employed	66.4%	71.5%
Not Employed: Retired	15.4%	5.4%
Home Ownership		
Own Home	70.4%	46.5%
Marital Status		
Married	56.8%	49.4%
Children < 18 Living at Home		
1+ Children in Household	41.7%	60.6%

Base: Magazine readers Source: MRI Fall 2006

Figure 7.11 Profile of Hispanic Magazine Readers

There is no doubt that the past five years have also been hard for Hispanic magazines, with the closure of about half a dozen Spanish-language titles, most notably *Reader's Digest's Selecciones* which had been in existence since the 1970s. The largest magazines in the Hispanic market today are geared toward women and entertainment, and there are really only four key players in this space: Editorial Televisa, Meredith Corporation, Time Inc., and Latina Media Ventures.

KEY PLAYERS

Editorial Televisa, the publishing arm of the multimedia conglomerate Grupo Televisa, is the undisputed king of the Spanish-language magazine industry in the United States and in Mexico, of course. Editorial Televisa is also a key player in many other Latin American countries with the exception, perhaps, of Argentina and Brazil. (In both of those countries there are other important media companies, Grupo Clarin, Globo, and Grupo Abril, respectively, with large publishing units.) This is one of the few media industries where Univision does not have a presence, although they did publish a family magazine in the 1990s called *Más*, but that's another story for another time.

In the United States, Editorial Televisa publishes nine Spanish-language magazines, including some well-known women's titles, like *Vanidades* and *Cosmopolitan en Español*. Editorial Televisa is the only magazine company that offers advertisers a one-stop shop with the ability to buy ads in Hispanic-targeted beauty, business, fashion, entertainment, general interest, health, and lifestyle magazines. However, Televisa's magazines have very low circulations. *Vanidades* is its largest title, with sales of 125,000 copies a month.

Perhaps the most exciting development in the Hispanic magazine world in the past five years is the entrance of Meredith Corporation, the publisher of well-recognized titles such as *Better Homes and Gardens, Ladies' Home Journal*, and *More* magazines. In 2005, under the brilliant leadership of Steve Lacy, President and CEO of Meredith Corporation, Meredith launched *Siempre Mujer*, as the first-ever lifestyle and shelter publication for Spanish-dominant women living in the United States. The new magazine was the brain-child of Hispanic marketing expert Ruth Gaviria, who was hired to start the Hispanic Ventures Group, which combined the company's existing portfolio of Spanish-language magazines under one umbrella, making Meredith the leading publisher of magazines reaching Hispanic women in every life stage. Meredith also publishes *Ser Padres*, the leading Spanish-language parenting magazine for the past twenty years as well as *Ser Padres Espera* and *Ser Padres Bebe*, magazines for expecting moms and new moms. In 2012, after only seven years in existence and with 550,000 copies in circulation, *Siempre Mujer* became the second-largest Spanish-language magazine in the market, dethroning *People en Español* with 540,000 copies in circulation. The leader in the circulation is *Siempre Mujer's* sister publication *Ser Padres*, which had a circulation of 850,000 in 2012.

Gossip continues to do well for Time Inc., which owns *People en Español*. I'm proud to say that I was part of the editorial team that developed and launched this magazine in 1996. It is still considered the most successful Hispanic magazine launch in the U.S. However, it continues to be the only Spanish-language title in the stable of this venerated magazine conglomerate. *Latina* magazine was also started in 1996, founded by Christy Haubegger, who now leads the multicultural practice at Creative Artist Agency. According to *Ad Age's* 2012 edition of the Hispanic Fact Pack, (see Figure 7.12), the two largest magazines in terms of gross ad revenue are *People en Español* and *Latina*. Note that the only other English title in the top ten magazine list is *Hispanic Business*, which in May 2012 converted to a digital-only platform. Both *Latina* and *Hispanic Business* are privately held titles.

HISPANICS ONLINE

Perhaps the biggest change over the past five years, in terms of Latinos and media, has happened in the digital space. Five years ago we were still talking about the digital divide that kept swaths of Latinos disconnected from the Internet. Today, the conversation has completely flipped, with Latinos leading in technology adoption and usage. According to the latest report (2011) from the Interactive Advertising Bureau (IAB), there will be 42 million Hispanics online by 2015, which will represent 73 percent of the Hispanic population and 16 percent of the total online users in the United States. Not surprisingly, Hispanic adult Internet users are a very attractive audience. Compared to non-Hispanics, they are younger—on average eight years younger—and they live in larger households. Hispanic Internet users are also twice as likely to live in households with three or more children and 77 percent more likely to live in households with three or more employed adults.[24] In terms of shopping online, the IAB research shows that almost two-thirds (61 percent) of Hispanic Internet users made a purchase in 2009, spending on average $746, which is very close to what the average Internet user spent ($851) online the same year. The fact is that that Internet has become part of Latinos' daily life, with 61 percent saying, "When I need information, the first

Largest Hispanic magazines by gross ad revenue

		GROSS ADVERTISING REVENUE		
RANK	MAGAZINE (PARENT)	2011	2010	% CHG
1	**People en Español** (Time Warner)	$69,351	$47,444	46.2
2	**Latina** (Latina Media Ventures)	32,588	27,888	16.9
3	**Ser Padres** (Meredith Corp.)	18,927	15,061	25.7
4	**Siempre Mujer** (Meredith Corp.)	18,054	11,994	50.5
5	**TV y Novelas** (Televisa Publishing)	17,616	14,190	24.1
6	**Vanidades** (Televisa Publishing)	16,318	12,807	27.4
7	**TV Notas** (Maya Publishing Group)	7,132	8,236	-13.4
8	**Ser Padres Espera** (Meredith Corp.)	4,916	4,514	8.9
9	**Cosmopolitan en Español** (Televisa Publishing)	4,616	3,304	39.7
10	**Hispanic Business** (Hispanic Business)	4,127	4,256	-3.0

Source: Measured magazine ad spending from Media Economics Group's HispanicMagazineMonitor. Figures exclude internet advertising and circulation revenue. Dollars in thousands. 1. Percent change at top based on total industry data from Latino Print Network.

Source: Hispanic Fact Pack 2012: Annual Guide to Hispanic Marketing and Media © 2012 Crain Communications Inc.

Figure 7.12

place I look is the Internet" and 29 percent saying "The Internet has become a primary source of entertainment for me personally," a 121 index over non-Hispanics, according to the IAB.

Although Hispanics are less likely to have Internet access at home compared to the U.S. average (62 percent and 76 percent respectively) according to Nielsen, Hispanics are three times more likely to have Internet access via a mobile device (9 percent versus 3 percent respectively).[25] In fact, Hispanics are 28 percent more likely to own a smart phone than non-Hispanic whites, which partially explains why they outpace all other ethnicities in terms of data services consumption (Figure 7.13). That, of course, is good news for the phone companies but also says a lot about the future of digital media and the important role Latinos will play in it.

Most important, 29 percent of Hispanics say that "the Internet has become a new way for me to socialize or meet people," with 48 percent of Latinos admitting to having a social network profile according to the IAB.[26] New digital technologies have enhanced the fundamentally social nature of Latinos, helping them amplify what is already culturally innate to them: socializing and what we used to call word of mouth. It's no wonder that when it comes to social media, Latinos are reigning supreme. In his article for *Media Post*, "Are Online Hispanics Part of Your 2012 Plans?" Lee Vann says, "Online Hispanics continue to be heavy users of social media, driven by their relative youth, need to stay connected with family and friends within and outside of the U.S., and desire to create and consume culturally relevant content in English or Spanish. Not only are Hispanics over-indexing in their usage of established platforms such as Facebook and YouTube, they are also flocking to new platforms such as Google+, Tumblr, and Pinterest."[27]

According to a 2010 study from the Pew Research Center's Internet & American Life Project, 18 percent of Latinos who use the Internet have accounts on Twitter, compared to only 5 percent of white non-Latinos, and 13 percent of African American non-Latinos. On Facebook the same thing holds true, with 54.2 percent of Latino Internet users on Facebook, followed by 47.7 percent of white non-Latinos and 43 percent of African American non-Latinos. Beyond socializing, Latinos are also

Mobile Data Services Used by Hispanics in the Past 30 Days

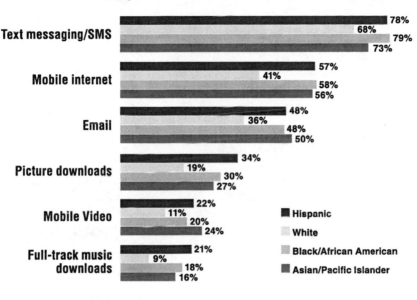

Source: Nielsen Q4, 2011 Mobile Hispanic Insights Report

Figure 7.13 Hispanics Outpace in Mobile Consumption

using these social media platforms to get and share information about issues that they care about most. For example, in 2011, Facebook and Twitter joined forces with the White House and Univision during the broadcaster's Education Town Hall with President Obama as part of their campaign called "Es el Momento" and in two hours its dedicated website, eselmomento.com was viewed by 90,000 online users and generated 6 million impressions on social media. Not only that, Univision phone banks fielded approximately 10,000 calls generated by the 2.7 million viewers who tuned in to the show, and that week 50,000 Latinos attended the education fair held in Los Angeles.

As with other media, language usage and preference is again something to consider when talking about U.S. Hispanics online. Depending on the study you read, you will get different data on language usage. Before jumping to conclusions about the data pre-

Top Ten Hispanic Sites

Among all Hispanics, from ComScore's Hispanic Ad Focus [1] category.

RANK	PROPERTY	UNIQUE VISITORS IN THOUSANDS	PERCENT REACH [2]	HISPANIC COMPOSITION PERCENT	INDEX
1	Univision Communications	2,744	8.4%	79.2%	538
2	Terra - Telefónica	2,045	6.3	55.7	379
3	Yahoo en Español	2,010	6.2	90.8	617
4	MSN Latino [includes Telemundo]	1,625	5.0	79.7	542
5	Prisa	934	2.9	75.8	515
6	Orange sites	738	2.3	53.7	365
7	Batanga	691	2.1	55.3	376
8	Grupo Televisa	534	1.6	77.5	527
9	Musica	489	1.5	75.4	512
10	ESPN Deportes (Walt Disney Co.)	355	1.1	73.2	497

Source: ComScore (www.comscore.com), May 2012. 1. Hispanic Ad Focus category measures the entire U.S. audience at sites and other ad-supporting entities oriented toward the U.S. Hispanic audience. Univision ranked as the top publisher site in the category with nearly 27 million Hispanic unique visitors. 2. Percent reach here is the percent of all Hispanic internet users (32.5 million). Rankings of largest sites continues on Page 32.

Source: Hispanic Fact Pack 2012: Annual Guide to Hispanic Marketing and Media © 2012 Crain Communications Inc.

Figure 7.14 Top Ten Hispanic Websites among All Hispanics

sented, make sure you are aware of the composition of the panels used to conduct research. Often, online panels tend to recruit more English-dominant Latinos, skewing results toward the English-language usage. The truth is that Hispanic Internet usage tends to skew more toward English than toward Spanish, partly because the Internet tends to attract younger people, who are more bilingual, but also because Spanish content online was hard to find in the beginning of the Internet boom and was only starting to develop when the bubble burst. Internet portal Starmedia, the pioneer in the Spanish-language Internet space that launched in 1996, was in the midst of a worldwide expansion when the Internet bubble burst in 2000. Just two years later, they sold what was left of the portal to France's Telecom Orange. Although late to the game, in 2002 Univision launched Univision.com and quickly became the leader of the redefined Spanish-language Internet space in the United States, in spite of the fact that several other portals had launched before them, namely Terra, Yahoo en Español and AOL Latino. Univision.

com continues to lead the pack online, as you can see from the list of top websites according to ComScore in Figure 7.14.

The AOL Latino Cyberstudy, conducted by Cheskin Research in 2010, said that 54 percent of online Hispanics were Spanish-preferred or bilingual in 2009. That represented about 19 million Hispanic online users. One of the things that the IAB study pointed out was that Spanish-preferred and bilingual online users outpace English primary users in buying power index across a variety of online activities, and that they were much more engaged online, spending more days online per month, more time per visit, and visiting Spanish-language online sites more frequently. Now that's what I call sticky! (See Figure 7.15.)

If Comscore is right, and we are indeed becoming "digital omnivores," consuming content at home, at work, and on the go through a

More days online per month
+6% average daily visitors
+20 average usage days per visitor

More time per visit
+24% total minutes
+19% average minutes per usage day
+35% average minutes per visitor
+7% average minutes per visit

More pages viewed
+20% total pages viewed
+15% average pages per usage day
+32% average pages per visitor

More frequent visits
+18% total visits
+30% average visits per visitor

Source: IAB, US Latinos Online, a driving force. IAB Hispanic Research Working Group, May 5th 2010.

Figure 7.15 Spanish/Bilingual Users Outperform English Users

growing number of connected devices led by smart phones and tablets, marketers must realize the growing importance of the younger, more highly connected, Latino consumer. After seeing how Latinos consume across all media platforms, it is easy to see how any marketing plan is incomplete if it does *not* include the Hispanic consumer. For that, let's go to the next chapter and see what the advertising landscape looks like.

Key Takeaways:

- Hispanics access media from every platform available and often lead the general market as early adopters of emerging technologies.
- 2012 saw a new flurry of activity with the announcement of five new network launches by the biggest players in the media world. Interestingly, all but one were in Spanish.
- Network, spot, and cable TV garnered almost 70 percent of the total Hispanic advertising spend, which totaled $7.14 billion in 2011.
- Spanish-language programming continues to connect. In 2012, twenty-two of the top twenty-five TV programs among Hispanic adults 18–35 were in Spanish.
- Because of their serialized nature and over-the-top storylines and characters, many people confuse telenovelas with Spanish soap operas—but the similarities are few.
- Telenovelas are ratings juggernauts. Their cliff-hangers and plot twists make novelas virtually DVR-proof, with 96 percent of Univision's primetime novelas viewed live by a highly engaged audience who tune in every weeknight for an average of four to six months.
- Radio is perhaps the most bilingual medium among Hispanics. It is also the most diverse, with a wide variety of English- and Spanish-language formats reaching more than 95 percent of all Hispanic listeners
- Seventy-five percent of all adult Hispanics read magazines— about eleven issues per month. Hispanic magazine readers are

also very desirable consumers with a median age of 33.6 and household incomes of $45,192, according to the MPA.

- Hispanic adult Internet users are a very attractive audience. Compared to non-Hispanics, they are younger, on average eight years younger, and they live in larger households.
- Digital technologies have enhanced the fundamentally social nature of Latinos, helping them amplify what is already culturally innate to them: socializing.

NOTES

1. *The State of the Hispanic Consumer: The Hispanic Market Imperative*, Copyright © 2012 The Nielsen Company.

2. *The State of the Hispanic Consumer: The Hispanic Market Imperative*, Copyright © 2012 The Nielsen Company.

3. The Nielsen Company, median age (P2+) and live viewing data based on broadcast prime Monday–Saturday 8 P.M.–11 P.M./Sunday 7 P.M. –11 P.M. (09/19/2011–01/29/2012), Live+7. Non-programming minutes data based on monitor plus via Lake 5 Media 10/31/2011–11/27/2011. Monday–Saturday 8 P.M.–11 P.M./Sunday 7 P.M.–11 P.M. Includes network and local commercials 1+ second duration, PSAs, promos, and direct response. Reflects New York DMA.

4. The Nielsen Company, National Hispanic People Meter (NPMH), All ad-supported broadcast and cable networks. All programming excluding breakouts and programs <30 minutes, plus pre- and post-sports programming. Live+7 data. Total day Monday–Sunday 7 A.M.–2 A.M. 2011–12 full season (09/19/2011–01/29/2012) bilingual reflects personal language (Mostly Spanish/Span-Eng Equal/Mostly English).

5. Vega, Tanzina and Bill Carter, "Networks Struggle to Appeal to Hispanics," *The New York Times*, August 5, 2012. Copyright © 2012 The New York Times Company. www.nytimes.com/2012/08/06/business/media/networks-struggle-to-appeal-to-hispanics-without-using-stereotypes.html?pagewanted=all&_r=0.

6. Kondolojy, Amanda, "Univision No. 1 Network in Primetime Among Adults 18—34 On Wednesday Nights and Reaches 8.1 Million Soccer Fans with USA Vs. Mexico Match," *TVbytheNumbers*, August 17, 2012. http://tvbythenumbers.zap2it.com/2012/08/17/univision-no-1-network-in-primetime-among-adults-18-34-on-wednesday-night-and-reaches-8-1-million-soccer-fans-with-usa-vs-mexico-match/145260.

7. The Nielsen Company. National People Meter (NPM) (09/19/2011-09/23/2012), Broadcast Prime Monday-Saturday 8 P.M.–11 P.M., Sunday 7 P.M.–11 P.M.,

Live +7. Shares based on sum of impressions among UNI, TF, GALA, TEL, AZA and ETV.

8. "Gross US Ad Spending," Hispanic Fact Pack 2012: Annual Guide to Hispanic Marketing and Media, published by *Advertising Age*, Copyright © 2012 Crain Communications Inc. http://adage.com/trend-reports/report.php?id=68.

9. Ryan, Joe, "U.S. Advertising Spend Increases Slightly in 2011," *Direct Marketing News*, March 13, 2012. Copyright © Haymarket Media, Inc. www.dmnews.com/us-advertising-spend-increases-slightly-in-2011/article/231864.

10. The Nielsen Company, National People Meter (NPM) Week in May 2012 (05/07/2012–05/13/2012), Monday to Sunday 7 A.M.–2 A.M. Based on 6+ minute qualified audience. Live + SD.

11. Market Survey Schedule and Population Rankings Spring 2012 (DMA), Copyright © Arbitron Inc. Unduplicated P12+ Cume Monday to Sunday 6 A.M.–12 Midnight (incl. PR and Spill). Unduplicated Cumes for competitor groups, include non UVN markets also. Entravision, Liberman, Clear Channel Hispanic and CBS Radio Spanish include Spanish-formatted stations only.

12. Univision.com US and PR-only traffic analytics MRC accredited, January 2011–December 2011; mobile visits = WAP (MIA+Futbol/Salud/Foros WAP) + APP (Futbol+Univision+Marcador+Scoreboard+Video+Radio), mobile web + APP January 2012–November 2012.

13. The Nielsen Company, NPower, NPM (05/07/2012–05/13/2012) Monday to Saturday 8 P.M.–11 P.M. and Sunday 7 P.M.–11 P.M., Live+7. Based on a qualified audience of 6+ minutes and on the percent of each network's prime-time audience who didn't watch any of the other listed networks. (E-L networks based on the top ten in prime time among adults eighteen to forty-nine for the week).

14. The Nielsen Company, National People Meter (NPM), Telemundo's *La Reina del Sur* final airing (05/30/2011) 10:00 P.M.- 11:00 P.M. Live +SD. Full-Run based on (02/28/2011-05/30/2011), 10:00 P.M.–11:00 P.M., Live + SD. http://tvbythenumbers.zap2it.com/2011/05/31/%E2%80%9Cla-reina-del-sur%E2%80%9D-draws-best-audience-ever-for-telemundo-entertainment-program-averaging-nearly-4-2-million-total-viewers/94284/.

15. Kang, Cecilia, "Federal Regulators Approve Comcast's Acquisition of NBC Universal, with Asterisks," *The Washington Post*, January 18, 2011. Copyright © 2011 The Washington Post. www.washingtonpost.com/wp-dyn/content/article/2011/01/18/AR2011011806440.html.

16. The Nielsen Company, National People Meter (NPM), Live +7 program based daypart . 2011–2012 STD (9/26/11–1/29/12). Monday to Sunday 7 A.M.–2 A.M.. Excludes breakouts.

17. M Street Journal 2003–2012 data.

18. Hispanic Radio Today–2011 Edition, Copyright © 2011 Arbitron Inc.

19. Hispanic Radio Today–2011 Edition, Copyright © 2011 Arbitron Inc.

20. Hispanic Fact Pack 2012: Annual Guide to Hispanic Marketing and Media, published by *Advertising Age*, Copyright © 2012 Crain Communications Inc.

21. Guskin, Emily and Amy Mitchell, "Hispanic Media Faring Better than Mainstream Media," The State of the News Media 2011: An Annual Report on American Journalism, released by the Pew Research Center Project for Excellence in Journalism. http://stateofthemedia.org/2011/hispanic-media-fairing-better-than-the-mainstream-media.

22. Guskin, Emily and Amy Mitchell, "Hispanic Media Faring Better than Mainstream Media," The State of the News Media 2011: An Annual Report on American Journalism, released by the Pew Research Center Project for Excellence in Journalism. http://stateofthemedia.org/2011/hispanic-media-fairing-better-than-the-mainstream-media.

23. The State of Hispanic Print, NAHP Annual Media and Legislative Summit, March 2011.

24. U.S. Latinos Online: A Driving Force, IAB (Interactive Advertising Bureau) Hispanic Research Working Group, May 2010. Revised May 2011. www.iab.net/media/file/USLatinosOnline_RevisedMay2011FINAL.pdf.

25. *The State of the Hispanic Consumer: The Hispanic Market Imperative*, Quarter 2, 2012, Copyright © 2012 The Nielsen Company.

26. Simmons NCS/NHCS Fall 2009 Full Year, Population Adult 18+ Full Year (Nov08-Dec09). "Online" defined as websites/search engines visited past 30 days, Mintel Report, "Hispanics Online" as cited in company press release, March 25, 2009.

27. Vann, Lee, "Are Online Hispanics Part of Your 2012 Plans?" *Media Post*, ENGAGE: Hispanics, March 8, 2012. www.mediapost.com/publications/article/169720/are-online-hispanics-part-of-your-2012-plans.html#ixzz25dcjF0yV.

8

THE HISPANIC
ADVERTISING INDUSTRY

The Hispanic advertising industry is undergoing a major transformation. On the one hand, the explosive growth of the Hispanic population has more and more businesses knocking on agency doors. On the other, the marketers and agencies are grappling with important issues that are unique to ethnic markets, such as how to properly deliver culturally relevant brand messages to Hispanic consumers and how to measure results with systems that do not properly track ethnic populations. Marketers and agencies are also faced with a quickly changing and complex target: Hispanic consumers who are constantly being redefined not only by their generation, but also by how they self-identify, where they live, whether they were born in the U.S. or not, and whether they predominantly speak Spanish, English, or both. Add to that a veritable explosion of media platforms in which to advertise goods and services, and you can see why the Hispanic advertising industry is in flux.

Perhaps the biggest game changer on the media side of the Hispanic advertising world came about between 2004 and 2006 when Nielsen Media Research decided to double the size of its national television audience sample by implementing "the largest-ever national sample expansion among African American and Latino households" in order to more accurately track the television audiences they measure on their national TV ratings service. The change was welcomed by

Spanish-language broadcast and cable companies who, until then, had been forced to use the National Hispanic Television Index, a separate panel created in 1992 to measure TV consumption of Spanish-speaking audiences in the U.S. In 2006, when the Nielsen national sample had been expanded, both Univision and Telemundo subscribed to the National Television Index (NTI) putting them on equal footing with all other major broadcasters in terms of apples-to-apples comparisons of TV ratings. Since then, Spanish-language media companies have been able to close more deals during the traditional television "upfront season" by showing reluctant media buyers the real power of Spanish-language television both in terms of ratings and reach.

As a matter of fact, in 2011 Univision proclaimed it was the number one network among adults 18–34, regardless of language, on ninety nights; and it also beat NBC in primetime against the prized 18–49 demo on 195 nights—that's one out of two nights in a year.[1] Likewise, Telemundo boasted about its 2012 Olympic coverage, which delivered a total cumulative viewership of 22.5 million viewers during the London Olympics—double the total viewers that tuned in to watch the 2008 Beijing Olympics on Telemundo. While the opening and closing ceremonies were universally panned, Telemundo's ratings were undoubtedly helped by the fact that the final match for soccer's gold medal pitted all-time international rivals Mexico and Brazil, making it the most-watched Olympic event in the history of the network, averaging 3.6 million total viewers.[2]

In this chapter I will try to give you a sense of where the Hispanic marketing and advertising industry is today, who the key players are, and how to properly think about your approach to Hispanic marketing. But let's first take a quick look back at how we got here.

HISTORY OF HISPANIC ADVERTISING

Although the birth of the Spanish-language advertising industry in the United States dates back to the 1950s, its focus early on was on helping American companies market their products in Latin America.

Interamericas was the first dedicated U.S. Hispanic advertising agency, founded in New York by Luis Diaz Albertini in 1962. But it really wasn't until the '70s and early '80s that major national brands started advertising to the Latino community in the United States. Among those early advertisers were Colgate-Palmolive, McDonald's, and Coca-Cola. The '80s and '90s were decades of tremendous growth for both the Hispanic population and Hispanic agencies that were launched to service the growing Hispanic market. With the exception of Young and Rubicam's (Y&R) Bravo Group, however, large multinational agencies were not interested in Hispanic marketing until the turn of the century. Now, of course, leading agencies realize that profitable growth depends on gaining the necessary expertise to tap into changing tastes of one of the most influential consumer segments in the United States: Hispanics.

Over the past ten years there has been some merger activity, as some of the more established independent Hispanic agencies have been gobbled up by large holding companies. According to *Advertising Age*'s 2012 edition of the Hispanic Fact Pack, five of the top ten largest Hispanic advertising agencies are now owned by large holding companies. In fact, Omnicom now owns three of the top ten Hispanic agencies, including the number one Hispanic agency, Dieste, whose estimated revenue was slightly over $39 million in 2011 (Figure 8.1).

Today you will find nearly one hundred specialized agencies in the directory of AHAA, the Voice of Hispanic Advertising, a nonprofit trade organization that was founded in 1996 to help champion corporate investments in Hispanic marketing. And while the Hispanic agencies that belong to huge multinationals lead the industry in terms of annual billing, more than half of the top fifty Hispanic advertising agencies are still independently owned. Contrary to what you might think, these independent agencies don't just pick up the leftover crumbs that fall off the large holding companies' tables. No, many of these minority-owned agencies have huge clients like Texas-based Lopez Negrete, who has had the Walmart account for almost twenty years now, or Zubi Advertising in Miami, which has managed the Ford account for as long as I can remember.

Ten Largest US Hispanic Agencies

RANK	AGENCY [COMPANY AFFILIATION]	HEADQUARTERS	KEY EXECUTIVES	2011 REVENUE	% CHG
1	Dieste* [Omnicom]	Dallas	Greg Knipp, CEO; Tony Dieste, chmn & co-founder	$39,024	5.5
2	GlobalHue*✓	Southfield, Mich.	Donald A. Coleman, chmn & CEO	33,970	-0.5
3	Bravo Group* [WPP (Y&R)]	Miami	Eddie Gonzalez, CEO; Eric Hoyt, pres & COO	31,500	5.0
4	Lopez Negrete Communications✓	Houston	Alex Lopez Negrete, pres & CEO	28,260	17.0
5	LatinWorks*✓ [Omnicom]	Austin, Texas	Manny Flores, CEO & mg ptnr; Alejandro Ruelas, CMO & mg ptnr	23,600	6.5
6	Conill* [Publicis (Saatchi)]	Torrance, Calif.	Cynthia McFarlane, CEO & chairperson; Carlos Martinez, pres	23,258	18.0
7	Zubi Advertising Services✓	Coral Gables, Fla.	Joe Zubizarreta, COO; Michelle Zubizarreta, chief admin officer; Joe Castro, exec VP	18,900	2.2
8	Alma* [Omnicom (DDB)]	Miami	Luis Miguel Messianu, pres & chief creative officer	17,180	-9.8
9	De la Cruz Group✓	Guaynabo, P.R.	Rene de la Cruz, chmn & CEO	16,594	5.6
10	Grupo Gallegos✓	Huntington Beach, Calif.	John Gallegos, pres & CEO	15,500	6.9

* Ad Age Estimates ✓ Denotes minority ownership
Source: Hispanic Fact Pack 2012: Annual Guide to Hispanic Marketing and Media © 2012 Crain Communications Inc.

Figure 8.1 Largest U.S. Hispanic Agencies

AHAA publishes a directory of its member agencies every year. This directory provides a detailed listing of each AHAA member agency's services and specialties, client rosters, capitalized billings, and key personnel and contact information, which is very helpful. Remember, not all agencies are good at everything, so ask questions and make sure the agency you hire knows how to do what you need it to do. Because the Hispanic consumer is changing so quickly, the one-size-fits-all mentality no longer works. Some agencies will be better at creative and strategic planning, while others excel at public relations or direct mail. So you see, you need to ask questions and find out exactly what they can or cannot do for you.

I know what you're thinking: I'm not big enough to work with an agency. I don't have a million dollars in my advertising budget. Well, first of all, you don't need lots of money to work with an agency. And second, if you have a small business and usually don't work with an agency, don't worry. You can still get help. Not every Hispanic agency is listed in the AHAA directory, so check your local listings as well to find out if there is a shop in your area that might be able help you out.

The growth in the number of Hispanic shops controlled by holding agencies can be attributed to a marketing trend that has been around for the past decade: big brands want a one-stop shop. Before, marketers would have to manage multiple agencies to get their job done, but with the demand for brand synergy and cost efficiency, and lack of time on the part of brand managers, in recent years there has been a trend toward consolidating all marketing efforts with one advertising shop . . . assuming they have the right expertise in-house. Frankly, I'm not sure that brands get better results with this one-stop shop mentality, but it sure does make the job of the brand manager easier! Between this trend and the rise of marketing accountability in the form of increased scrutiny of advertising costs from procurement, the traditional advertising compensation model has been turned on its head. As a result, larger holding companies now seek a piece of the Hispanic ad pie that they had ignored for so long. In fact, some big advertising shops think that they can "fake it" by hiring a few token Latinos and calling that a "specialized discipline" . . . but faking it only gets them so far. After one or two failed efforts, clients can see right through these façades and are now demanding that their agencies build proper ethnic expertise around their brand needs. It is interesting to note that some very well-known agencies don't have the expertise in-house and have recognized the difficulty in developing it. So they will often partner with a Hispanic agency to deliver the expertise needed for a client. This is a recognized alternative that can work, but only when the ethnic shop has a real seat at the table. African American, Asian, and LGBT specialty shops are also partnering with established agencies in this manner.

In spite of the fact that over one-third (36 percent) of all consumers in the United States and over 41 percent of all young adults (eighteen- to thirty-four-year-olds) are multicultural, ethnic marketing efforts continue to get the short end of the stick (not to mention budgets). Ethnic agencies are often left out of the *critical* strategic planning process but are often asked—at the last minute—to "adapt creative." This approach is often destined to fail, since the creative is based on a consumer insight that may not resonate with Hispanics or touts brand benefits that Hispanic consumers simply don't care about. Anything can be translated into Spanish, but if your message doesn't resonate, or worse, doesn't even make sense, Latinos probably won't buy your product. This is the ugly truth. The problem is that far too often, this is the process for Hispanic marketing campaigns. Then, when the results come in—if they are tracked at all—and they don't look so good, everyone is quick to say Hispanic marketing doesn't work. We've come a long way, no doubt, but we still have a longer road ahead. What gives me hope, however, is that some leading companies are starting to change the way they approach their brand marketing by adopting a more holistic view of their consumers and asking their agency partners to come up with a "total market strategy."

Some people have confused total market strategy with what I call "rainbow marketing," which is an effort to mainstream multicultural marketing. These efforts are often driven by simple casting choices in commercials—let's make sure we have one of each color in the ad and voilà, there's your *cross-cultural* spot. In my opinion, this does not work because it is based on a superficial approach, not a strategic approach.

On the other hand, total market strategy is a seven-step process that, if done correctly, can yield incredible results. This is a process that is starting to be used by leading marketers and media planners who recognize the need to reach *all potential consumers* who fall within a brand's target market, regardless of race, ethnicity, or language preference. You see, the concept of "multicultural marketing" was born in the '90s when ethnic segmentation tools became sophisticated enough to really help marketers and agencies better understand who was consuming their products. But over the years, the term *multicultural* became a way of "segregating" consumer segments by size: if they weren't big enough, they didn't matter. The reality is that the so-called "general market" really became a euphemism for "whites." Smart marketers now recognize that ethnic consumers, whether Hispanic, African American, or Asian, are an increasingly important part of the mainstream, the *new* mainstream, as Guy Garcia called it in 2004.

Glenn Llopis, founder of the Center for Hispanic Leadership, got it right when he recently said, "Many organizations want to make Hispanics part of the 'mainstream'—but they must know how to integrate their intentions with proper intelligence and know-how." In the same article written for *Forbes* magazine in November 2012, he adds, "Ignoring the Hispanic market represents slow death. On the other hand, those who invest wisely will dominate their industry for the next twenty years! Those who don't are putting their businesses and brands at risk. The Hispanic market can no longer be viewed as a tactical option, but rather must become a strategic imperative. The Hispanic market must stop being managed and approached as if it were a diversity initiative. You must either be in or out. There is no gray area here."[3]

I truly believe that total market strategy is the right way to execute successful marketing initiatives for Latinos or any other ethnic community. Let me share with you the following roadmap to total market strategy, which was developed by Graciela Eleta, who for more than eight years headed up the Hispanic marketing efforts for Procter & Gamble and is widely recognized as an authority on marketing to Hispanics.

TOTAL MARKET STRATEGY ROADMAP

By Graciela Eleta

1. **Leverage Consumer Research to Define Your Strategy.** A brand should always stand for the same equity in consumers' minds, be they Hispanic or not. However, if consumer research shows that category penetration, brand awareness, habits, or practices are different between Hispanic and non-Hispanic consumers, you should consider a different communication strategy. Brands may need to go back to their introductory strategies to "launch" with Hispanics as they would if entering a new market.

2. **Ensure Product and Packaging Are Relevant.** This does not mean that you need heritage brands or products created specifically for Hispanics to win in the market. In fact, it means just the opposite. It is best to have a single innovation stream that addresses Hispanics along with non-Hispanic consumers. This will allow you to develop products, packaging, and services that are equally relevant to your

diverse consumer base. Many brands are finding that they can benefit from Hispanic-inspired product innovation—such as Hispanic
ingredients, flavors or fragrances—to delight all consumers.

3. **Develop Culturally Relevant Creative.** Ads developed or
adapted with Hispanics in mind, rather than straight translations,
generate higher enjoyment, believability, and persuasion among Hispanics. The best way to engage with Hispanics is with "in-culture"
messages in contextually relevant media environments. There are
many ways to do this, including touching on Hispanic passion points
like music and food, driving emotional benefits as opposed to only
functional ones, and emphasizing cultural values such as family and
the American Dream. If you integrate Hispanic insights into your
creative brief from the start, you will save time, effort, and money in
developing an entirely new commercial.

4. **Drive Concurrent Launches of New Initiatives.** When it comes
to new product or service introductions, make sure you are launching your Hispanic efforts concurrently to maximize the trial and
awareness lift among Hispanics. When you go to market at the same
time, you are not only more cohesive, you're also maximizing your
return on investment. Concurrent launches allow you to take full
advantage of English-language media spillover, public relations,
social media, in-store merchandising, and grassroots efforts in the
"general market" that touch Hispanic consumers.

5. **Support Brands with Sufficient and Consistent Funding.** Total
market strategy suggests that you maximize your overall U.S. media
reach by including Hispanic media from the start. Your Hispanic
media plan should be reflective of the Hispanic contribution to your
overall sales. So, if 18 percent of your sales come from Hispanics,
18 percent of your marketing budget should ideally be devoted to
reaching this consumer. And consistently supporting your Hispanic
messaging is essential to building a long-term relationship with
these consumers. Ideally, you should mirror your English-language
reach, frequency, and weeks on air. In instances where your brand or
category is underdeveloped, you should consider introductory media
levels to drive Hispanic trial and awareness.

6. **Customize Retail Distribution, Assortment, and Services.**
Whether shopping for groceries or a car, Hispanic consumers need
to feel welcomed at your point of purchase. To delight Hispanic shop-

pers, you should consider taking a holistic approach in your high Hispanic outlets that includes targeted distribution of your most relevant Hispanic offerings, bilingual support services—website, warranties, signage—and bilingual customer service. Investing in shopper insights is another important step to ensure that your brand remains relevant to these shoppers throughout their path to purchase.

7. **Define and Track Success Metrics Across Disciplines.** Ineffective measurement of results is a common reason for cutting budgets and subsequent loss of market share. In a total market strategy, senior management holds all functional and business leaders accountable for results, not just the multicultural managers. It is also important to benchmark against your competition and to look beyond short-term ROI as a way to define success. Metrics such as category and brand growth coming from Hispanics, category incidence, and purchase frequency gaps, regional and national market share gaps, as well as trial and equity trends must all be consistently monitored and analyzed to assess progress against Hispanic goals.

For more great insights on Hispanic marketing and the Hispanic consumer visit: www.univision.net/the-hispanic-consumer.

WHO'S GOT GAME?

Every year, *Advertising Age* publishes a list of the top advertisers in the U.S. Hispanic market (Figure 8.2). Invariably, Procter & Gamble is always at the top of the list. This consumer product giant has been a leader in this market for the last forty years, and as its investment in Hispanic marketing increases, so does its share of the U.S. Hispanic wallets. It is rare to find a company that has such a dedicated Hispanic marketing team. Far more common is to find Hispanic marketing efforts falling in the hands of the "token" marketing person who may happen to be a person of color but may not have actual experience in ethnic marketing. In fact, you would be shocked at how many large corporations still "look into" this huge opportunity by assigning the market analysis to a summer intern. I swear it is true and obviously shameful. That's why Hispanic advertising agencies *still* play such an important role. They can help your company properly size your opportunity in the Hispanic mar-

Largest Spenders in Hispanic Media

Companies ranked by U.S. measured-media spending. Dollars in thousands.

RANK	MARKETER	U.S. MEASURED-MEDIA SPENDING 2011	2010	% CHG
1	Procter & Gamble Co.	$220,552	$197,655	11.6
2	Dish Network Corp.	154,745	90,430	71.1
3	Verizon Communications	114,613	137,919	-16.9
4	McDonald's Corp.	114,164	117,301	-2.7
5	AT&T	110,388	132,086	-16.4
6	General Mills	97,023	91,814	5.7
7	Broadcasting Media Partners [1] (Univision)	87,516	119,198	-26.6
8	Toyota Motor Corp.	86,178	79,947	7.8
9	Kraft Foods	83,675	36,334	130.3
10	General Motors Co.	79,384	102,470	-22.5
11	L'Oréal	77,796	50,392	54.4
12	Deutsche Telekom (T-Mobile)	77,442	79,369	-2.4
13	State Farm Mutual Auto Insurance Co.	73,898	91,762	-19.5
14	Sprint Nextel Corp.	73,173	73,468	-0.4
15	Ford Motor Co.	62,500	36,539	71.0
16	Walmart Stores	60,875	65,579	-7.2
17	DirecTV	59,766	128,911	-53.6
18	Fiat (Chrysler Group)	58,049	18,118	220.4
19	Comcast Corp.	56,321	51,989	8.3
20	Sears Holdings Corp.	55,185	53,916	2.4

Source: Hispanic Fact Pack 2012: Annual Guide to Hispanic Marketing and Media © 2012 Crain Communications Inc.

Figure 8.2 Largest Spenders in Hispanic Media

ket, guide research efforts to determine actionable consumer insights, and then develop marketing campaigns around these insights. Some can even help with media planning and buying, although those two areas in particular have, over the past decade, moved to larger specialized agencies that provide cost efficiencies driven by the total size of their clients' investments. The good news is that the leading Hispanic media buying and planning agencies have invested the necessary time and money in talent to create the right specialized teams to properly manage those areas beyond your creative agency.

While *Advertising Age* tracks the top fifty companies advertising in the Hispanic market, Figure 8.2 shows you the top twenty. A quick look at this list confirms what I discussed in Chapter 4 about the industries that are poised to benefit most from the growth of the Hispanic population in the next five years. Among the largest advertisers in the Hispanic market you will find CPG and food companies, mass retailers, automotive companies, and some consumer electronics. However, you'll notice that many big companies in those sectors are still blatantly missing and that companies in other sectors like entertainment, education, real estate, or financial services are just getting started. If your company is not listed here, you'd better hurry up and figure out how to start capitalizing on the Hispanic market, or risk being left out of the biggest growth opportunity this country has seen in the last fifty years.

Another interesting thing to note about the list of top advertisers in the U.S. Hispanic market is that every year you'll see some high-flying new entrants that, more often than not, quickly fade away. Don't be a flash in the pan. Remember the AHAA study on maximizing impact in the Hispanic market that I spoke about in Chapter 1? Their analysis, conducted by the Santiago Solutions Group, found that best-in-class companies, allocating one-quarter of their ad spend to Hispanic media over five years, would generate annual revenue growth of 6.7 percent. Consistency has paid off for P&G, McDonald's, General Mills, and others, so why shouldn't it work for you, too?

In spite of the Great Recession, the total amount of money invested in Hispanic media has nearly doubled from $4.3 billion in 2002 to $7.14 billion in 2011 (Figure 8.3).

What is stopping more investment? A combination of fear, lack of internal alignment, tools to properly measure ROI and, finally, a historic lack of commitment, which has resulted in on-again, off-again efforts by even some of the largest global brands. Actually, it's hard to watch sometimes how a company will get a CMO who "gets it" and pushes hard to invest in the Hispanic market for two or three years. Then, just as things are starting to take off, that leadership changes, someone new comes in and all of a sudden, you are back at square one. The commitment to the

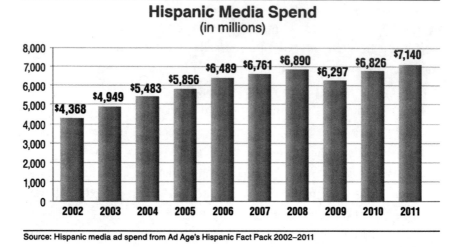

Hispanic Media Spend
(in millions)

Source: Hispanic media ad spend from Ad Age's Hispanic Fact Pack 2002–2011

Figure 8.3

Hispanic consumer needs to come from the very top—the CEO and the board of directors—and needs to be part of the long-term plan, not just an opportunity for short-term gains.

The good news is that Latinos *like* advertising more than their Anglo counterparts, and research studies show they also are more open to, and engaged with, brand messages on every media platform. Remember, this is *not* about language. This is about culture and respecting your consumer by knowing what cultural levers to pull in your marketing messages. For the record, let me just say that in order to effectively reach *all* the Latino community you should advertise in *both English and Spanish*. Hispanic marketing isn't an either/or proposition between Spanish- and English-language media. Depending on your target market, chances are you'll need both to properly reach all the Latino community. "Spending in almost all Spanish advertising mediums increased from 2010 to 2011, further evidence that marketers will continue to invest in this growing marketplace as the economy recovers," says Nielsen. "While not quantifiable, there is also some media spending allocated to English-language initiatives by advertisers mindful of English-speaking Latinos," they add. The bottom line is this: today

Spanish-language media continues to be the most efficient way to reach the majority of Latinos in this country. However, as more and more second- and third-generation Latinos, who are more English-dominant, enter their peak spending years, it is likely that English-language media vehicles that are Hispanic-oriented could also become more efficient for marketers to reach Latinos in the United States, but we've got a long way to go on that front.

The key to reaching Latinos in any language is respect and authenticity. According to the Univision webinar *Meet Hispanic Millennials, Your Culture Driven Consumer,* Hispanics value brands that respect them. Based on research conducted by Burke Inc., this study set out to understand how connected Hispanic millennials were to Hispanic culture and ranked them in terms of high, medium and low connection.[4] Hispanics want to know that a brand "gets" them, recognizes their Hispanic identity and culture, and understands them enough to know how the brand would fit into their lives. Respect seems like something older/first-generation Latinos might gravitate toward, but it's interesting to note that 72 percent of high-culturally connected Hispanic millennials said they prefer purchasing from brands that "treat me with respect" vs. 70 percent of Hispanic non-millennials. Part of that "respect" comes from authentic representation in ads. As noted in the Yahoo/Mindshare Ethnodynamics study, "Marketing to Hispanics," half of all Hispanics feel as if most ads don't target them. While the need for ethnic representation was higher among first-generation Hispanics (Figure 8.4) than second-generation Hispanics, this study found that diversity in advertising is consistently important for all generations, with 65 percent of first-generation Hispanics and 62 percent of second-generation Hispanics strongly agreeing that they "prefer ads that show diversity rather than a single ethnicity."[5]

This concept of respect and authenticity applies to all ethnic minorities and goes to the heart of what David Burgos and Ola Mobolade from Millward Brown call urban mindset consumers in their excellent book, *Marketing to the New Majority.* "Today's young adults live in a world where the walls between African American, Asian, and Hispanic iden-

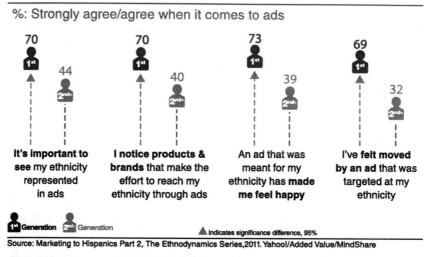

%: Strongly agree/agree when it comes to ads

70	70	73	69
44	40	39	32
It's **important to see** my ethnicity represented in ads	I **notice products & brands** that make the effort to reach my ethnicity through ads	An ad that was meant for my ethnicity has **made me feel happy**	I've **felt moved by an ad** that was targeted at my ethnicity

1st Generation   2nd Generation   ▲ indicates significance difference, 95%

Source: Marketing to Hispanics Part 2, The Ethnodynamics Series, 2011. Yahoo!/Added Value/MindShare

Figure 8.4 Importance of Ethnic Representation in Advertising

tity have become permeable, so much so that individuals can construct and live out multicultural personal identities made up of the culture(s) they are born into, marry into, socialize with, or with which they simply have a strong affinity." So brand respect is closely tied to the ability for brands to be relevant and authentic with these complex consumers, who are extremely influential. Brand cultural relevance and authenticity is important for African Americans and Asians, but as you can see in Figure 8.5, for Hispanics it matters even more.

As mentioned earlier, another reason to court Hispanic consumers is that they are open to your advertising messages. According to *The Cultural Connection: How Hispanic Identity Influences Millennials,* 57 percent of high-culturally connected millennials sign up via e-mail or text messaging to get alerts from their favorite brands on things like store sales. More important, Hispanic millennials are significantly more likely to share information about your brand via social media platforms. Figure 8.6 shows how 51 percent of High CCI Millennial Latinos shared information about a product or brand using a social media platform such as Facebook or Twitter vs. 15 percent of Hispanic non-millennials. By gaining Latinos as customers, you are gaining brand ambassadors and

%: Strongly agree/agree when it comes to ads

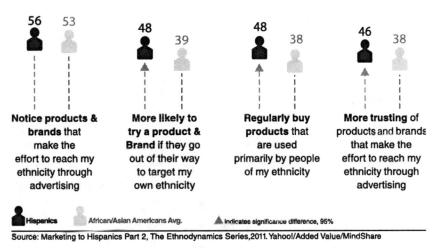

56 53	**48** 39	**48** 38	**46** 38
Notice products & brands that make the effort to reach my ethnicity through advertising	**More likely to try a product & Brand** if they go out of their way to target my own ethnicity	**Regularly buy products** that are used primarily by people of my ethnicity	**More trusting** of products and brands that make the effort to reach my ethnicity through advertising

Hispanics   African/Asian Americans Avg.   ▲ Indicates significance difference, 95%

Source: Marketing to Hispanics Part 2, The Ethnodynamics Series, 2011. Yahoo!/Added Value/MindShare

Figure 8.5 Importance of Cultural Relevance and Authenticity in Advertising

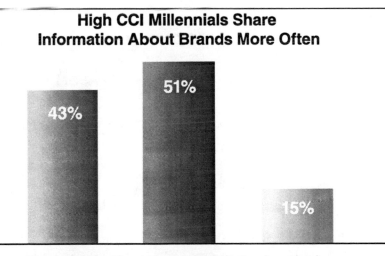

High CCI Millennials Share Information About Brands More Often

Shared information about any product or brand using any social media platform like Facebook, Twitter, etc

■ **Millennials**   ■ **High CCI Millennials**   ■ **Non-Millennials**

Source: 2012 Univision's Cultural Connection Study, conducted in collaboration with Burke Inc.

Figure 8.6

influencers, people who will spread your messages to their not-so-small circle of friends and family. Everyone knows this goes a long way in the close-knit Hispanic community.

Now, there is a reason why television commands such a large share of the Hispanic advertising pie: because it works. According to *Meet Hispanic Millennials, Your Culture Driven Consumer*, more than half of Hispanic millennials have gone online to learn more about the product after seeing a commercial on TV. This means you have an opportunity to engage Hispanics with deeper conversations online. Remember what Graciela Eleta told us earlier: focusing your messaging on culturally relevant brand attributes or benefits may help you connect better with your potential Hispanic consumers.

Finally, when it comes to the impact your advertising messages have with Hispanic consumers, research shows that language *does* play a role. Many studies support this fact, but let me just quote Nielsen's TV Brand Effect study. "Language influences advertising's ability to connect with the Hispanic audience on a number of levels, from likeability to recall," says Nielsen. According to them, the following key information can serve as guidelines for advertisers interested in reaching the Latino community:

1. Hispanics remember English-language commercials as well as the general population.
2. The same commercial shown in Spanish bumps up ad recall by as much as 30 percent.
3. Latinos like ads 51 percent more if viewed in Spanish rather than English.
4. Hiring Spanish-speaking talent to deliver the script resonates 30 percent better with Latinos."[6]

WHAT ABOUT CREATIVE?

When it comes to creative, there's the strategy part, which as we've already discussed is critical, and then there's the execution part. Best-in-class Hispanic creative should align with your brand's overall equity and character, address Hispanic trial barriers, use relevant Hispanic insights, demonstrate cultural affinity, and create emotional engagement. Easier said than done, no doubt. But the effectiveness of targeted ads is proved through the work that David Burgos and Ola Mobolade do everyday at Millward Brown. According to them, "targeted" advertising is more likely to work better than general market creative across the board, especially in terms of consumer engagement and believability—that is, in catching the attention of consumers. In fact, targeted ads also have a positive effect on message relevance and persuasion.

Of course, "targeted" ads are those that are developed for Hispanics specifically using Hispanic insights to achieve cultural relevance and "non-targeted" are those ads that were created for the population at large.

Before you embark on any creative effort, however, you should ask yourself how much do you know about *your* brand vis-à-vis the Hispanic consumer. Here are some questions you need to consider before getting started.

1. How developed is the category in general, and your brand in particular, among Hispanics?
2. Are Hispanic consumer practices and habits different?
3. How recognized is your brand among Hispanics?
4. Does your brand enjoy heritage among Hispanics?
5. Will your brand be the first in the category to advertise to Hispanics?

Results Confirm that Cultural Relevance Counts

Source: Millward Brown

Figure 8.7 Cultural Relevance Increases Ad Effectiveness

As we discussed earlier, in our section on total market strategy, it all starts with the creative brief, where you must include Hispanic data in the discovery and research phase and Hispanic insights in strategic development so that you can *recognize similarities and acknowledge differences*. Once you have done that, it's all about execution. Here, you have several options to pick from that vary in terms of cost and lead times. Figure 8.8 shows you the different creative options available today. On the top of the pyramid, adapting or translating English-language or global creative is still the cheapest and the most common creative execution in the Hispanic market. Unfortunately, it is also the least effective. The most effective but most expensive creative execution is total-market creative which allows you to deliver culturally relevant, in-culture, and in-language messages for each of your total-market audiences.

Throughout the year there are conferences where you can go and see best-in-class Hispanic creative and learn how other marketers are handling their Hispanic efforts. In the resource guide at the end of the book, you can find a list of conferences I recommend.

Creative awards are one way the advertising industry recognizes best-in-class work. Over the past five years we have seen a rise in recognition of Hispanic creative even in the most prestigious advertising awards shows, like the Cannes Lions International Festival of Creativity, where last year U.S. Hispanic creative shops won six golden Lions. From 1998 until 2010, *Advertising Age* ran the Hispanic Creative Awards, which recognized excellence in the Hispanic advertising world and were part of the annual AHAA Conference. Here's a link to the last Hispanic Creative Advertising Awards given out by *Advertising Age*: http://adage. com/article/special-report-hispanic-creative-advertising-awards-2010/ hispanic-creative-advertising-awards-2010/146370/.

In February 2012, AHAA announced plans for a new Hispanic Creative Advertising Award, this time in partnership with Circulo Creativo, a nonprofit organization founded in 1999 with the sole objective of promoting creative excellence and communication among creative professionals who work in the United States. "In partnership with Círculo Creativo, we have created an award uniquely designed for the U.S. Hispanic indus-

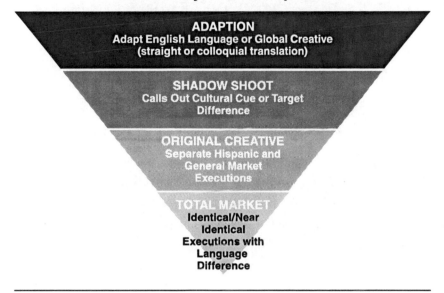

What Are My Creative Options?

ADAPTION
Adapt English Language or Global Creative
(straight or colloquial translation)

SHADOW SHOOT
Calls Out Cultural Cue or Target
Difference

ORIGINAL CREATIVE
Separate Hispanic and
General Market
Executions

TOTAL MARKET
Identical/Near
Identical
Executions with
Language
Difference

Figure 8.8

try one that is organized, judged, and awarded by top Hispanic advertising creatives," said Roberto Orci, chair of AHAA and CEO of Acento, a Hispanic advertising agency in the U.S. "The U.S.H. Idea Awards will become the standard to showcase the best work from our industry and elevate it to compete on an international level." In 2012, more than three hundred entries for the Idea Awards were received from creative talent in the U.S. Hispanic market and twenty-two winners were selected, representing the best of the field following a rigorous review, according to a press release posted on their website. The U.S.H. Idea Awards were presented at a gala marking the end of the AHAA 2012 Annual Conference at the Arsht Center in Miami on May 4, 2012. The top five creative executions of 2012, selected as "Best in Show" were:

- "Volvo in Every Car," Volvo, La Comunidad
- "Forgot your Password?," Alzheimer's Association, Grupo Gallegos

- "Keep it Legendary," Heineken, The Vidal Partnership
- "El Spooky Show," MTV3 / Comedy Central, La Comunidad
- "Maricopa," Border Action Network, Bravo Group/Y&R

To see all of the 2012 U.S.H. Idea Award winners, or learn more about these awards, please go to: http://www.ushideaawards.com/

THE RISE OF CONTENT MARKETING

Advertising is, in essence, brand storytelling. Whether that story lasts thirty seconds (as in a traditional TV spot) or thirty minutes (as in an infomercial), the reality is that brands are constantly telling stories and looking for the right media in which to place their stories. Media companies, of course, are the ultimate storytellers and for the past fifty years have controlled the content we consume mainly because of the extremely high cost of producing media, but also because the platforms on which their stories were distributed were limited by devices on which one could receive their signals—basically TV, through broadcast or cable signals.

However, over the past five to ten years, technological advances have allowed for brands to also have the ability to "create and distribute content" via Internet platforms which can provide their potential or existing customers with highly targeted information, creating a whole new kind of advertising and marketing effort. Traditionally known as custom publishing, these kinds of specialized marketing efforts are mainly produced either by highly specialized agencies (servicing clients in the automotive, health care, financial industries, and the like, which require communicating lots of detailed information to their customers) or by media companies who create dedicated teams to help brands craft and distribute customized media (magazines, white papers, informational kits, and videos) that help deliver a brand's message to a select group of consumers.

The cost of these programs is usually quite high, but for certain industries, the ROI and customer loyalty are worth it. A few examples of custom publications are the airline magazines you find in your seat pocket every time you fly or the monthly magazine you get from your health insurance company or from your 401K provider. Direct marketing is not new to the advertising industry, it's been around forever. However, the creation of brand-specific content marketing programs or custom media has been on an huge upward swing since it started getting cheaper to produce and easier to disseminate. According to a 2011 study published by the Custom Content Council, today content marketing is a $40 billion industry.

Technology that facilitates low-cost, high-quality content creation coupled with the ubiquity of the Internet and the rise of social media platforms have given brands the ability to create their own "content" like never before. But the ability to create content doesn't necessarily mean that your customers will engage with it. If it is not good content and/or on-brand, chances are you are alienating your customer base while damaging your brand image. So tread very carefully. Storytelling is a lot harder than you think, and where brands often fail is truly understanding what their "brand story" is and how to tell it in an authentic way. There's art and science to creating content that helps brands sell more and that's why you need the help of experts if you want to go that route. The Custom Content Council and the Direct Marketing Association are also excellent resources for you to get all the information you need to move forward with these kinds of initiatives.

The top reason to create custom content is to "educate consumers," with 49 percent of companies citing this reason in the 2011 Spending Study published by Contentwise and the Custom Content Council. Customer retention was named as the second leading primary reason, in both the business-to-business space and the business-to-consumer space. In fact, John Obrecht, the editor of *BtoB* magazine wrote an opinion piece in October 2012, in which he declared that "content is king" and that content marketing was "rapidly gaining critical mass."[7] There are several great examples of branded content in the Hispanic marketing space, like *Comida Kraft,* which is the largest customized-content program in the Hispanic market. This platform includes a custom published magazine, a dedicated Spanish-language website with videos and experts answering customer questions, customizable e-mail programs, as well as easy to use apps with recipes and shopping lists for busy moms. Unilever has a similar program called *Vive Mejor* and General Mills created one under the name of *Que Rica Vida*, all of which have had success in reaching Hispanic moms who are looking for more sources of information on food and healthy tips for their families. The advantage you have with these kinds of programs is that you can surround your target consumer and achieve scale. By bundling several brands together, custom programs like these are more cost-efficient—on a brand-by-brand basis—while allowing each to tell its own story. At the same time, it provides the consumer with a great product that is entertaining and easy to use while building customer loyalty. This is an area where I do see a lot of potential for growth in the next five years. There are some specialized companies, such as Meredith Hispanic Ventures, and many Hispanic agencies with the necessary expertise in the content-marketing area that can help you out. Again, the beauty of it is that it is a measurable marketing investment that more often than not results in positive ROI and brand loyalty.

A FINAL THOUGHT

Now let's talk for a moment about acculturation and assimilation, terms that have been so overused and misused that I and others in this space no longer think they are useful. As Burgos and Mobolade say in their book, *Marketing to the New Majority*, "Segmenting ethnic consumers by acculturation has been problematic because it based on the zero-sum assumption that all immigrants are on the steady path to becoming fully American in their lifestyle, behavior, and preferences, thereby becoming less ethnic with time . . . . Given the history of African American targeted marketing, it's surprising that the old Hispanic assimilation model went unchallenged for as long as it did. After all, African Americans have been in this country for a number of generations, yet race-based distinctions still exist. It stands to reason that the same thing will happen with the Hispanic population."[8] Amen. I would only add that acculturation and assimilation cannot be truly measured and if they can't be measured, then they shouldn't be used to categorize your potential consumers. It is a losing proposition and I urge you to stay away from them both. There are other measurable and actionable ways to segment Latinos, so I encourage you to use them instead.

Of course, metrics are hugely important, and for far too long they have been put aside in ethnic marketing efforts mainly because the syndicated tools used by many companies to measure marketing campaigns have been very slow to adopt the proper panels and models to truly reflect the diversity of the American consumer market in general and effectively track Hispanic marketing in particular. But thankfully, things are changing, which is why in the next chapter I will give you five simple rules to follow in order to ensure that you are setting yourself up for success in this marketplace.

Key Takeaways:

- Marketers and agencies are grappling with important issues that are unique to ethnic markets, such as how to properly deliver culturally relevant brand messages to Hispanic consumers and how to accurately track results with systems that do not properly track ethnic populations.
- Total market strategy is a process used by leading marketers and media planners who recognize the need to reach *all potential consumers* who fall within a brand's target market, regardless of race, ethnicity, or language preference.
- Latinos like ads 51 percent more if viewed in Spanish rather than English. The same commercial shown in Spanish bumps up ad recall by as much as 30 percent.
- Best-in-class Hispanic creative should align with your brand's overall equity and character, address Hispanic trial barriers, use relevant Hispanic insights, demonstrate cultural affinity, and create emotional engagement.
- Latinos are looking for brands to treat them with respect and that means being culturally relevant and authentic in their advertising messaging.

- Custom content production for Hispanics is on the rise, but make sure you work with experts who will know how to tell your brand story properly.

NOTES

1. The Nielsen Company, National People Meter (NPM), 12/27/10–12/25/11, Monday to Saturday 8–11 P.M./Sunday 7–11 P.M., Live + SD, A18-49(000).

2. Kondolojy, Amanda, "Telemundo Media's 2012 Olympic Broadcast More than Doubled 2008 Beijing Olympics among Total Viewers," *TVbytheNumbers*, August 13, 2012. www.tvbythenumbers.zap2it.com.

3. Llopis, Glenn "America's Corporations Can No Longer Ignore Hispanic Marketing Like Mitt Romney Did," *Forbes,* Nov. 11, 2012. www.forbes.com/sites/glennllopis/2012/11/12/americas-corporations-can-no-longer-ignore-hispanic-marketing-like-mitt-romney-did.

4. Univision Communications, Inc. https://us.reg.meeting-stream.com/univisionmanagementco_060712.

5. Marketing to Hispanics, Part 2 of the Ethnodynamics series, Mindshare Added Value and Yahoo! http://advertising.yahoo.com/article/marketing-to-hispanics-20120329.html.

6. Nielsen TV Brand Effect, *The State of the Hispanic Consumer: The Hispanic Market Imperative*, Copyright © 2012 The Nielsen Company.

7. "Content Ascends to Marketing Throne," *BtoB* magazine, October 8, 2012.

8. Burgos, David and Ola Mobolade, *Marketing to the New Majority, Strategies for a Diverse World*, Copyright © 2011 Millward Brown.

9

YOUR ROADMAP TO SUCCESS

L ike I said in Chapter 1, Hispanic culture becomes more mainstream every day. All you have to do is walk outside to witness how the country embraces Latino culture. Jennifer Lopez has become a household name, helping brands sell everything from cars to fashion and beauty. Around the corner from where you live or work, you can enjoy my favorite new lunch dish, a Chipotle burrito bowl. In fact, the long lines at Chipotle, the hottest fast-food chain in the country, are a testament that you can have tasty and healthful meals that just happen to also be Mexican. And at every good bar or restaurant worth its salt, you can order a killer Mojito or classic Margarita. All of these things have become part of the fabric of America.

My experience—and the experience of millions of Hispanics in this country—is that for us, culture is additive, not subtractive. I can be 100 percent American *and* 100 percent Latino at the same time. I don't have to give up any part of my culture in order to become more American. I am bilingual and bicultural, and that duality is part of my reality every day. It gives me more choices, and hopefully I am smarter for it. Ultimately I control what I consume and in what language I choose to consume it. Smart companies are already using unique Hispanic insights like this in their marketing campaigns and are quite successful. Take, for example, the current L'Oreal campaign for True Match foundation, the most popular foundation brand with over 200 million units sold since it launched in 2004. What made it the market leader was the fact that, for the first time, L'Oreal had created the most ethnically diverse range of shades in the market. But by 2011 they started losing ground to their competition, according to Erica Bowen, the Vice President of L'Oreal, who spoke to a roomful of marketers last fall during the ANA Multicultural Marketing & Diversity Conference held in Miami Beach. To reverse their declines, they conducted research that led to the development of eight new shades of foundation for African American women and six new shades for Latinas. Then they put some marketing muscle behind a 360-degree path-to-purchase plan to keep Hispanics and African American women at the heart of their "true match" campaign, with in-culture and in-language creative that resonates both with ethnic consumers and non-ethnic consumers. The TV commercial featuring Beyoncé starts off with this line: "There's a story behind my skin. It's a mosaic of all the faces before it," celebrating the singer's mixed-race heritage of African American, Native American, and French that makes her so drop-dead gorgeous. The Hispanic creative is equally powerful using Jennifer Lopez as their spokesperson; the copy simply reads: "The Story Behind My Skin: The 100% Puerto Rican," with creative executions running both in Spanish- and English-language media.

The campaign extends from print to TV, online, and mobile (where Hispanic and African American women over-index) with similar simple messages but packs a punch because it is empowering to Latina women who have been taught that beauty means "making the most of what we have." In this case JLo is selling foundation, something Latina women think they don't really need, given their beautiful brown skin tones. Therefore, it uses the Hispanic insight of being proud of one's heritage and addresses the purchase barrier right upfront. The message is clear and simple, yet demonstrates cultural affinity. Most important, it creates emotional engagement by featuring the talented Ms. Lopez, to whom all Latina women can relate, as she has become the Liz Taylor of our times. According to Erica Bowen, the campaign has been a huge success, lifting company sales by 15 percent since the campaign started in early 2011. Ms. Bowen also acknowledged that, in fact, sales in the African American and the Hispanic markets were outperforming the growth seen in the general market. L'Oreal is just one of many smart companies that are leading with ethnic insights and seeing growth across the board, such as Walmart, Kellogg, and McDonald's, among others. If you think multicultural marketing is something for the future, I've got news for you: the future is here.

FIVE RULES FOR THE ROAD

1. Don't ignore the Hispanic opportunity. Embrace it!

If you think you can bury your head in the sand and ignore Hispanics, think again. It's wishful thinking to simply hope that somehow your mass-market strategy will reach your potential Hispanic consumers. As you have already seen in previous chapters, this is not happening, so wake up and smell the McCafé. As the so-called general market becomes more and more fragmented, understanding how to sell your products and services to the emerging minorities (Black, Hispanic, or Asian) has become a business imperative. Your new reality is this: minorities represent one-third of all consumers in America. Now ask yourself, are 30 percent of your sales coming from these markets? If your answer is no, in order to thrive, and possibly even just to survive, you must embrace this opportunity for growth. Make no mistake— the future of your business will depend on your ability to penetrate an increasingly fragmented, multicultural marketplace. Remember that by 2040, minorities will make up half of the total population, 25 percent of which will be Latino. So, the first thing you need to do is embrace your Hispanic opportunity and set yourself up to successfully sell them your products. In order to do that, however, you must start thinking differently about your business.

Let's say you are a magazine publisher looking to expand your most successful brands into the Hispanic market. The knee-jerk reaction might be to simply translate your magazines into Spanish and put them on the newsstands. With this approach, you will most probably sell some magazines in Spanish, but for you to really succeed, you'll need to better understand who your audience is and what stories resonate with them. Don't make the assumption that they will read anything you deem important as long as it is in Spanish, as this may be completely wrong. Let me illustrate this point further with an example. Let's assume you have a celebrity magazine. Everyone likes celebrity gossip, right? Sure. But not all celebrities have crossover appeal. Of course there are Hollywood celebrities who have worldwide appeal, but not all TV stars, sports stars, or even royalty who appeal to you also appeal to Latinos. Thanks in large part to the success of Spanish-language media in this country, the Latino community has, in fact, created a parallel universe in the world of entertainment. So, how do you define who is a celebrity for Latinos? It depends on who your target audience is. If your target readers are Latin women thirty-five to fifty-five who watch Spanish-language TV, you'd better know what is important to them: telenovelas. Can you name one telenovela star? I'll give you a hint. He danced his way into many American households in 2012 with his appearance on *Dancing With the Stars*. That's right, one of the most famous telenovela stars of Spanish-language TV is today a rising star in Hollywood. I'm talking about William Levy, of course.

The same is true for sports stars. Men in the United States are mainly obsessed with football, basketball, hockey, NASCAR, and baseball. But if you are not covering soccer, wrestling, and boxing, your magazine probably won't have much appeal to a Hispanic male reader.

Okay. Now, let's assume that you do have a staff who can help you identify the right celebrities to cover in these new Hispanic magazines. How do you treat your celebrities in print? In Latin America and Spain, celebrity magazines rarely talk badly about their celebrities. Sure, they love their gossip, cover celebrity tragedies and indiscretions, but Latin celebrities are treated like royalty—you never say anything bad about them. Mean-spirited, tabloid-style articles will not go over well with Hispanic readers. If you don't know who your target audience is, you will inevitably fail to reach them by simply translating your product into Spanish. Never make assumptions about what Hispanics (or any other minority group, for that matter) know or like about your product. The best thing you can do before embarking on any marketing strategy for Hispanics is to spend some time and money to find out what your target market thinks about your product, which takes me to your second rule for the road: Do your own research.

2. Do research, but know whom to include and what questions to ask.

Understanding the differences between your current consumer and your new Hispanic consumer can make or break your project. You would *not* believe how many companies have launched "Hispanic initiatives" into the marketplace without doing any market research at all. Also, don't assume that just because your product is well known in the mainstream market, it is known or recognized in the Hispanic market. Quite the contrary, it is a safer bet to treat any new Hispanic effort like a new product launch, with all that that entails. Would you launch a product in Canada without doing research? I hope not. You must first find out what people know or think about your product. How do they feel about the product category in general? Are there cultural or linguistic nuances that you need to be aware of? The classic example here is the Chevy Nova. Back in the seventies when Chevrolet was launching this car in Latin America, they could not figure out why sales were so terrible until someone told them that the words *no va* in Spanish means "it doesn't work"!

I know what you're thinking. Market research is expensive, it takes time, and your boss is pushing for you to just get it done. Well, unless you want egg on your face, you'd better push back and do some research.

Speaking at the ANA Multicultural Marketing & Diversity Conference last fall, the president of Kellogg for North America, Brad Davidson, shared with the audience some lessons they learned from their own Hispanic marketing efforts. According to Davidson, Kellogg had been supporting nine different brands between 2005 and 2009. But their Hispanic marketing efforts were "disparate" and there were no KPIs to measure against. By the time he took over, they were only putting 1 percent of their advertising spend behind one brand and, more important, by not properly supporting their Hispanic marketing efforts, Kellogg had lost three percentage points to their competition. In any business, losing three share points is a big deal. In the cereal business, it is huge.

"We had no market data on Hispanics," said Davidson, who realized the first thing he needed to do was to invest in research that allowed his teams to recognize the similarities Latina moms have to other moms, but more important, helped them understand the differences, too. As a result, they figured out that the strategy they had taken from their mass-marketing campaign was not resonating with Hispanic moms. So with unique insights from the new research, they were able to develop a new strategy that was more culturally relevant and has driven their recent success with Hispanic moms. "This is about total market, and it's about path to purchase. Whether it is an Anglo mom or Hispanic mom, it's about getting on their list, in the cart, and in their heart," he added. For Kellogg, the refocus on how to win with Hispanics has been driving growth across the board. According to Davidson, the change in marketing strategy for the Eggo brand alone lifted its sales by ten share points in 2012.

A WORD OF CAUTION ABOUT RESEARCH

If you are conducting national research, make sure you pick neutral markets that mirror the Hispanic marketplace, such as Chicago, where you get a good mix of Mexicans, Central and South Americans, and Latinos from the Caribbean. If you are doing research on Mexicans, don't do research in Miami or, for that matter, in East Los Angeles, because you will get a distorted picture. If your business has stores only in Texas, keep in mind that a Mexican living in San Antonio may be completely different from a Mexican living in El Paso or Houston or McAllen. In many ways, Hispanic consumers are the same as any other consumers, but understanding the little things that can turn them on or off will make the difference between success and failure when you launch your product in the Hispanic market.

The accuracy of any quantitative research will also depend on the quality of the sample you use. As a rule of thumb, the sample should match the composition of the Hispanic population across demographics. Besides the usual demographic indicators of age and gender, marketers should make sure the sample represents accurate language usage. Even though today the majority of Hispanics are bilingual, researchers recommend that every sample have an adequate representation of Spanish-dominant Hispanics, who are usually harder to find. While this segment can be found online, you must be careful, because the Hispanic online population tends to skew toward English-dominants and therefore may not be representative of the total Hispanic market. That is why it is common for a research supplier to add a quota of phone interviews to ensure that the sample is representative. Figure 9.1 shows you how different the online populations are for both the general market and the Latino market.

In the past, Hispanic online panels have not been very good. But today there are several online panels that claim to have solved this issue by making specific recruitment and maintenance efforts with their Hispanic samples. One more word on mobile: although Hispanics over-index in mobile, it has limited usage for survey research, so don't even go there.

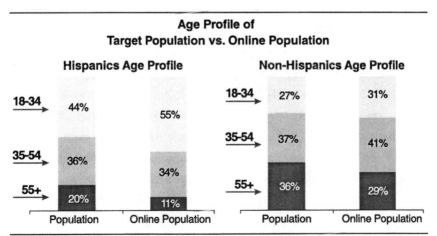

**Age Profile of
Target Population vs. Online Population**

Hispanics Age Profile

18-34 → 44%

55%

35-54 → 36%

34%

55+ → 20%

11%

Population | Online Population

Non-Hispanics Age Profile

18-34 → 27%

31%

35-54 → 37%

41%

55+ → 36%

29%

Population | Online Population

Source: Simmons NCS/NHCS Fall 2011, Base: Online users in the last thirty days

Figure 9.1

Also, keep in mind that culture matters, so make sure you (or your research vendor) do not apply a general-market view to your research. Cultural cues, family values, holiday celebrations, and attitudes toward a host of things—from food to fashion and entertainment—are different for Latinos, regardless of whether they are U.S.-born or foreign born. Make sure your research vendor knows this and applies it properly to your research. Finally, when conducting research, make sure that the vendor you work with has had experience working with Hispanics in the U.S., not in Latin America. If they don't, you could end up paying for their mistakes, and your research will most likely suffer. In the resource guide, I list a number of vendors who can help you conduct whatever research you need.

3. Make a commitment to Hispanic marketing.

One of the reasons I have worked on so many Hispanic projects is that often the company behind the start-up did not make a real commitment to the project. Without the commitment in terms of time and money, you will always fail. If you have taken the time to understand your target market and have done your research, the worst thing you can do is "test the waters" with a halfhearted effort. I'm all for testing, but leave your market wanting more, not disgusted with their experience when trying you out for the first time. You only have one chance to make a good impression, and Latinos are savvy consumers.

Once you've made a commitment, you must be careful not to hold the Hispanic market to a higher standard of business success. If it takes five years for a company to break even with the launch of a new product in the general market, why do these same executives think they can launch a new product in the Hispanic market and break even, or even make money, in just one year? This expectation of a higher return on investment in this market truly dumbfounds me, but I encounter it all the time. You must respect this market as much as you respect any other consumer market; your commitment to the Hispanic market must go beyond what your company is going to get out of the Hispanic market and include efforts to give back to the community. For example, you can support the Hispanic Scholarship Fund or your local soccer league. Latinos are weary of companies that are looking to make a quick buck on them. If you want their support and loyalty, you must support the Latino community in other ways that are meaningful to them. If you give back to the community, they will take note, and you will see that they will always give back to you, too.

Unfortunately, shortsighted executives—who tend to worry more about the price of their stock from quarter to quarter—dominate the world of business. It takes a strong, visionary leader to realize that the only way to deliver the long-term growth that Wall Street has become accustomed to is by expanding into new markets and giving them time to fully develop. Clearly, the emerging minorities in the United States are becoming a bigger and more important piece of the nation's economy. Among these minorities, Hispanics already represent the largest segment and are growing faster than any other minority in the United States. The continuous flow of legal immigration coupled with our high birth rates means that the Latino population grows by approximately 1.5 million persons *each year*. These are big numbers and they demand real commitments.

Walmart, the largest retailer in the country, made headlines in 2011 when it announced that it would decentralize its multicultural marketing group and turn everyone in the marketing department into a multicultural marketer. It was a bold and innovative move that really helped start the conversation about the total-market approach, and one that seems to be paying off, according to Tony Rogers, the senior vice president for brand marketing and advertising at Walmart. Keep in mind that Walmart has been marketing to Latinos for almost twenty years, but their efforts had been isolated and not always in sync with the broader enterprise. A year after their experiment in multicultural marketing, Rogers said, "I think this total-market approach has an opportunity to make our marketers better, helping our teams really understand who our customer is, what the key entry barriers are, and what's the most compelling way to talk to that customer. In today's marketplace, you can't do just a good old-fashioned blocking and tackling from a marketing perspective without fully engaging yourself with the multicultural customer."

Walmart's new commitment to multicultural marketing is no doubt pushed by the fact that, according to their analysis, 100 percent of their growth in sales over the next five years will come from the multicultural marketplace in the United States, so they are doubling down on this new approach and have committed to grow their spending against multicultural consumers "by at least 100%."[1]

4. Don't forget to get your message out.

If you have spent time and money understanding your Hispanic consumer, and you have created a new product or tweaked your old product to make sure it works for the Hispanic market, why would you not let people know that? If you don't have an advertising budget, and you're not planning any special promotions or public relations campaigns, how on earth do you expect to sell your product? Any product launch in the Hispanic market must be treated as a new product launch, even with recognizable brands. Brand arrogance will get you nowhere.

During his session at the ANA Multicultural Marketing & Diversity Conference, "Walmart's Multicultural Journey: One Year Later," Rogers also shared four key learnings:

1. Make multicultural part of everything you do, rather than projects in silos.
2. Train people.
3. Set goals and keep score.
4. Build partnerships and leverage people outside your company.

If your Hispanic marketing budgets are limited, then you must think of other ways to get the word out. I recommend you either hire a public relations specialist with experience in the Hispanic market, or make sure the Hispanic advertising agency you are working with provides that service. If your company has a public relations department, chances are it doesn't really know what to do in this market. Again, simply translating a press release won't do. You need Hispanic press lists, contacts in Hispanic media, and the know-how to pitch your story for this market. Find out what's important to this market about your product. A well-thought-out public-relations campaign is probably the cheapest way to get your message out. Give yourself time to create some brand awareness in the community and, most important, keep the buzz going. Of course if you have an advertising budget, proper media planning will be critical to your success. This is an area where holding companies have really made incredible inroads, with the top media buying agencies developing dedicated teams to help marketers optimize their advertising dollars. The leaders in this space are Tapestry Partners and MV42, both part of the Starcom Media Group, which is owned by Publicis. They are followed by MEC Bravo, owned by WPP, and OMD Latino, owned by Omnicom.

In today's growing and complex Hispanic media market, in-depth knowledge of network programming schedules and program demographics is required. You'd be surprised how much more you can get out of your advertising dollars if you spend them in the right places. If you've got a great product and a great message, what good does it do if it doesn't reach your audience?

5. Measure what matters.

I asked my good friend Roberto Ruiz to share with us his thoughts on the need for proper tools to measure the effectiveness of your marketing campaigns to Hispanics. He's on the leading edge of this subject through his work with the largest advertisers and marketing vendors in the United States. Here's what he has to say about measuring what matters.

THE RISE OF MARKETING ACCOUNTABILITY

By Roberto Ruiz, SVP Strategy & Insights,
Univision Communications Inc.

> Marketers have come a long way since John Wanamaker's famous claim that he knew half of his ad investment was a waste—he just did not know which half. The 2008 recession served as a booster to a trend already

in motion: the demand for increased corporate accountability. Two factors have played a pivotal role in the importance of marketing accountability. First, the demand for higher overall corporate accountability, and second, the increased importance of digital marketing, specifically search engine optimization, where the impact of marketing activity can very effectively be measured. In 2002, Congress enacted the Sarbanes-Oxley Act as a result of the corporate malfeasance of large corporations such as Enron, Tyco, and Adelphia. While the main culprits of these debacles were on the finance side, the result was a government-imposed need for corporate accountability that ended up affecting all areas of business, including marketing. Faced with increased scrutiny, chief marketing officers demanded more and better tools to measure the impact of their marketing investments. At the same time, the rise of Google at the vanguard of digital marketing also pushed marketers to start comparing the efficacy of their different marketing activities. If Google could prove the power of search to drive revenue, why should other mediums escape measurement?

According to a survey published by the Association of National Advertisers (ANA) in 2009, marketers showed a significant year-over-year increase in their efforts to measure the impact of marketing campaigns using cross-functional teams, which included finance and analytics. Bob Liodice, president of the ANA said, "With marketers, CFOs, and CEOs paying more attention to each dollar spent, marketing accountability processes have become strategic imperatives." As a result, marketing accountability is now a key element of most marketers' activities. And, of course, Hispanic efforts have not escaped this trend. Moreover, given that Hispanic marketing activities are, for many brands, frequently new initiatives, they face increased scrutiny compared to other campaigns or programs that brands have done for several years.

BRAND MEASURES

One way marketers look at the impact on a specific target of their activities is by tracking changes in measures related to brand health. These include unaided and aided brand awareness, recall, consideration, and others. These are frequently the easiest to measure, given that most tools rely on interviews either via phone, online, or in some rare instances, in person. Successful marketers always include a sample of Hispanics in their regularly scheduled brand-tracking efforts, as opposed to doing one-time-only efforts or separate measurements. All mainstream vendors such as Millward Brown, Polk, GFK, and others now have Hispanic expertise and will produce reliable measures. Once these measures are in hand, marketers can compare their performance in the Hispanic segment vs. the non-Hispanic segment and have an indication of how the brand is performing, as well as uncover potential opportunities.

An alternative to brand metrics—and one that is frequently used as a first approach to understand the brand situation in terms of penetration with Hispanic consumers—is to use syndicated research tools such as Simmons or MRI. Both are panel-based measurements and have robust Hispanic consumer samples. Using Simmons, for example, brands can understand measures such as the category development index (CDI) and the brand development Index (BDI) and map where the brand stands vs. its competitors. Over time these tools can provide high-level perspective on how the brand is progressing. However, these tools are only updated quarterly and brands would need a year to read any meaningful change.

CREATIVE EFFECTIVENESS

I once heard a Nielsen executive say that almost 70 percent of advertising success hinged on the quality of creative. Maybe that is an exaggeration, but, as Chiqui mentioned earlier, creative quality is a critical factor in campaign success. Many marketers use copy testing as an initial vetting tool before airing a campaign. This should apply to Hispanic efforts as well. Proper sampling is critical here. Once creative is on air, Nielsen IAG provides a robust tool to measure critical brand measures linked to advertising campaigns. The IAG panel includes a Hispanic sample that is representative of language breaks. Marketers can understand the impact of both ads and in-program integrations, as long as the ads run on prime time in the main networks (Univision and Telemundo). IAG results prove the positive impact of Spanish-language advertising among Hispanics, and specifically among bilingual Hispanics.

Figure 9.2 shows a comparison of ads aired during 2011, and compares the brand and message recall, as well as ad likability among

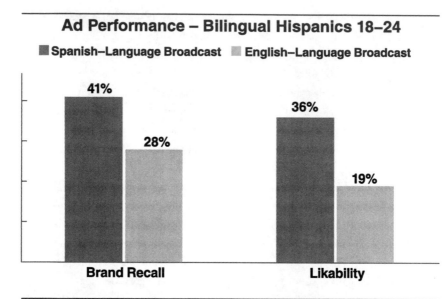

Ad Performance – Bilingual Hispanics 18–24

■ Spanish–Language Broadcast ■ English–Language Broadcast

41%

28%

36%

19%

Brand Recall　　　　　**Likability**

Source: Nielsen TV Brand Effect (IAG) 7.1.11 to 12.31.11. Limited to prime time non-sports programming.
Limited to same brands on Spanish-language broadcast and English-language broadcast.

Figure 9.2

bilingual Hispanics watching ads for the same brand in English and in Spanish. Note that all measures—and especially likability—are significantly higher for ads in Spanish, even though these consumers are bilingual. IAG attributes the difference to a few factors, including the emotional connection to the Spanish language, less clutter in Spanish-language networks, and the fact that usually ads in Spanish have been created using specific Hispanic insights based on research, which can easily contribute to higher effectiveness.

SALES METRICS—OPPORTUNITIES AND CHALLENGES

While brand measures are important, they always come second to the ring of the cash register. Sales are the ultimate objective of a campaign and as such, success and permanence of Hispanic efforts hinge on being able to prove the campaign is resulting in incremental sales. For some categories this is relatively easy. Wireless providers, for example, track new additions by surname and have a relatively accurate picture of how many new Hispanic consumers they have signed. Firms such as Geoscape or Ethnic Technologies help marketers analyze customer databases and help identify which among them are Hispanics, even eliminating the Filipinos, who given similar names and sometimes surnames, can be confused with Hispanics. In general, any product that requires consumers to register their names offers a better opportunity to track sales to Hispanic consumers.

For consumer packaged goods, Nielsen and IRI have built proprietary tools that provide an estimate of sales to Hispanics. IRI's tool, Ethnic Workbench, uses demographic information around the store location to assign scanner data to Hispanic sales. This is a blunt instrument but definitely better than nothing. The challenge is that not all Hispanics shop near where they live, and the IRI and Nielsen databases do not account for outlets with less than $2 million in sales. Nielsen's tool Nielsen Target Track II is more sophisticated, designed and tailored to every brand they measure, which adds Hispanic item velocity to the algorithm. In other words, if a store is selling a fair amount of a Hispanic product (say Harina Pan, a white corn flour mix purchased by Venezuelans and Colombians), the system will recognize that Hispanic consumers are shopping at the store and will assign a percentage of the sale of other items in the store to the Hispanic segment. The good news in CPG is that vendors continue to develop new tools, and the measurement is getting better.

Categories such as consumer electronics or retail in general are the hardest in which to accurately measure sales to Hispanic consumers. Walmart and JCPenney, for example, rely on a cohort of stores deemed Hispanic and track sales changes at these stores as a proxy for the success of their Hispanic efforts. The same technique is applied by many restaurant chains such as McDonald's, which also has a cohort of Hispanic stores. In the overall U.S. market, retailers and manufacturers use NPD, a New York-based company that has a panel of consumers who report purchases. Except for quick-service restaurants, where NPD recently added a Hispanic sample, in these other categories the panel does not accurately represent the Hispanic market. The panel is polled online, and it skews to English-speaking Hispanics.

Once brands have determined a methodology for tracking sales, there are a number of measures that can be looked at to both establish marketing objectives and track progress. Figure 9.3 lists a number of options for marketers to consider.

TEST MARKETS—DO'S AND DON'TS

In the context of determining the impact of marketing to the Hispanic consumers, many marketers choose to test before rolling out national initiatives, which is smart. But there are a number of considerations in setting test and control markets.

1. Demographics

The first step in selecting test and control markets is to find matching demographics. The main variables to consider are population, country of origin, and income. Markets such as Miami, with an average income significantly above the national average and a Hispanic population that, while changing, is still mostly of Cuban origin, should not be used as a test market. Depending on the brand, cities in Texas or California can easily be paired.

2. Brand and Category Development and Distribution

Marketers should look at category development to make sure mar-

---

Success Metrics to Consider

Hispanic Sales as % of Total

Hispanic Market Share Gap vs. GM

% of Category Growth driven by USH

Regional Market Shares

% of Concurrent Launches

HH Penetration and Purchase Frequency vs. GM

Quantify Upside and Impact of Inactivity

Hispanic BDI & CDI

Awareness/ Trial/Loyalty vs. GM

Brand Average Value

Source: Simmons NCS/NHCS Fall 2011, Base: Online users in the last thirty days

Figure 9.3

kets to be compared have similar CDI. If the brand is already present, BDI should also be considered. For CPG and retail brands, distribution in high-density Hispanic areas are also important factors. It is critical that the brand has adequate levels of distribution in order for the media to have maximum impact on sales.

3. Media Planning and Purchase Cycle

Local media weights and investments—and the relationship of the local media plan to a potential national plan—are critical to make sure that the test is successful. Media agencies and media companies can collaborate with marketers in creating a national theoretical plan linked to the local test. Media cost is also a factor to be considered carefully in test situations. While Los Angeles is a great test market, cost and media availability can be factors playing against it. Another key factor for successful testing is matching the media plan to the purchase cycle of the product or service. This is especially critical for brands with longer purchase cycles, where the expectations of sales lift must be aligned with the number of weeks of media and its impact. If a soap brand has a purchase cycle of, say, ten weeks, one cannot expect that a six-week media plan will have a huge impact.

4. Measurement

Before embarking on a test, the brand team must agree on metrics and how results will be measured. It is critical to determine expectations based on other brands of the same relative size and distribution. One option for consumer packaged-goods brands is a matched panel test. Both IRI and Nielsen offer these tools, and they have processes designed to find matching stores (similar area, income composition, pricing strategy, etc.) in test and control markets, and evaluate lift. The result can then be compared to norms for equivalent brands.

PUTTING IT ALL TOGETHER

Over the last five years, sophisticated marketers in multiple categories have adopted Marketing-Mix Modeling (MMM) as one of the key tools to understand the impact of their marketing efforts. In general, MMM models look to isolate marketing activities and link these to incremental sales. The process is done via complex multivariable statistical regression. Nielsen, IRI, the Hudson Group, and others are players in this space. The challenge in determining the Hispanic ROI results from our previous discussion on measuring Hispanic sales. By definition, when we try to measure sales to Hispanics by using a cohort of stores defined by a demographic composition of the store—or even if we employ some sort of algorithm—we will be missing a certain portion of the sale, as all Hispanics do not shop in the Hispanic cohort. Even if we did a linear progression, where we would assign a percentage of sales based on the percentage Hispanic population around the trade area, we would still be missing a portion of sales. For this reason, Hispanic sales lift is generally half of total-market lift. Depending on the cost of media, the ROI will also be lower. In a presentation at the 2010 Nielsen Consumer Conference, executives from General Mills stated that if a brand was able to reach ROI parity by year three of targeting Hispanics, that should be considered a huge success.

I am not implying here that MMM tools should not be employed. What I am saying is that results should be analyzed in the context of these challenges and compared to results for other Hispanic efforts for similar-size brands. To help you and your team overcome some of these challenges, ask yourself the following questions when reviewing marketing/media mix results:

1. Was the Spanish-language advertising copy-tested? How did it perform relative to norms? Weak creative can undercut even strong media plans.
2. Was research conducted to track awareness and attitudes among consumers? Was the advertising successful in building awareness and positive intent-to-buy? Conducted in tandem with sales analyses, usage and attitudes studies can be useful leading indicators of future buying, especially when media runs late in the period being measured.
3. Does the product have strong distribution and low out-of-stock in high-index Hispanic stores? Were there relevant supporting Spanish-language materials (packaging, signage) at retail? If relevant to the category, does the research firm capture sales in the outlets where Spanish-speaking consumers are more likely to shop (e.g., bodegas)?
4. Was the product new to the market or new to the Spanish-language market? As in the general market, new products generally

take longer to show positive financial payback as trial and repeat tends to build over time.

5. How long is the product-purchase cycle vs. the period for which ROI was calculated? A mismatch (i.e. a short burst of advertising for a long purchase-cycle product) is unlikely to show a positive ROI in the short term. Longer purchase-cycle products generally fare better with longer, continuous plans.

6. Was the initial investment sufficient to generate impact? Media investment is often visualized as an S-shaped curve, with a minimum CRP/investment threshold required before results kick in. Too small an investment will have challenges in registering on the ROI screen.

Roberto's insights on measurement are based on his extensive experience with clients over the past 25 years and I want to thank him for sharing them here. ¡*Gracias*!

Key Takeaways:

- If you think multicultural marketing is something for the future, I've got news for you: the future is here. Smart companies like Walmart, Kellogg, and L'Oreal, among others, are leading with ethnic insights and seeing growth across the board.
- Marketing accountability is now a key element of most marketers' activities. Since Hispanic marketing activities are, for many brands, frequently new initiatives, they face increased scrutiny compared to other campaigns or programs that brands have done for several years.
- Once brands have determined a methodology for tracking sales, there are a number of measures that can be looked at to determine if Hispanic marketing objectives are being met and to track progress.
- Marketing-Mix Modeling tool results should be analyzed in the context of the challenges the Hispanic market currently faces with measurement tools and compared to results for other Hispanic efforts for similar-size brands.

NOTES

1. Wentz, Laurel, "Walmart's Tony Rogers: 100% Growth is Multicultural," *Advertising Age*, Oct. 31, 2012, Copyright © 2012 Crain Communications Inc. http://adage.com/article/hispanic-marketing/walmart-s-tony-rogers-100-growth-multicultural/238051.

10

~~~

THE BIG PICTURE

"By embracing the diversity of human beings, we will find our way to true happiness."

Howard Moskowitz

Malcolm Gladwell ended his February 2004 TED Talk, "Choice, happiness and spaghetti sauce," with this quote from Howard Moskowitz, a market researcher and psychophysicist who is perhaps best known for the "horizontal segmentation" work he did for Prego thirty years ago. Thanks to the pioneering work of Moskowitz, today food companies develop a much greater array of flavors or varieties within each product line. But when Moskowitz started working for Prego, Americans basically had three kinds of spaghetti sauce to choose from: plain, spicy and chunky. What he discovered is that one-third of Americans really wanted something else. They wanted *extra*-chunky spaghetti sauce. So Prego developed a new line of extra chunky, and immediately their sales went through the roof. According to Gladwell, that line of *extra*-chunky Prego sauce eventually generated $600 million in sales and knocked their competition, Ragu, off its feet. Why is this important? Because thanks to this breakthrough, Prego was able to increase both their customers' satisfaction and their bottom line. This doesn't mean that one spaghetti sauce was better than the other. It was just different. The *extra*-chunky simply satisfied a need of a segment of the population that was not being met by other sauces and Prego was able to capitalize on this opportunity and make people happy.

I believe the Hispanic community offers the same opportunity to make American businesses happy. If you are looking for growth and are willing to understand the needs of the Latino consumer in order to win their loyalty and share of wallet, then Latinos will buy your products, you will grow your business, and we will all be happier, no? The key point here is that you need to start thinking that change isn't necessarily bad. Change can be good. In fact, change is necessary in order to grow. As we saw in the example of Prego, in an effort to satisfy the needs and tastes of more Americans by adding unique and distinct ingredients to everything from spaghetti sauce to ice cream and vinegar, food companies have, over the last three decades, grown their businesses by capturing a larger overall market share in each category.

In his speech last summer to the Nielsen Consumer 360 Conference in Orlando (http://www.youtube.com/watch?v=BXYfdrBa3vk), Gladwell talked about how America is undergoing a new paradigm shift similar to the one it experienced fifty years ago when the first baby boomers came of age. Their ideas and ideals set the tone for America for the last fifty years and they will continue to play a role as Boomers enter their golden years. Today's generational paradigm shift is being shaped by the Millennial Generation and their radically different set of ideas about how the world should look and operate. You see, according to Gladwell, the baby boom generation is used to working within a hierarchy, whereas the millennials prefer to work as a network. The hierarchical approach is one in which there is a centralized management structure that is closed and disciplined enough to follow one strategic direction. The Millennial Generation's networked approach is the complete opposite: it is open, decentralized, and flexible. So, when you have a generational paradigm shift like this, what happens? According to Gladwell, they initially clash but eventually adapt . . . and as a result you get the "best of both worlds."

It's funny that Gladwell would choose those words to describe the ideal state coming out of this generational paradigm shift, because for years that's how we in the Hispanic marketing world have described what Latinos bring to America: the best of both worlds. On the one hand, Latinos pride themselves on truly upholding the foundational principles that make the United States the greatest country in the world: a belief in hard work, family, and the opportunity to have a better life without letting go of the best of our cultural heritage. That melding is exactly why I believe that Hispanics, over the next fifty years, will make America happy.

THE FOUR Ps

By now, I hope you feel a lot smarter about the Hispanic community and the important role we have played and will continue to play in the future of America. If I have done my job right, you also now have a better picture of *how* to approach this huge opportunity Latinos represent. As you have seen already, this is a very dynamic marketplace. I expect many things will change over the next five years, and I will have to write another book. But I want to leave you with some final thoughts on what *you* can do to help elevate the conversation about Latinos in the United States. I call them the four Ps, and if you remember nothing else, please remember this: people, press, politicians, and presidents.

PEOPLE

One of the things that drives me crazy about the conversation around the Latino community in the U.S. is that we are not thought of as American *people*. The anti-Latino rhetoric around illegal immigration makes most Americans think of Latinos as "aliens" or "invaders" and not as American people. But the truth is that the overwhelming majority of Hispanics in the United States are here legally. We are citizens of the United States. We are your colleagues, your friends, and often your next-door neighbors. This sense of alienation stays alive partly because we continue to be thought of as the "latest immigrant group" to come to America. And while it is true that every year, more than 500,000 Hispanics *legally* immigrate to this country, the Latino population grows more by natural births than through immigration. In fact, every year over 1 million Latino babies are born in the U.S. We *are* the people of the United States of America.

In fact, we are the people who helped re-elect President Barack Obama in 2012. We are the people who defend the frontlines of America's current wars in Afghanistan and Iraq and who have served honorably in many more wars before. We are the people who are starting businesses, starting families, and joining the American workforce in droves. Our children fill America's classrooms from kindergarten to college, and our youth help set trends in fashion, food, and music. We are the people who find nobility in any job we can get and will work hard in order to buy food, clothes, cars, and homes, helping to keep America's economy going strong. We are the doctors and nurses and civil servants who will help take care of the baby boomers as they deservedly start to retire, and we will keep America growing for the next fifty years.

PRESS

The reason Americans in general have such a distorted view of the Latino community is that the media coverage and entertainment portrayals are completely distorted and stereotyped. Even during an election year, when the Latino community got more press than I have ever seen before, many conservative talk radio hosts and Fox News personalities were off-the-charts out of control. *And nobody in the rest of the media called them on it.* In fact, a recently released poll by the National Hispanic Media Coalition concludes that their vitriol has actually been shaping the opinions and attitudes Americans have toward Latinos more than anything else. "Negative portrayals of Latinos and immigrants are pervasive in news and entertainment media. Consequently, non-Latinos commonly believe that the media-promoted negative stereotypes about these groups are true."[1] Comedy news shows like Jon Stewart's, *The Daily Show with Jon Stewart,* or Stephen Colbert's, *The Colbert Repport,* seem to be the only ones that will pick up on some of the stuff that these extreme right pundits are saying, because what people like Ann Coulter, Michael Savage, and Bill O'Reilly say about us is just so incendiary, it's ridiculous.

For example, on his radio show, Michael Savage stated that Americans are "being displaced by the people of Mexico. This is an invasion. The illegal aliens come here not to work, but to work the system, sell drugs, rape, and kill on contract." The examples of blatant hate talk abound, but I will not give them any more room in my book. But the reality is that insidious misinformation like this happens on a daily basis in the media. Just last December, in her column for the *Huffington Post*, "America Nears El Tipping Pointo," Ann Coulter portrays Latinos as unskilled workers looking for a government handout by having illegitimate children, when the fact of the matter is that Latinos actually use less than their fair share of government benefits. In his column for *Latino Voices*, Roque Planas sets the record straight. "According to a study released this year by the Center on Budget and Policy Priorities: Non-Hispanic whites accounted for 64 percent of the population in 2010 and received 69 percent of the entitlement benefits. In contrast, Hispanics made up 16 percent of the population but received 12 percent of the benefits, less than their proportionate share—likely because they are a younger population, and also because immigrants, including many legal immigrants, are ineligible for various benefits."[2]

In pointing out the absurdities in the right-wing media, the *Daily Show* and the *Colbert Report* actually do a better job covering Latino issues than all the other broadcast news shows and cable networks. But beyond correcting absurdities, the news and entertainment media have to do a much better job of including Latinos in *all* their stories and not just focus on the Latinos when the subject is immigration or drug wars. How can you do a story about education without talking about Latino children, when in some states they represent 50 percent of the student population? The truth is that media organizations still only have token Latinos on staff, and nobody who is powerful enough cares enough to make a difference.

POLITICIANS

Adapting to change is something both parties need to embrace, *pronto.* This past election cycle we saw very clearly how one party thought they could win the Hispanic vote by simply doing the same thing they had done for years. Nowhere was this more telling than in Florida, where the Romney team sincerely believed that they had the state squarely in their column and lost the Hispanic vote 60 percent to 39 percent. With Cuban-American voters swinging further left than ever before—Obama won 49 percent of their vote, up from 35 percent in 2008—many in the GOP saw their worst fear come true: Florida going blue for the second time in a row. What's next, Texas? The Latino vote also helped Obama win three other swing states that were too close to call the day of the election, Colorado, Nevada, and New Mexico. "In each of those states, Latinos significantly increased their share of total voters, gaining influence that could be decisive in future elections," reported Julia Preston and Fernanda Santos for *The New York Times* on Nov. 7.[3] Whether the GOP will be able to change their game enough to truly attract Latinos back to their party is yet to be seen, but it seems to me that they did more things wrong than Obama's team did right.

To their credit, the Obama team knew they had to change their approach in order to win the Latino vote. They had their work cut out for them, too, with many Latinos saying they were disappointed in the president, unhappy with his performance on many fronts, from jobs to deportations. Latinos were among the hardest hit during the past recession, and Obama had promised to tackle immigration reform but instead focused on health care. However, the Obama team did their homework. They listened and changed the way they campaigned in the Latino community, starting with getting his message out as early as March of 2012, nine months before the election. As everyone now knows, he won the Latino vote by big margins, but that does not mean that the Democratic Party can sit on their laurels either, as survey after survey shows that Latino voters are, in fact, true swing voters.

"Latino voters confirmed unequivocally that the road to the White House passes through Latino neighborhoods," Clarissa Martinez De Castro, a top official at NCLR, the Hispanic organization also known as the National Council of La Raza, told *The New York Times* the day after the election. But much work needs to be done to keep the Latino electorate happy. As Eliseo Medina, international secretary-treasurer of the Service Employees International Union, said to *The New York Times*, "The sleeping Latino giant is wide-awake and it's cranky. We expect action and leadership on immigration reform in 2013. No more excuses. No more obstruction or gridlock."

What's interesting is that when you look at the electoral map, you'll notice that the states with the largest populations (California, Texas, New York), and many of the so-called "swing states," are the same states that businesses are focusing on for growth with multicultural consumers. And for the foreseeable future, these states will continue to be battlegrounds for both business and politics as the graying and the browning of America continues. On the political front, this generational mismatch, or "cultural-generation gap," as demographer William Frey of the Brookings Institute calls it, will continue to play out in terms of the tension between the graying, white population who are resistant to increasing taxes and public spending; and a younger, minority population who are expecting more government help in education, health care, and other public-sector programs that are critically important to them as they get ready to enter the American workforce.

The clock is ticking, and politicos on both sides of the aisle need to find some common ground so we can all move forward or we will all get left behind. The future of America hangs in the balance.

PRESIDENTS

I want to end by talking about businesses and the people at the very top—the presidents, CEOs and CFOs who are the leaders of today's corporations. It is really up to you, your boards of directors, and your senior leadership to set the vision and strategies for your company's future growth. And as you do your business planning every quarter or every year, I encourage you to ask yourself and your senior leaders one simple question: What about Hispanic? I think I have laid out clearly how the opportunity is in front of you to rethink your business, to rethink your approach to certain things in order to make them better and satisfy the needs of not so few in this country. Yes, it may turn out that in rethinking your business, you may have to do things differently. It will take some adjusting, too, but the results—as Walmart, McDonald's, and P&G have seen already—could be tremendous. By implementing a total market strategy and expanding the way you approach the marketplace, you are not only satisfying the needs of a growing number of new consumers, you may also be expanding your bottom line with innovations that you would have never thought about if you continued to focus only on the same customers you have had for years, even decades.

America is changing and so must you. You need to understand that marketing your products and services to Latinos or other multicultural consumers is not better or worse, it's just different. Find a need, create a product to satisfy that need, and then go out and sell it. That's the golden rule in business, right? But any new effort will take time and money to work properly, so you must also make a commitment to doing things right. Just because your advertising efforts need to be done in a different language doesn't mean it's harder to do, it's just different. If you were expanding your business to Canada, China, or Africa, you would be doing things a little differently, so don't keep on ignoring your Hispanic opportunity. I encourage you to get out there and catch the biggest demographic wave since the baby boom!

NOTES

1. Barreto, Dr. Matt A., Dr. Sylvia Manzano, and Dr. Gary Segura, The Impact of Media Stereotypes on Opinions and Attitudes Toward Latinos, implemented by Latino Decisions for NHMC, September 2012.

2. Planas, Roque, "Ann Coulter Attacks Latinos in Column, As Conservatives Seek to Reach Out to Hispanic Voters," *Huffington Post*, December 7, 2012. www.huffingtonpost.com

3. Preston, Julia and Fernanda Santos, "A Record Latino Turnout, Solidly Backing Obama, "*The New York Times*, November 7. 2012. Copyright © 2012 The New York Times Company. www.nytimes.com/2012/11/08/us/politics/with-record-turnout-latinos-solidly-back-obama-and-wield-influence.html?_r=0.

RESOURCE GUIDE

RESEARCH COMPANIES

Arbitron
9705 Patuxent Woods Drive
Columbia, MD 21046
Phone: (410) 312-8000
www.arbitron.com

Burke Inc.
500 West Seventh Street
Cincinnati, OH 45203
Phone: (513) 241-5663
www.burke.com

Cheskin-Added-Value
116 West Twenty-Third Street,
Suite 500
New York, NY 10011
Phone: (917) 860-0517
Contact: Stephen Palacios
www.cheskin.com

ComScore Networks
4000 Shoreline Court #200
South San Francisco , CA 94080
Phone: (650) 244-5400
www.comscore.com

Creative & Response Research
    Services Inc.
500 North Michigan Avenue
Chicago, IL 60611-3781
Phone: (312) 828-9200
www.crresearch.com

Cultural Access Group
445 South Figueroa Street
Suite 2350
Los Angeles , CA 90071
Phone: (213) 228-0300
Fax: (213) 489-2602
www.accesscag.com

Geoscape
2100 West Flagler Street
Miami, FL 33135
Phone: (888) 211-9353
http://www.geoscape.com/

GfK Custom Research
75 Ninth Avenue, 5th Floor
New York, NY 10011
Phone: (212) 240-5300
www.gfkamerica.com

Global Insight—IHS
321 Inverness Drive South
Englewood, Colorado 80112
http://www.ihs.com/index.aspx

Horowitz Associates
1971 Palmer Avenue
Larchmont, NY 10538
Phone: (914) 834-5999
http://www.horowitzassociates.
   com/

IBIS World
401 Wilshire Blvd, Suite 200
Santa Monica, CA 90401
Phone: (800) 330-3772
http://www.ibisworld.com/

Kantar Media
New York City, NY - HQ
11 Madison Avenue
12th Floor
New York, NY 10010
Phone: (347) 748-9551
http://kantarmediana.com

Latino Decisions
15 South Grady Way, Suite 620
Seattle, Washington 98057
Phone: (425) 271-2300
www.latinodecisions.com

The Latinum Network
2 Bethesda Metro Center
Suite 300
Bethesda, MD 20814
Phone: (240) 482.8260
www.latinumnetwork.com

Millward Brown
11 Madison Ave.
12th Floor
New York, NY 10010
Phone: (212) 548-7200
www.millwardbrown.com

Mintel Group Ltd.
351 West Hubbard Street
8th Floor
Chicago, IL 60654
Phone: (312) 932-0400
www.mintel.com

The NPD Group, Inc.
Foodservice Hispanic CREST
900 West Shore Road
Port Washington, NY 11050
Phone: (516) 625-0700
(866) 444-1411
www.npd.com

Roslow Research Group
79 Main St # 301
Port Washington, NY 11050
Phone: (516) 883-1110
http://www.roslowresearch.com/

Simmons Market Research
1501 SW FAU Research Park
   Blvd., Suite 100
Deerfield Beach, FL 33441
Phone: (800) 551-6425
www.simmonssurvey.com

Symphony IRI Group
150 North Clinton Street
Chicago, IL 60661-1416
Phone: (312) 726-1221
http://www.SymphonyIRI.com

The Nielsen Company
770 Broadway
New York, NY 10003-9595
http://www.nielsen.com/global/
    en.html

TNS Media Intelligence
Headquarters 100 Park Avenue,
4th Floor
New York, NY 10017
Phone: (212) 991-6000
www.tns-mi.com

The Santiago Solutions Group
800 South Victory Blvd.
Suite 205
Burbank, CA 91502-2427
Phone: (818) 736-5661
http://santiagosolutionsgroup.
    com/
The Futures Company
11 Madison Avenue, 12th Floor
New York, NY 10010
Phone: (212) 896-8112
http://thefuturescompany.com/

NONPROFIT RESEARCH CENTERS

The Pew Hispanic Center, based in Washington, DC, is a nonpartisan
research center supported by a grant from the Pew Charitable Trusts
of Philadelphia. The Center is a project of the University of Southern
California Annenberg School for Communication. The Pew Hispanic
Center's mission is to improve understanding of the diverse Hispanic
population in the United States and to chronicle Latinos' growing
impact on the nation. The Center strives to inform debate on critical
issues through dissemination of its research to policy makers, business
leaders, academic institutions, and the media.

Pew Hispanic Center
1615 L Street NW, Suite 700
Washington, D.C. 20036
Phone: (202) 419-3600
www.pewhispanic.org

Selig Center for Economic Growth. Created to convey economic
expertise to Georgia businesses and entrepreneurs, the Selig Center
for Economic Growth is primarily responsible for conducting research
on economic, demographic, and social issues. Through its range
of projects—major economic impact studies, economic forecasts,

publications, information services, and data products—the Center's efforts help to guide business decisions and the direction of public policy.

Terry College of Business
310 Herty Drive
Athens, GA 30602
Phone: (706) 542-8100
http://www.terry.uga.edu/

TRPI—The Tomás Rivera Policy Institute (TRPI) is a freestanding, nonprofit policy research organization that has attained a reputation as the nation's "premier Latino think tank." The research mission of the Tomás Rivera Policy Institute is to help resolve policy challenges arising from demographic diversity in the 21st century global city.

The Tomás Rivera Policy Institute (California Office)
University of Southern California
School of Policy, Planning & Development
650 Childs Way, Lewis Hall, Suite 102
Los Angeles, CA 90089-0626
Phone: (213) 821-5615
www.trpi.org

GOVERNMENT OFFICES

US Bureau of the Census—The best source of information for just about anything in the United States. The Bureau of the Census carries the latest demographic, economic, and geographic information in the United States.

US Bureau of the Census
4600 Silver Hill Road
Washington, DC 20233
Call Center (301) 763-4636 or (800) 923-8282
www.census.gov

USHCC—United States Hispanic Chamber of Commerce
Since its inception, the USHCC has worked toward bringing the issues

and concerns of the nation's more than 1.6 million Hispanic-owned businesses to the forefront of the national economic agenda. Through its network of more than 130 local Hispanic Chambers of Commerce and Hispanic business organizations, the USHCC effectively communicates the needs and potential of Hispanic enterprise to the public and private sector.

US Hispanic Chamber of Commerce
1424 K Street NW, Suite 401
Washington, D.C. 20005
Phone: (202) 842-1212
https://www.ushcc.com/index.cfm

HISPANIC MARKET PUBLICATIONS

Hispanicad.com
1 Chardonnay Road
Cortlandt Manor, NY 10567
Phone: (914) 734-8264
Fax: (914) 737-3234
www.hispanicad.com

Hispanicbusiness.com
5385 Hollister Avenue, Suite 204
Santa Barbara, CA 93111
Phone: (800) 806-4268
www.hispanicbusiness.com

Hispanic Market Weekly
2332 Galiano Street
Coral Gables, FL 33134
Phone: (305) 448-5838
www.hispanicmarketweekly.com

Media Economics Group
7427 Mathews-Mint Hill Road,
Suite 105-364
Charlotte, NC 28227
Phone: (704) 841-2030
info@media-economics.com

Multicultural Marketing
   Resources Inc. (MMR)
150 West 28th Street, Suite 1501
New York, NY 10001
Phone: (212) 242-3351
www.multicultural.com

TRADE ASSOCIATIONS

AHAA—The Voice of Hispanic Marketing (formerly the Association of
Hispanic Advertising Agencies)
AHAA (Headquarters)
8201 Greensboro Drive, Suite 300
McLean, Virginia 22102
Phone: (703) 610-9014
www.ahaa.org

CAB—Cabletelevision Advertising Bureau
830 Third Avenue
New York, NY 10022
Phone: (212)508-1200
www.cabletvadbureau.com

MPA—Magazine Publishers of America
810 Seventh Avenue, 24th Floor
New York, NY 10019
Phone: (212) 872-3700
www.magazine.org

NAHJ—National Association of Hispanic Journalists
1050 Connecticut Avenue NW
Washington, DC 20036
Phone: (202) 662-7145 / (888) 346-NAHJ
http://www.nahj12.com/
nahj@nahj.org

NAHP—National Association of Hispanic Publications
National Press Building
529 14th Street NW, Suite 1126
Washington, D.C. 20045
Phone: (202) 662-7250
www.nahp.org

HISPANIC ASSOCIATIONS

ASPIRA
The mission of ASPIRA is to empower the Puerto Rican and Latino community through advocacy and the education and leadership development of its youth.

ASPIRA (National Offices)
1444 I Street NW, Suite 800
Washington, D.C. 20005
Phone: (202) 835-3600
http://www.aspira.org/en

CHCI—Congressional Hispanic Caucus Institute
The mission of the Congressional Hispanic Caucus Institute (CHCI) is to develop the next generation of Latino leaders. CHCI seeks to accomplish its mission by offering educational and leadership development programs, services, and activities that promote the growth of participants as effective professionals and strong leaders.

Congressional Hispanic Caucus Institute
911 2nd Street NE
Washington, D.C. 20002
Phone: (202) 543-1771
www.chci.org

HACR—The Hispanic Association on Corporate Responsibility's mission is to advance the inclusion of Hispanics in corporate America at a level commensurate with our economic contributions. HACR focuses on four areas of corporate responsibility and market reciprocity. They are: employment, procurement, philanthropy, and governance.

Hispanic Association on Corporate Responsibility
1444 I Street NW, Suite 850
Washington, D.C. 20005
Phone: (202) 835-9672
http://www.hacr.org/

HSF—The Hispanic Scholarship Fund (HSF) is the nation's leading organization supporting Hispanic higher education. Its goal is to strengthen our country by advancing the college education of Hispanic Americans. Its mission is to double the number of Hispanics earning a college degree.

Hispanic Scholarship Fund (Headquarters Office)
1411 W. 190th Street, Suite 325
Gardena, CA 90248
Phone: (877) HSF-INFO (877-473-4636)
www.hsf.net

Immigration Policy Center (IPC) is the research and policy arm of the American Immigration Council. IPC's mission is to shape a rational conversation on immigration and immigrant integration. Through its research and analysis, IPC provides policymakers, the media, and the general public with accurate information about the role of immigrants and immigration policy in US society.

American Immigration Council
1331 G Street, NW, Suite 200
Washington, DC 20005-3141
Phone: (202) 507-7500
http://www.immigrationpolicy.org/

LULAC—League of United Latin American Citizens. The mission of the League of United Latin American Citizens is to advance the economic condition, educational attainment, political influence, health, and civil rights of the Hispanic population of the United States.

LULAC (National Office)
1133 Nineteenth Street, NW, Suite 1000
Washington, D.C. 20036
Phone: (202) 833-6130
www.LULAC.org

MALDEF—Mexican American Legal Defense and Educational Fund. MALDEF is the leading nonprofit Latino litigation, advocacy, and educational outreach institution in the United States. Its mission is to foster sound public policies, laws, and programs to safeguard the

civil rights of Latinos living in the United States and to empower the
Latino community to fully participate in society.

MALDEF (National Headquarters)
634 South Spring Street
Los Angeles, CA 90014
Phone: (213) 629-2512
www.maldef.org

NALEO—National Association of Latino Elected Officials. The
National Association of Latino Elected and Appointed Officials
Educational Fund is the leading organization that empowers Latinos
to participate fully in the American political process, from citizenship
to public service.

NALEO Educational Fund
1122 West Washington Blvd., 3rd Floor
Los Angeles, CA 90015
Phone: (213) 747-7606
www.naleo.org

NCLR—National Council of La Raza. The National Council of
La Raza (NCLR) is a private, nonprofit, nonpartisan, tax-exempt
organization established in 1968 to reduce poverty and discrimination
and improve life opportunities for Hispanic Americans. NCLR is the
largest constituency-based national Hispanic organization, serving all
Hispanic nationality groups in all regions of the country.

NCLR (Headquarters)
Raul Yzaguirre Building
1126 16th Street, NW
Suite 600
Washington, DC 20036-4845
Phone: (202) 785-1670
www.nclr.org

NAA -- New America Alliance is a non-profit organization dedicated
to advancing the economic development of the American Latino
community. The Alliance is organized on the principle that American
Latino business leaders have a special responsibility to lead the process
of building the forms of capital most crucial to Latino progress—

economic capital, political capital, human capital, and the practice of philanthropy.

New America Alliance
1050 Connecticut Avenue, NW, 10th Floor
Washington, DC 20036
Phone: (202) 772-1044
http://www.naaonline.org/index.html

RECOMMENDED CONFERENCES (In Alphabetical Order)

ADCOLOR® Diversity Summit

The mission of ADCOLOR is to celebrate and champion diversity in the advertising, marketing, media, and public relations industries. ADCOLOR strives to create a network of outstanding diverse professionals and champions of diversity and inclusion by honoring their accomplishments and leveraging their stories as a road map for others to follow.

Advertising Week

Advertising Week is the world's premier annual gathering of marketing and communications leaders in New York City. With more than 200 distinct events, the Week is a hybrid of thought leadership seminars featuring the industry's best and brightest and engaging special events which galvanize targeted constituencies.

Association of National Advertisers (ANA) Multicultural & Diversity Conference

The conference is constantly evolving to meet the needs of attendees. Features keynote sessions by senior-level client-side marketers as well as sessions devoted to the most important issues facing these markets.

Association of Hispanic Advertising Agencies (AHAA) Annual Conference

AHAA is committed to promoting the common business and professional interests of industry members. Encouraging study, discussion, and education regarding the Hispanic-specialized marketing and advertising industry are among AHAA's strategic initiatives.

Geoscape New Mainstream Business Summit

This conference will provide you with actionable intelligence, hands-on workshops, inspiring keynotes, and case studies from companies that are leading the movement toward the New Mainstream.

Hispanic Retail 360

Hispanic Retail 360 Summit is a three-day event for retailers and marketers who want to learn how to tap into the $1 trillion Hispanic market and grow their business.

Hispanicize: Hispanic PR & Social Marketing Conference

Hispanicize brings brands, media, marketers, celebrities, filmmakers, innovators, and bloggers together in a unique creative environment focused on creative ideas and best practices.

IAB Mixx Conference

The IAB educates marketers, agencies, media companies, and the wider business community about the value of interactive advertising. Working with its member companies, the IAB evaluates and recommends standards and practices and fields critical research on interactive advertising.

NAMIC

Founded in 1980, the National Association for Multi-Ethnicity in Communications (NAMIC) is the premier organization that educates, advocates, and empowers for multiethnic diversity in the communications industry.

NCTA – The Cable Show

NCTA is where leaders from every sector—from content to devices to applications to education—come together to spark ideas and create partnerships that keep cable ahead in today's digital media revolution.

New Generation Latino Consortium (NGLC)

The NGLC conference is an organization dedicated to hosting business conferences and fielding innovative research studies focused on the bicultural, bilingual, and media-savvy Hispanic consumer.

Nielsen Consumer 360 Conference

Nielsen's Consumer 360 brings you innovative thought leaders and industry experts who will share exclusive insights and help you develop business solutions that are fueled with punch and ingenuity. These industry trailblazers will share their uncommon approach to cutting-edge solutions and bring to life ideas that illuminate consumer behavior.

Social TV Summit

Social TV Summit focuses on the use of technologies that allow a viewer to interact, socialize, search, share, and purchase around content they are watching on TV, or online, with one screen or a second screen like a laptop, tablet, or smart phone.

ACKNOWLEDGMENTS

This book would not have been possible without the input and help of many, many people. First I must thank Jennifer Knight, who encouraged me to write the first *Latino Boom!* book and has patiently listened to me talk about this market for the past fifteen years. Thanks must also be given to my fearless leaders, Randy Falco and Ruth Gaviria, who not only gave me the time to write this book, but who also encourage all of us at Univision to spread our thought leadership about the Hispanic consumer. Special thanks go to my colleagues in research, Elizabeth Ellers, Debbie Shinneck, Belia Jimenez, Beth Bachrach, Myra Rivera-Alvear, but most especially to Ingrid Carrete, who pored over seemingly endless reams of data to create many of the charts in this book and always kept me honest with the other data I quote. A huge debt of gratitude goes to my good friends and colleagues Roberto Ruiz, Cynthia Ashworth, Linda Ong, and Graciela Eleta, who so graciously contributed to the book.

My warmest thanks go to Monica Talan, Rosemary Mercedes, Joe Del Grosso, Kathy Whitlock, Enedina Vega Amaez, Georgia Galanoudis, Horacio Gavilan, and Ronald Mendez, whose help, feedback, and comments made the book much better. Much gratitude goes to Richard Zuluaga, who designed numerous covers for this book.

Of course, I couldn't have done any of this without the guidance of my good friend and mentor, Fred Ciporen, my former agent, Alfredo Santana, and my lawyer, Charles Knull. At Strauss Consultants, a huge *abrazo* to Karen Strauss for believing in this book from the get-go and guiding me each step of the way. But there aren't enough words in English or Spanish to thank the team at Worthy Shorts, especially

Otto Barz, Louis Neiheisel, Susan Peterson, David Snidero, Darlene Swanson, and my copy editor, Victoria Wright, who patiently corrected my manuscript and asked all the right questions. Thanks must also go to my favorite photographer in the world, Emérito Pujol, for taking my picture for this book. Last, but certainly not least, *muchos gracias* to my colleagues, Natalia Munoz, who created my beautiful website, www. latinoboom.net, and Mary Patierno who edited my author video. And finally, thanks to all the people and institutions who graciously allowed me to use their data for this book.

CPSIA information can be obtained at www.ICGtesting.com
Printed in the USA
BVOW02s1025211013

334134BV00004B/54/P